From Mimetic Translation to Artistic Transduction

From Mimetic Translation to Artistic Transduction

A Semiotic Perspective on Virginia Woolf, Hector Berlioz, and Bertolt Brecht

Dinda L. Gorlée

ANTHEM PRESS

Anthem Press
An imprint of Wimbledon Publishing Company
www.anthempress.com

This edition first published in UK and USA 2023
by ANTHEM PRESS
75–76 Blackfriars Road, London SE1 8HA, UK
or PO Box 9779, London SW19 7ZG, UK
and
244 Madison Ave #116, New York, NY 10016, USA

© 2023 Dinda L. Gorlée

The author asserts the moral right to be identified as the author of this work.

All rights reserved. Without limiting the rights under copyright reserved above, no part of this publication may be reproduced, stored or introduced into a retrieval system, or transmitted, in any form or by any means (electronic, mechanical, photocopying, recording or otherwise), without the prior written permission of both the copyright owner and the above publisher of this book.

British Library Cataloguing-in-Publication Data
A catalogue record for this book is available from the British Library.

Library of Congress Control Number: 2023939250
A catalog record for this book has been requested.

ISBN-13: 978-1-83998-908-7 (Hbk)
ISBN-10: 1-83998-908-4 (Hbk)

This title is also available as an e-book.

To my son Jorrit,
a fine reader of semiotic rhetoric

CONTENTS

1. Forked Tongues: Theory from Translation to Transduction … 1
   Exploring New Avenues of Translation … 1
   Jakobson's Concept of Poetry in Translation … 18
   From Translation to Transduction … 31
   Sebeok's Transduction … 39
2. Wave after Wave: Wagner's Waves Eclipsed by Virginia Woolf … 47
   Play Within Play … 47
   Three Waves … 58
   Wagner's Water Music … 68
   Virginia Woolf's Brain Waves … 76
3. War and Love: The Parabolic Retranslation in Berlioz's Opera … 89
   Berlioz's Poetical Drama … 89
   Olympic Odyssey … 100
   Hunt and Storm … 119
4. The Threepenny Opera: Jakobson's Poetics Retranslated in the Spirit of Brecht's Work-Plays … 129
   New Tongues for Brecht's Language … 129
   Brecht Juggling with Gay's *The Beggar's Opera* … 143
   From Speech to Criminal Slang … 163
   Epic Epilogue … 171

Bibliography … 175

Index … 189

Chapter 1

FORKED TONGUES: THEORY FROM TRANSLATION TO TRANSDUCTION

Exploring New Avenues of Translation

A word of explanation is needed for those readers who have not previously been introduced to the idea of a greater understanding of the evolution of translation into transduction. Transduction is beyond translation: it moves beyond the transferal of one language to another to signify speculative attempts at examining and executing the belief, concepts and meaning of the different arts. The art of translating means engaging in the analytical exercise of transferring, rotating and twisting one language into another art; but for literary translation, the objective of retranslation or self-translation is to create through translation the poetic and lyrical terms of transduction, which is the main concept discussed in this book.

Translation (including retranslation and self-translation) seems to be an ancient and contemporary process of attempting to unite science and art in order to communicate information through incomplete changes and reforms of coded language determined in space or time. In today's world, an understanding of human culture can expand translation into the unexpected force linguistic retranslation into coded and uncoded music, conveying the "expressive melody, the rhythmic experimentation, the coloristic use of harmony and instrumental timbres, [and] the relaxation of and uncertainty about formal canon" (Longyear 1969, 3). The extension of translation over the ages is called transduction, which concerns the "arts of incompletion" (Bernhart and Englund 2021) of words-and-music as illustrated and exemplified in the present book *From Mimetic Translation to Artistic Transduction: A Semiotic Perspective on Virginia Woolf, Hector Berlioz, and Bertolt Brecht*.

Transduction expands informational (that is, highly meaningful) language into an inventory of the literary dialects, idioms and jargons of other fine and applied arts. To judge the evolution of translation to transduction, if the operational conclusion arising from the evidence introduced in the examples of this book is a true metaphor, Peirce's "interpretants" in transduction can signify that the details of the artistic signs are not necessarily seen as harsh and static target units but are sent forth in the fluid patterns given to received source signs. Peirce's interpretants are called "reactor" signs, explained in terms of the stimuli, responses, needs and satisfaction of the categories of the source sign (Sebeok 1994/1999, 64–65).

If the translator's mind develops toward the art of transduction, the new version can be improved over the previous translation. The transduction can be reworked from linguistics into encoding the continuous processes engaged in by the audience as sign users to interpret and transform one form of energy into another. If the translator's mind develops toward the art of transduction, the conditions are improved and can be extended from linguistics to embrace a completely different art or non-art with a different meaning. However, if interdisciplinary sign-action is a step to promote the technique of the sciences, the possibilities of transduction can be true for the cultural perspective of the human sciences. The mimetic process that transforms translation into transduction involves the interrelated encoding and decoding of the humanities, including translation studies (Nida and Taber 1969/1982, 199–200; see for methodology de Groot 1969, 203–209).

The traditional terminology for translation originated in the exegesis of literary translation, with the first model being the translation of the Bible into modern languages (Nida 1964). The translation of the philological, linguistic and communicative medium of the Christian religion created sacred writings that were translated into many languages to make the biblical text known to believers around the world (Nida 2001, 494–497). The *philological* retranslation of the Bible started as a circular history of text transmission from old to new languages, in which the sense of the sacred writings has priority over words understood by everyone. These new translations were stylistically more in line with the contemporary usage of the target language rather than the old language. Nida's *linguistic* approach was instrumental in the rapid expansion of Bible translations into hundreds of major and minor languages to support missionary work. Many aboriginal populations had no written medium and relied on an oral literary tradition. The task of the missionary translators was to attempt to "formulate alphabets, analyze complete grammars, determining the meanings of words in quite different cultures, and learning to appreciate some of the remarkable features of oral literature" (Nida 2001, 495; see Nida 1950).

Nida's (1964) work served as practical help for missionary Bible translators, enabling them to draw from Cherry's modern communication theory (1957/1966). Translation performs the social function of serving the sign-receptor, moving away from employing technical means for translating ornate biblical language to accepting the common usages of words so as to reflect the origin myth of translation studies in simple words. The language of the sacred scriptures had to be socially restricted to formal units, without violating the aesthetic quality of the biblical words. Communicative translation was not concerned with finding a "circular" synonym between source and target texts but focused on the functional or pragmatic parasymmetry intermediating between synonyms. In the activity of translation, the meaning of words, grammar and paragraphs needs to possess a certain and clear parallelism with the figurative, even poetic, language of the "holy scriptures," but the equivalence depends on the translator's own personal style in their treatment of the language.

Literary translators continued this poetic tradition by applying the "literature" of the Bible to other languages and other literary works, but they treated the activity of translation as the origin myth of the "other Babel, that impossible tower" (Barnstone 1993, 3; see also 135–152). Since the diverse languages create a multilingual chaos, translatable and even untranslatable works of literary art were idealized in Burton Raffel's *The Forked Tongue: A Study of the Translation Process* (1971) in the historical context of Homer's *Iliad* and *Odysseus*, Cervantes' *Don Quixote de la Mancha*, old Chinese verse, and the Anglo-Saxon chronicles of *Beowulf*. Thereby, the activity of making literary translations was expanded from the circular version of Nida's formal translation (philological translation) into the less formal (indeed, poetic or poeticized) shapes of diverse languages. While biblical metaphors speak of literal and figurative (that is to say, for religious purposes, "good" and "evil") thoughts of meaningful (that is, not neutral) forms of translation,[1] literary translation admitted rhetorical speech, poetical metaphors and a variety of figures of speech to decode the hidden meanings and embellish narrative discourse.

A "code" is defined by Thomas A. Sebeok as the "agreed formulation, or set of unambiguous rules, where messages are converted from one representation into another," so that "encoding" is the "transformation [of codes], whereby, by operation of code rules, a source alters a message from one representation to another"; at the same time, "decoding" is the "transformation [of codes], whereby, by operation of rule codes, a destination alters an incoming message from one representation into another" (1984a, 29). A literary code can be read, spoken, recited or even sung, as treated here in this book. This investigation of the interplay of brain and voice is more complex in design, examining the different codes that generate Sebeok's "emblem," defined as a "highly formalized symbol, usually in the visual modality" (Sebeok 1984a,

---

[1] See Gen. 10:5; Ps. 34:28, 50:16; Job 33:2; 1 Cor. 2: 12:10–30, 13:1, Acts 2:1–13; Rev. 16:10.

29). The emblematic sign expresses the formalized symbol of religious language (Sebeok 1984a, 35–36).

In the parable "The garden of forking paths" (written in Spanish in 1941, translated into English in Borges 2000, 44–54), Jorge Luis Borges zigzags himself in a contrary act away from the source text. His act of translation was not one of copying, but of creating a new way of seeing through retranslation and/or self-translation. Literary translation is not a circular procedure of translating word-for-word but is a continuing challenge to reread the source and surpass it with a rich network of subjective signs that overplay and underplay the source term to form the target poem, novel or stage play bearing the personal mark of the translator. Borges's "tortuous method [...] forked, broke off [...] the meanderings" (2000, 53) of the source text to embrace the poetical metaphors and periphrases of his own target text. The retranslated target text was not the myth of a radical circle of synonyms but re-formed the source text into the compound signs of art. Regarding the semiotic aspects of translation, Roman Jakobson was initially cautious in his criticism about the overflow of the grammatical models of poetry into the hypersigns of the "growing, dizzying net of divergent, convergent and parallel times" (Borges 2000: 53). Later, Jakobson realized that poetic verse is a different genre that invites literary translators to translate, retranslate and even self-translate the artistic signs of literature into the bifurcated tongues of language in their own time and space.

In the course of time, the activities of translation have broadened from dealing with literal translation, retranslation and self-translation to the horizon of wider frontiers. The goal was to bridge the gap between literature and science outside mainly literary translations. Legal or juridical translation, official or diplomatic translation, technical translation, commercial or business translation, philosophical translation, vocal (or operatic) translation, as well as other mixed forms of translation, each with their own qualities of equivalence or functional shifts in detail between the cultural natures of source with target texts, were acceptable disciplines. Translation studies in the twentieth century evolved into the multi-project of contemporary translation studies. The view of translating old literature into new translated versions developed from the ancient formal experience of scientifically transferring units of word sounds, meter and versification into multidisciplinary fragments and blended with literary translation to transform translation into a modernized field. In the humanities, the ideas and concepts of the literary translator were expanded from orthodox to unorthodox, from normal to anomalous, or even from subliminal and traumatic minds to flow from source text into elliptic, parabolic and hyperbolic versions and plot twists in the target poem, novel or theater play. The curves and turnings of the converging steps of Peirce's new terms and sentences are the main topics discussed in this book.

To find new steps and meanings, the puzzle is to put together how literary translation studies are a challenge for the translator. Translation allows transformation into the final stage, where the content of life is unraveled as the genesis of signs in a mixed discipline in science and art. The symbolic commitment to translating literary texts exchanged the dimensions of the "sacred" experience into the relatively "free" and secular events of popular translation. The cultural approaches of the literary translator can remove the constraints imposed by the skill of authoritative translation allowing the translator to serve as a provisional sign-maker of other arts. The translator produces a multidisciplinary replica as a token of culture (Johansen 1993, 151), which can be supplemented by the translator with extensions and paraphrases (Gorlée 2020). Peirce's prefix quasi- provides the sign, mind and thought of the translator with the quasi-sign, quasi-mind and quasi-thought. The translator plays on words by moving his/her mind away from the conventional mathematical or statistical source grammar and rephrasing the single words and sentences in the critical, but subjective, pictures of the target culture.

Peirce alternated with a highly idiosyncratic terminology. For example, quasi- is his preferred prefix to thrive on the hard work of speculative grammar. Prefix quasi- is loosely attached to the preparatory action described in Peirce's quasi-sign, quasi-mind, quasi-thought and other human possibilities. Originally, the prefix quasi- indicates "seeming," "as it were" to resemble "that what it qualifies is not the real thing but has come of its qualities" (*Brewer's Dictionary of Phrase and Fable*, see Evans [1870]1989: 901). A quasi-sign is seemingly a perfect sign but is imperfect; the quasi-mind is partially a logical mind but is illogical; and the quasi-thought is not present in real logic but in human quasi-forms of reasoning. The foundation of Peirce's reasoning was that the logical algebra has been pursued to lead more directly from the graphs to "the ultimate analysis of logical problems than any algebra yet devised" (CP: 3.619). Peirce's logical analysis was seemingly accurate, but the logical analysis of quasi-forms with an understanding that is missing was not really a logical procedure but an informal quasi-dialogue (Johansen 1993, 247–247). The prefix quasi- was intermixed with illogical turns and inferences to be understood by the quasi-scientific and quasi-public audience with a casually popular terminology.

The transfer of the literary translator has a certain artistic freedom, but with a caveat. The subjective replica from the quasi-translator is a "chemical" copy of the simple code with cells flowing from the positive to the negative sides in the opposite direction to the target text, moving away from the old literal translation to become the emblematic sign. In the secondary cell, can one reverse the chemical reactions and even state that the final piece can be considered as a parody. The literary translator seems to navigate the old rules of translation and untangle the quasi-questions to be answered by new quasi-propositions in time (CP: 2.309). Moving away from the old rhetorical reversion of cross-switching two languages, the literary translation has become the anonymous technique of building an alternating current of electricity with the dramatic liberty to produce a thermoelectric field (*replica*) of the source text (Sheriff 1984/1991, 78, 246) in *"ordinary"* language (talking *in* language), so that metalanguage provides fertile territory to play the rich game of fulfilling literary ideas and lyrical thoughts.

Literary translation is not a geological method of teleprocessing (Sheriff 1984/1991, 245) like taking an exact measurement of the encoding process to decode the communicative data and encode it in a different language. The map of literary translation is an object of great beauty, so the translation must depict the emotional types of colors, strata and tints, echoing them as equal in the target variations. Translation gives a vision of the world, and the effect is not that of an old-fashioned optical instrument but one of a telescope conversing with nature and the world (Emre 2020). In the seventeenth century, the invention of the telescope changed the view of the world. The telescope can provide a magnified picture of the military battlefield of the enemy, or it can serve as an eyeglass to follow a play performed in the theater. The lens of the telescope gives a reasonable, but imperfect, mirror image. However, it must not be forgotten that literary translation is not a rational observation of the landscape but involves a subjective conversation with the translator's reason and feeling. The translator is like a televiewer of the fractures, cavities and breakpoints of the source message to transpose this geological network into the target text. As an artisan, the translator makes an artistic (re)translation from cross-switching (Sheriff 1984/1991, 23, 245).

The translator's task is to be, in Jakobson's parlance, a decoder working as an artist of the landscape of language. The translator's task is to rectify or remedy the "inner" features of speech sounds so they become the "outer" features of phonemes and variants for producing the codes of the target text. In his analysis, Jakobson endows the multiple codes of the mentalistic, code-restricted, generic, fictional and algebraic views with new information (Jakobson and Halle 1956/1971, 22–30). In the translation of literature, Jakobson reorganized the psychophonetic features of words and sentences that give the incomparable art of poetic emotion a new flavor. The translator works at lyrical translation as an analytical native "decoder," but at the same time, as an artisan, the translator acts as Jakobson's "cryptanalyst." The cryptanalyst is "a detached and external onlooker," but simultaneously he or she works at remaking the "recipient of messages without being their addressee and without knowledge of the code" (1961/1971a, 174–175). Further, Jakobson's cryptanalyst

[...] attempts to break the code through a scrutiny of the message. As far as possible, this level of linguistic investigation must be merely a preliminary stage toward an internal approach to the language studied, when the observer becomes adjusted to the native speakers and decodes messages in their mother-tongue through the medium of the code. (Jakobson 1961/1971a: 175)

Examples of the artisan's analytical-and-emotional invention language are the double signs of semiotranslation coming from the semiotics of Charles S. Peirce (Gorlée 1994, 2004). Umberto Eco gave semiotics the *"ratio facilis"* for modifying the *"congruence, projections, and graphs"* to arbitrarily alter linguistic and non-linguistic signs (1985, 180), Eco's emphasis). Translation scholars, including Jakobson himself, abandoned the semiotic structure of Saussure to embrace the method of Peirce, so that "any concept with any image can create a sign, a meaning-effect [...] to mystify the automatism of the signifier/signified relationship" (MacCannell and MacCannell 1982, 132–133).

The literary inventor follows the "chemical" reaction of the sign to feel the tone of beauty, which is based on proportional rules, giving it a new tune. The rules do not draw on Saussure's fixed circle (producing synonyms) but on the dramatic clues of the "similitude between triangles where the length of the angles and the proportions between sides are made pertinent, irrespective of the size of the triangles" (Eco 1985, 182). This contrast moves away from Peirce's tone and token (the agent working on the activity) into type (the ideal information) of translation. Literary translation, with the help of Peircean semiotics, has found its way out of the old versions of translation to bemuse the readers with the beauty and wonder of meaningful clue-words transformed into transduction.

The complex machine of translation is the first step in the chain of the interpreter's events that lead, through conduction, to the verbal and non-verbal codes of transduction. In my previous book, *From Translation to Transduction: The Glassy Essence of Intersemiosis* (Gorlée 2015), the theoretical part was analyzed through the semiotic doctrine of Charles Sanders Peirce (1839–1914). Peirce's anatomy of the "circuitous roads" (Gorlée 2015, 32–47) moves through, between and even beyond the "flesh and bone" (Gen. 29: 14; Jer. 8: 1,2) of the original author's ways, from the source text to the "good" or "bad" texture of the target signs to suggest the "theory" of translation. The geometrical arrangements determine the way in which the sign-reader, agent, interpreter or translator sets a value on the Borgesian tortuous paths leading from backward forward to Roman Jakobson's poetic signs to make a fictional novel (Jakobson and Halle 1956/1971, 24–25). The logical method of semiotic translation comes from the more complex action of the translator's brain in reaction to the "situational reflexivity" (Chambers 1984, 24–25) of the translator reading, formulating and thinking the source text in order to reformulate, rewrite and remake it into the literary replica (token) of lyrical poetry (Weissbort 1989).

Peirce's active and emotional involvement in the form, function and process of linguistic signs was transformed into the modern process of translation to interconnect language, culture and mind into one whole. Peirce proposed that his three categories (firstness, secondness, thirdness) were varieties of feeling, force and thought. The categories are in the triadic elements of self, power and knowledge or meaning, value and information. Peirce's categories are not seen as individual elements but take part in the quasi-semiosis of firstness and secondness to end the process in the total meaning of final semiosis as thirdness (CP: 5.484–5.489). Jakobson's concept of poetic language showed that harmony includes the acculturation of the disharmony of connecting with different cultures. He displaced the fragmented literary authors in the various languages (for Jakobson, Russian, Czech, French and English) to "play" with the semiotic involvement of literary translation. The theory of the crisis of language appears on the horizon of translation studies to (re)adapt music, painting, photography, film, sculpture and other arts to be harmonized with the metaphors of language. The connection of translation from disharmony to harmony creates acoustic and visual types of transduction. The downplay and overplay of the literary translator have changed the translator from an artist into artisan.

Peirce's argument was about giving possible meanings to the cryptic clues of linguistic signs. In Peirce's abstract doctrine of semiotics, the meaning of language is not about creating a circular element with a patterned orbit; language is spiraled around the interaction between formal and elliptical shapes,[2] in which the information is not a direct curve of constant information but like a point moving around a fixed center of reasoning giving the indirect information available at the time rather than the direct. In the logical telescope of the world of language, the approach of the translator is not one of perfect vision but an imperfect one in subjective quasi-semiosis. The vision of the world "could never be absolute, bounded, complete, or fixed by a single, logical perspective" (Emre 2020, 32). The process of logical semiosis in language is "man's fancy, framed in his own mind, according as he pleases" (Emre 2020, 32). Translation forces the translator to see his or her world in a cultural shift of perspective.

---

2 See Peirce's paragraphs CP: 1.249, 1.548, 4.367, 5.541, 5.543, 6.303, 5.582, 7.300, 7.303, 7.310, 7.475–7.483, 7.474–7.475.

James H. Bunn's "field" theory in his book *The Dimensionality of Signs, Tools, and Models* makes the revolutionary shift from the artist to the artisan looking through a semiotic telescope to see and even measure the dimensions of the linguistic text, (1981, 134–141). The translator's task is to interconnect Peirce's triadic category from the quasi-semiosis of translation enacting real semiosis for the time and place. The spiral curve of translation describes the circular meaning given to linguistic signs, but the imperfect telescope can be transformed into various extralinear variations leading the private curves of the translator's emotions away to the logical form of reasoning. Translation follows the relative and absolute motion of the source text but can be displaced by replacing the elliptical rotation of meaning from Saussure's fixed rule with the Peircean double parabole on the way to the definitive hyperbole.

The human activity of translation forms an empirical path to discover how the artisan may "filter" the organic force of nature not in the synonyms of translation, but in the series of invariants in parasynomyms (Sheriff 1984/1991, 41). The free narratives stand for Peirce's three interpretants, which multiply and transform sign-and-object into multiple reactions (called "interpretants"), giving the received sign its multiform meaning depending on time and place. Peirce's target interpretant replies to the source signs to interpret in the target language using several variants and invariants. The artisan provides the readers with a free variety of meanings equal to or different from other interpreters (Johansen 1993, 145–185).

Ellipsis rotates from the fixed circle of tunes to focus on the quasi-construction of variant tokens; ellipsis gives vagueness and indecision to the sign-receivers (Scheffler 1997, 51–54). In Eugene Nida's *Toward a Science of Translating* (1964), the *dynamic equivalence* of the circular translation can be changed into various shades of the ellipsis, which departs from the linear form into experimental movements of vocabulary and grammar. In literary translation, however, the *formal equivalence* of the sign cannot be measured without solving problems of circularity of the real meaning. The target speech must be equivalent to the source speech to provide the average interpretation of one fixed point of the ellipsis, but the whole meaning abandons the "closed" source text to stylize into the metaphorical applications of the "open" target sign in the translation (Nida 1964, 159–160, 223–225; Nida and Taber 1969/1982, 22–24). In logical reasoning, the geometrical spiral of the curves issues from the center of the ellipsis to express the transverse or opposite actions of the spiral, offering the straight or curved lines of scientific vocabulary and grammar. However, the omitted and shortened form of the ellipsis forms arbitrary points between the center and the axes of the literary translation, so that the ambiguous connections and contrasts with straight or curved lines are necessary tools for parabole and hyperbole.

Changed into the *informal* design of the arts, the ellipsis is not constructed as a solid and circular pattern of language-switching in strictly organizing variable word lengths, breadths and heights into strict synonyms. In the ellipsis, some information can be omitted from the original, but the "patterned omission" expresses the meaning (or meanings) by focusing on the formula of emotional and logical metaphors (Nida and Taber 1969/1982, 200; see Scheffler 1997, 85–88). The ellipsis can leave out long or short signs in order to associate the meaningful structure, construction, or shape in a different pattern, emulating the intercultural angles in order to create changing wavy cycles (Sheriff 1984/1991, 81; see 40). Translation has the effect of creating new "wave forms" (Bunn 2002) handled by the interpreter (sign-user; see Chapter 2). Nida's dynamic equivalence helps the translator to translate the formal communication of language into the "wavy" and "multi-dialectic" discourses of theater, dance, sculpture, painting, opera and other arts, thus changing the nature of source signs into cultural target signs (Nida and Taber 1969/1982, 128–133).

Ellipsis considers the ideally beautiful ideas and thoughts of artistic movements by applying the translator/artist's distorting stress with invariants in order to realize the meaning differently in the electrical circle. It seemed that "beauty" in fine arts

> […] cannot be described by a compass, and it changes direction at every point of its points. This is easily said but hard to learn: no algebra can determine which line, more or less elliptical, will mold the various parts into beauty. But the ancients knew it, and we find it in their human figures and even in their vessels. Just as there is nothing circular in the human body, so no profile of an ancient vessel describes a half circle. (Winkelmann qtd. in Arnheim 1971, 50; see Arnheim 1954)

The figure of artistic ellipsis involves following the usual circuit of cross-switching, but literary translation provides new extensions to the lyrical metaphor. Literary translation changes from a circle into complete overstatement and understatement and moves the translator into the opposite or reverse direction (Goodman 1976/1985, 82–83) to give a different cultural meaning. The metaphorical spirals of ellipsis, parabole and hyperbole illustrate the three-dimensional effects of transduction applied to the arts. These dimensions roll like brain waves across the semiotranslational translation subjects treated in this book.

Peirce regarded the elliptical, parabolic and hyperbolic waves as "weakened" signs, seen in semiotic terminology as not full but "degenerate" signs (CP: 6.303; Gorlée 1990, 2004, 110–112, 119, 133, 183, 229). The pragmatic system of the empirical action would possibly achieve the effect of the final symbol (thirdness), but the translator's prototype has the human effect of not projecting the real truth, instead stagnating into the relative sign-version of the translator's usual mind and behavior. The translator is characterized by the practical biases of secondness (index) and the imaginative picture of firstness (icon), but thirdness (symbol) is hardly attainable (Gorlée 2004, 137). Beyond the three-forked knowledge of Peirce's categories (firstness, secondness, thirdness), the meaning intended by the literary translator has the amplitude of personal intuition and human action that may possibly end in the final insight of the translator in constructing metaphors of "procreation." These metaphors generate "the expression of a similitude when the sign of predication is employed instead of the sign of likeness—as when we say this man *is* a fox instead of this man is like a fox [...]" (CP: 7.590, Peirce's emphasis). The activity of translation is still defined as the old category of the conservative force of the grammar and vocabulary, although translation has been restructured and reorganized into the translator's elliptical, parabolic and hyperbolic metaphors to interpret the logic of science into mediated signs of culture (Esposito 1980, 93–99).

The objectives of translation can "degenerate" the source signs to "regenerate" the vague feelings of infinite signs as new references. This weakening involves the translator's personal or local culture in stressing the technical and cultural details of the target text (see Nida and Taber 1969/1982, 120–162). The translator attempts to "regenerate" the uncertainty of the quasi-symbol existing in double replicas (Peirce 1976a, 248) to focus the translation. Although the replicas are not meaningful signs but directionless copies, they are single elements of quasi-semiosis involved in starting the process of genuine and definitive symbols to achieve the real sign-action in the process of semiosis (Peirce 1976a, 248; CP: 3.425–3.455; see Gorlée 2004, 66–67, 129–132, 148).

To reach the hypertranslation of literary translation, the ellipsoid form brings the uncertainty of Peirce's "weak" stress of oneness (ellipse) and twoness (parabola) to transform them into thirdness (hyperbola). In *The New Elements of Mathematics* (Peirce 1976a, written in 1902–1905), Peirce's triadic category moves from a "line" to a "surface" to generate a "solid" figure of transformation. Transferred to language, Peirce's *"degrees of freedom* [...] speak, as geometers usually do, of moving points, lines, and surfaces" (Peirce 1976a, 369), Peirce's emphasis). Peirce's science of Symbolic Logic (described in 1902, Peirce 4.372–4.392) was a subject not generally accepted by mathematicians in his time and was barely represented in the edited *Collected Papers* (CP) of Peirce's writings. However, it was included in *The New Elements of Mathematics* (1976a, vol. IV). Peirce's new logic opened up pure mathematics to logic and the pedagogy of mathematics, so that the formalism of calculus achieved a high *"degree of freedom* in the associative algebra of the moving points, lines, and surfaces," transforming Peirce's vision of categories (Peirce 1976a, 369, Peirce's emphasis). In Figure 1.1, Peirce's three graphical and algebraic figures cut the circle into the

> *ellipse* (of which a circle is a special variety), or a curve which reaches to infinity, but has only one branch, and seen in perspective appears to be an ellipse, called a *parabola*, or a curve consisting of two parts either the possible shadow of an ellipse, the two approximating closer and closer as one goes away to two intersecting rays [...] which curve is called a *hyperbola*. (Peirce 1976a, 380, Peirce's emphasis)

In Figure 1.2, Peirce's three curves are plane sections of an "endless series of more and more constricted" points, but in the third section, the hyperboloid,

> we see how if a ray be drawn in the plane of this section so as to cut the curve, and be then moved, the two points in which it cuts the curve may run together, and for an instant coalesce, and how in a moment the two points disappear [...]. (Peirce 1976a, 381)

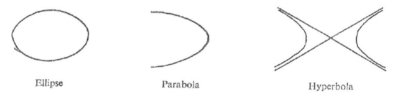

Figure 1.1 Ellipse, parabola, hyperbola. Source: (Peirce 1976a, 380, Figure 58).

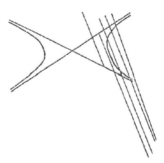

Figure 1.2 Hyperboloid. Source: (Peirce 1976a, 381, Figure 59).

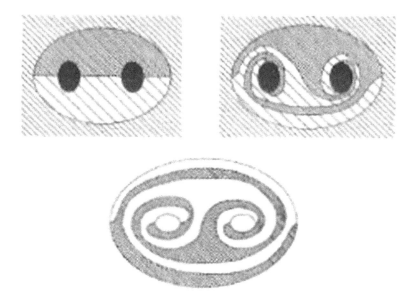

Figure 1.3 Boundaries. Source: (Peirce 1976a: 67).

The transductor distorts the ordinary translator's "free" or "authoritative" speech-habit into "scientific romances," as argued in the three examples in this book: Virginia Woolf's *The Waves* as *ellipsis*, Hector Berlioz' *The Trojans* as *parabole* and ending with Bertolt Brecht's *The Threepenny Opera* as *hyperbole*. This general principle underlies the three notions of literary translation in Peirce's "fragmentary" classification.

Peirce's three categories transform the vague and singular signs of linguistic categories into the pseudo-languages of "Qualities, Occurrences, and Meanings" (Peirce 1976a: 51). The artistic or fictive signs are musical tone, token and type,[3] the alternative signs of the fine arts. They were originally called "Quality, Relation, and Representation," but Peirce also called them "Flavor, Reaction, and Mediation" (Peirce 1976b, 18). These series convey essentially the same meaning as the general signs icon, index and symbol. Peirce's general categories are denominated oneness, twoness and thirdness, but now observed from the cultural level, we have the tone, token and type. The tone is the first possibility of pure feeling involved in a simple word (CP: 4.537, 8.363), the token embodies the dynamic statement of fact in real

---

3 See Peirce's CP: 3.360, 4.537, 8.363–8.364; MS 292:18-20; MS 339C: 499; MS 339D: 533–535.

sentences (CP: 3.360, 4.537, 8.363–8.364), while the type is the goal of meaningful final thought with logical connections (CP: 4.537, 8.363).

Peirce's terms tone, token and type classify how esthetics and ethics bear upon logic and mathematics. Tone, token and type are used for the arts, correlating mathematical science to the "Practical Sciences, or Arts" (Peirce 1976b, 19). The arts more definitely remake the general formula of Peirce's categories in terms of the peculiar "flavors" of arts (Peirce 1976b, 29–30). Peirce's three manifold varieties of the categories of firstness, secondness and thirdness (Gorlée 2012: 227–230) reach from the actual feeling and place of quasi-semiosis (firstness and secondness) to full intellectual semiosis (thirdness). In Peirce's semiotics, however, literary translation can play a game in the mind of the quasi-interpreter or quasi-translator (CP: 4.551). This game crosses from the emotional tone of language to the dynamic energy of the token to finally redouble the source text (type) into the target text.

Translation resolves (or solves) the problem of the vagueness of the categories in the "Practical Sciences, or Arts" by englobing linguistic units into the logical and emotional consistency of Peirce's "weak" linguistic signs: this results in Peirce's variety of habits-of-speech-in-arts (Gorlée 2016). Resolving the elements of prefixes, words and sentences from the source text into the practical and functional use of the target speech form is, in the first place, the syntactic activity that gives literal meaning to the nonliteral, even anomalous and eccentric, vocabulary and grammar of the source text to generate accordingly the semantic quasi-semiosis of the target text. The quasi-semiosis is just the relative truth changing the forms and shapes of translation into other (even unexpected) forms of artistic translation (Gorlée 2012: 132–135).

Abandoning the circular pattern of the translator's detachment from the source text, literary translation defines and expands the many-sided subjectivity of Wagner's poetic waves as they played into Woolf's elliptical underplaying and overplaying. Ellipsis transforms literary translation into a dramatic performance, "crystallizing" the target world into the ideas of the translator transformed into transductor. The art of translation involves the re-creation of the new cultural, aesthetic and spiritual textuality in order to remake, according to the transductor's mind, a new fixed "world" of the source text to express the world of the commentator (sign-receiver) rather than the real world of the original artist (Goodman 1976/1985, 88; Scheffler 1997, 194 fn. 6). The three patterns have the effect of creating a new drama that plays out in the target text (Jones 1989). During the activity of translation, the translatable object is reshaped into another language (dialect, speech or idiom), providing the original work with a different cultural (that is, spiritual and psychological) background, creating a new version from the original "world" (Scheffler 1997,163–209) and forming a new culture.

The ellipticity of Peirce's effort to ensure translatability displaces the basic untranslatability of Saussure's linguistic signs. The sign-receiver (translator, reader) is the first outside critic of the new message. His/her personal version is really invented and observed in the human interplay in the electromagnetic artifact to be a true messenger (or not) of transduction. The creative and inventive mind of the interpreter or translator seems to convey the symbolic idea from the target text to the interpretive choice of the source text (Sheriff 1984/1991, 80–81). The "weak" emotional and energetic interpretant of the translator's quasi-mind can interweave the degeneracies of the sign with a stronger narrativity to reach the continuous universe outside translation and thus to be processed in other arts or non-arts.

The process of Peirce's semiosis (Gorlée 2004, 66–67, 129–132, 148) shows how literary translation can abandon the weakened quasi-semiosis of secondness-and-firstness to achieve Saussure's intellectual attempt at real thirdness. For Peirce, the quasi-semiotic version gives translation into semiotic combinations of degenerate signs which unfortunately do not succeed in becoming the symbols of final thirdness. The anticipations and surprises of translation are reformulated in the quasi-translator's "Real Tendency" (CP: 8.361) to change and improve the "Actual Occurrence" of firstness (tone) and secondness (token). Peirce's "Beautiful and the Ugly, Right and Wrong, Truth and Falsity" (Peirce 1976b, 19) outlines the physical and emotional thrill of improving the cultural performance of this cultural form of translation which transfers the pre-established subcodes and code into the meaningful signs of literary beauty.

In my book *From Translation to Transduction: The Glassy Essence of Intersemiosis* (2015), I argued that the teaching of the American biologist and writer David Thoreau (1817–1862) committed a literary theft. During his solitary stay in the forest of *Walden*, he transcribed the natural scenery of Concord, Massachusetts, in the pages of his botanical research. He interweaved the action of man and woman, animals and plants with the mythology of Homer's story material to create new epics (Gorlée 2015, 139–171). Thoreau had a passion for the complex beauty of nature, but his walking paths into the woods near Walden Pond created living adventures in his mind. By decoding the creatures of nature into Homeric verses, the flock of birds, a wild lily, a lynx, a salmon, a Native American Indian and even a sunken boat were inventively transformed (that is, retranslated) by Thoreau backward into old episodes of the Greek original of the *Iliad* and the *Odyssey*. The evolutions of nature during the art of the four seasons of the year were intertextualized from botanical and agricultural experiments into archeological and even magical idioms of Homer's poems. Thoreau's forward retranslation into English served to alienate the elliptical variety of the landscape of Walden into the new poetic vision. Thoreau self-dramatized his book *Walden* into the transfiguration of real nature, thereby "transcribing" (in his own words) Homer's Greek poetry into the "modern tongue" of American civilization, including the past of the local Native Americans (Thoreau 1971, 103).

Another example in Gorlée (2015) illustrates how the Norwegian composer Edvard Grieg (1843–1907) crafted his musical path to "forward-translate" the Nordic folk life of Henrik Ibsen's play *Peer Gynt* into the instrumental and singing interpretation of Grieg's eponymous opera (Gorlée 2015, 171–201; see Gorlée 2016a). Grieg intertextualized the folk songs, folktales and witchcraft tales into different musical romances. Grieg's music refreshed Ibsen's poem, which had had no success with the audience at the National Theater of Oslo. Grieg reworded and rephrased Ibsen's high-level poetry into the folksy troll-world of Griegian music using arias and chorus to compose a "romantic" opera (or better, operetta) to please the audience.

In Gorlée (2015), I also explored the play of Spanish painter and sculptor Salvador Dalí (1904–1989), who desexualized his erotic desire into what can be called the striptease of male fear. Dalí self-translated the famous sculpture *Venus de Milo* from a beautiful statue into an asexual, even fetishistic, small-scale depiction of womanhood (Gorlée 2015, 201–230). His polemical translation into *Venus de Milo with Drawers* turned Venus into a pop-art figure, since Dalí adorned the front of the art-lady Venus with comical and unerotic boxes with pom-pom tufts of fur attached. This novelty (1923) created a chest of drawers to symbolize the polemical emotionality of Dalí's subterranean traumas. His homo- or hetero-erotic illusions became openly public. Venus' elegant body was adorned with furry decorations to the front, breasts, body and knee. Dalí used the rugged material to symbolize the plastic arts of feminine beauty as erotic indifference. Dalí's sculptural composition draws on the cultural codes of the experimental interfield or transfield to visualize his strange imagery of womanhood.

The "science fictional" futurology of literary translation shifted from retranslation and sped forward to self-translation. The free will of the translator's poetic mind engages in a cognitive and emotional evolution to ventilate linguistic or artistic signs of semiotranslation (Gorlée 1994, 2004, and elsewhere). The ways of knowing drive the translator into a "good" or "bad" form of translation. In itself, semiotranslation is a flat and meaningless activity without value, but it deconstructs the morphological rules of syntax to construct the performative semantics of music, dance or sculpture. The applied linguistics of literary translation transacts the constructive and deconstructive degrees of semiotranslation resulting in Peirce's values of fallibility and infallibility. Semiotranslation performs both "good" and "bad" translations, while transduction displays more than the literary, intracultural forms of "ordinary" translation, but stands for the theatrical, musical and sculptural gestures of seeing, hearing, tasting and feeling the artistic quality of the linguistic and non-linguistic codes of the song, story or scripture (Raffel 1971, 154–162; see Weiss 1961; Miller 2001).

Literary translation is having the imagination to envisage the reality and unreality of fiction. Fiction, based on experience and observation, changes the original source sign into the mental thoughts and judgment of the sign-receiver (translator). The quality of fiction creates a travesty of the source reality in the cultural target signs. The experimental senses of what the translation of reality into fiction may signify are explained in hypothetical experiments to build a "good" (or possibly "bad") texture of literary fiction. However, after dealing with the experimental premises of conservative translation, semiotranslation can unite the thousands of tongues of the Bible (Ps. 140:11; Acts 2:4; and other examples) in the spirit and mind of different cultures. Fiction exists to retell the culture of all countries in Raffel's "forked tongues" (1971, see Gorlée 2020a, 163–171).

We can conclude that the metaphor of the "forked tongues" puts fictive language to good use, but the double reading provides no truth. After weighing the substantial amount of evidence, fiction abandons the conservative activity of translation to improve the unconventional assemblage of words and sentences. The goal of fiction is to invent the poetic qualities of the literary art of meaning, sound and rhythm, as shall be discussed in Virginia Woolf's novel (Chapter 2). Since the danger is that the reality of making fiction is what easily gets lost in translation, fiction is characterized as being

> [...] as dubious as the idea [of arts] itself. A translation is an assemblage of words, and as such it can contain as much or as little poetry as any other such assemblage. The Japanese even have a word (*chōyaku*, roughly "hypertranslation") to designate a version that deliberately improves on the original. (Hays 2017, 58)

Hypertranslation is "not footnotes, is not definitions" (Raffel 1971, 115), but must be "read and evaluated and evaluated—with the inner ear, unaided by dictionaries, grammar, annotations, and scholarly disputes" (Raffel 1971, 115). Literary translation results in refreshing the valuable synonyms as the asymmetrical performance "full of twists and turns" (Hays 2017, 58). The target performance imitates the original vocabulary in the source text but stands out in a theatrical performance. Double lines of thought were the musicocentrist and logocentrist approaches of Hector Berlioz's operatic fiction (Chapter 3).

Semiotranslation focuses on the semiotic art of linguistic signs, but Peirce's philosophical-literary essays exposed dynamic arguments to stress new memories and opinions in the twentieth century. Peirce's triadic structure of linguistic terms transformed the syntactic speculation about translatability into the semantic cases of re- and self-translatability. Jakobson's contrastive concept of linguistic signs was reworked with Derrida's *différence* (or *différance*) of meanings. The contrastive features can deconstruct new ideas in speech and writing to create beauty. The shift from the deconstruction of literary signs with a new referent shows that the semiotic sign never constructs a parallel or neutral meaning, but it can play a game of difference. This game transforms confessional messages into a shared, democratic process of giving semiosic meaning (Derrida 1985, 93–161; on Derrida's deconstruction, see Norris and Benjamin 1988). For Jakobson, the Cubist freeplay of interpretative translation creates subversion of the common meaning of the sign, now clothed in the geometry of film, growing from short "shots" and "close-ups" to be remade into the "set-up" of the "montage" (Jakobson and Halle 1956/1975, 92). This results in the creation of an artificial code to bring poetic words (subcode) to the forefront, as seen in Bertolt Brecht's poetical-narrative transduction (Chapter 4).

The extralinguistic forms of meaning of the sign take part in the unending network of Peirce's quasi-semiosis to enjoy full semiosis. Jakobson and Derrida argued about the classical oppositions of words and sentences in translation, both of them using the unconventional referent to capture the equivalent (source) and opposite (target) circular forms in order to offer a dynamic interpretation. This shift in paradigm follows Peirce's *trompe l'oeil* concept of the interpretant, which works as a reversible sign giving different back-and-forth directions of intuition and reasoning. The interpretants synthesize the neural stimuli of narrative language articulating the multilingual process from source to target. Mimesis creates a new evolution in the translator's brain enabling the brain to react with free variables, thus making energetic and emotional invariables of language a real possibility. But the old, even biblical, shape, form and content of the sign in translation can be retranslated and reproduced in the story of transduction to demonstrate the intercultural and intersemiotic codification of modern fiction.

Jakobson's Concept of Poetry in Translation

The old anatomy of circular translation was rewritten by the literary scholar Roman Jakobson (b. Moscow, Russia, 1896, d. Cambridge, MA, 1982), who promoted a new spirit of literary communication in poetry. Jakobson started in Moscow as a Russian linguist but later emigrated to Prague (1920). In 1939, Jakobson was forced to leave his professorial chair at the University of Brno as a result of Nazi pressure due to his Jewish origins. After a number of temporary stays in Scandinavian countries, he arrived in the United States in 1941. Jakobson became a key figure in linguistics by broadening the surface grammar of language to include the abstract paraphrase of poetic literature. He energized the account of the diversity of languages to make literary translation an actual possibility for doing and theorizing for his contemporary readership. Dominated by the "poetic" analysis of multicultural languages, Jakobson remade Saussure's twofold meaning of linguistic signs to understand the transferal of linguistic signs into the dynamic intercultures of dialectology, folklore, painting and film. In the United States, Jakobson abandoned formalistic and conservative analysis and turned to the endeavor of breaking through in literary translation. In his revolutionary article "On linguistic aspects of translation" (1959/1966), Jakobson promoted the cross-disciplinary context of poetry-with-language combined with other domains of the arts to form a new art of literary translation.

Jakobson turned linguistics into a poetical craft applied in the art of translation. In Jakobson's early works, translation was the aesthetic project for transfiguring the poetic form. The irregular coherence of linguistic parts and elements is transferred by the fixed system of grammatical categories. In the United States, Jakobson transformed the linearity of language in Saussure's phonology to give space to his speculative grammar of Peirce's three types of translation. By extending one source sign into another target sign, Jakobson created the fruitful perspective of promoting literary verse anew thanks to the "poetic" temperament of the translator. From the classical iconography of "interpreting a verbal sign" through the syntax of linguistic or non-linguistic (or quasi-linguistic) signs, Jakobson proposed a triadic diagram in which:

1) Intralingual translation or *rewording* is an interpretation of verbal signs by means of other signs of the same language.
2) Interlingual translation or *translation proper* is an interpretation of verbal signs by means of some other language.
3) Intersemiotic translation or *transmutation* is an interpretation of verbal signs by means of signs of nonverbal sign systems.
   (Jakobson 1959, 233, reprinted in 1971, 266, Jakobson's emphasis)

Jakobson's categories of intralingual and interlingual translations were well-known classifications applied to the activity of translation and other forms of translation such as retranslation and self-translation. Intralingual translation is the linear action exemplified by the "rewording" of summaries and paraphrases taken from the same language (Gorlée 2020). The objective is to reinterpret and re-edit the flexible code-units of natural language with each other to make synonymous signs. The goal is to reach a close or clear equivalence between the subcodes of words and styles of one language. Interlingual translation according to Jakobson is the secondary action of building a bridge between two languages to cover the encoding and decoding activities of linguistic codes functioning in various languages. This results in quasi-synonyms or parasynonyms or even antisynonyms, which are not perfect synonyms, connecting source and target texts, but which express the multicultural opposition of elementary ambiguity between coded languages, dialects or idioms (Scheffler 1997, 25–49). Interlingual translation corresponds to the *proper* action of "traditional" translation, where the two codes stand for two different, independent expressions. For Jakobson, however, interlingual translation remained the ambiguous and unclear code system for transforming the source text into the target text.

Jakobson's third level, intersemiotic translation, offered new theoretical art forms to decode and encode the seemingly neutral or "formless" text-sign into art (Gorlée 1997, 240–244). The agreed codes can be analyzed by the translator, now in the role of artistic translator, or transductor, to make a cultural judgment of which target skills, crafts or arts should be integrated into creating meaningful codes or subcodes in arts. The translator is promoted from the role of strict translator to that of the free transductor, raising this aspect of linguistics to the status of other cultural experiences of what Jakobson called "poetic" arts. The language of poetry is a double articulation of language, different from ordinary speech but willfully used to adorn literary prose and verse. The "expressive, sorcerous, and mythopoeic tasks" of Jakobson's "poetics" (1979, 231) are characterized in the first place by parallelism in sound, verse and meaning to generate the "immediate" signification; but secondly by using figurative language removed from neutral synonyms to mediate literary language through meaningful metaphors and experiment with Jakobson's "mediate" way of giving creative signification. Literary verse is a game played by making precise, concise and condensed signs and parasigns (pitch, volume, pauses and intonations of speech) to color the literary genres of poems and songs. Poetic languages do not offer conceptual or functional information, as in the scientific, medical and legal signs of cognitive messages, but render a figurative and subjective, more fictional form to express the imaginative finesse of what Jakobson proposes as aesthetic diction of verse in patterned sound-meaning. Poetic verse provides readers with the contextual ambiguity of romantic poetry that characterizes the new term "hypertranslation."

The poetic verse of hypertranslation subdivides the classical tripartition of lyrical, dramatic and epic literature into poetry, drama and narratives. Poetry is the hypertone effect of the emotions of the writer translated into the sensuous expression of sound and rhythm. The lyrical effect for the translator lends new imagery to words and structure. While poetry stands for the emotional images of poems, ballads and personal diaries reflecting the dreams of the writer, drama is the dialogue of communicative interaction transpiring in time and space between two or more voices: the original author and the half-professional and half-personal roles "played" by the literary translator. The dramatic mode is the translator's token of experience, effort and struggle found in the genres of theater, opera and other music dramas. The story of the epic type is the narrativity transpiring in many working forms, combining theatrical drama with the causal and chronological definition to lend the romantic images a specific cultural context. Intertwining plots and episodes within rational and picaresque stories, the impressionistic novels can be detective stories, love stories, science fiction or any other genre of ideas and thought. Most literary genres are intertwined in form and content to encode a new cultural clue to surprise the readers. For example, myths, hymn tunes, ritual formulas and religious novels illuminate each of the three poetic compositions of human cultures, but each genre gives cultural rules a context of love, romance or even crime.

Hypertranslation was proposed by Jakobson (1956/1971) as a third type of translation that transforms an object into the same object but with a poetic quality. He gave literary poetry the intercultural signs beyond language to deal with personal and collective forms of artistic culture. Intersemiotic translation was defined as "transmutation," meant to develop, for example, poetic signs into musical verse to play a role in the theatrical performance of concerts, church, opera, church hymns and oratorios. Jakobson had an early interest in music combined with poetry. In his early article "Musikwissenschaft und Linguistik," written in Prague and published in 1932 (reprinted in *Selected Writings II: Word and Language*, 1971a, 551–553), vocal tones are for him not part of the "natural" environment but serve as technical signals of verse-tones to be performed as linear signs of chromatic sounds. The target chromatic sounds are rearranged in the target musical performance to read the metamorphosis from source to target.

For Jakobson, the positive effect of musical signs lay not so much in the technical change in the linguistic signs but in the audience's judgment of the active performance of the sung and played musical signs, that is to say in the audience's literary criticism of the hypertranslation. Jakobson compared the situation of translating musical into linguistic signs to propose how the cultural (that is, linguistic and musical) elements of words, phrases, clauses and sentences form the narrative genre of drama (Chambers 1984, 28). Jakobson's concept of pancultural strategy followed Saussure's analytic system of phonology to analyze the vocal sounds in music as "poetic" signs in language. Jakobson was aware of the sound patterns of language in musical signs, as in the two lines of music and text of opera, but the fluctuation of three sound waves was rephrased into Jakobson's general categories of tone, tonality and tonicity of musical sign. For him, Peirce's triad was evocative of the rhythmic, harmonic and dynamic process of singing and reciting to achieve the lyrical singing of musical fragments (Pike 1948; Ostwald 1973, 162–165).

Jakobson's interest in musical drama had a long history. His early personal history is one of political emigration. He wrote "What is poetry?" in 1933–1934 to deliver as a lecture in Prague, and then he continued the debate about music with the lecture "The dominant" (written in 1935, both articles reprinted in Jakobson 1981, 740–750 and 751–756). In his articles, he discusses the specific trait of his specialty of "poetics" in terms of having discovered the sound and meaning of linguistic and non-linguistic (that is, mainly musical) poetry. The "dominant" quality of poetic works is not the simplicity of the syllabic scheme of words, nor the rhyme of "ordinary" language, but in Jakobson's view, music in theater is inspired by a vision of poetry which is complexified into the aesthetic role and ethical function of meaningful signs. It creates in words, sentences and verses the emotional integrity of psychological emotions to appeal to the fashion of the twentieth century.

The personal emotions of the readers (hearers, translators, dramaturgs, singers and so forth) were Jakobson's personal addition to reformulate the "technical" sign of music-with-poetry. As the readers listen to the narrative and dramatic poetry, an emotional reaction is embodied in them in response to lyrical poems. The *Princeton Encyclopedia of Poetry and Poetics* defines the melodic expression of poetry in dramatic and epic poetry as the "brevity, metrical coherence, subjectivity" of the linguistic and musical signs, combined with the "passion, sensuality, and particularity of image" (Preminger 1965/1974, 46). Hypertranslation consists in the poet interacting lyrical words with music. This interaction of music with lyrical texts expands the lyrical text itself, displacing, altering and redeveloping it through the fashion of past ages, but the lyrical use of music has merged the two levels into one, as characteristic of the general processuality of transduction.

Particularly as illustrated in the troubled times of 1930s European politics, standard language can be displaced into various emotional lyrical genres to give rise to what Jakobson called "transitional genres" in his article "The dominant" (1935/1981: 755). The artistic form of political meanings can illustrate how the "*arrythmia*" of free verse can transform itself into the lyrical trend of modern ideological poetry in prose or verse (1935/1981, 751, Jakobson's emphasis). By mentioning the reasonable and sensible "transitional genres," Jakobson impregnated the contemporary process of literature with his new version in his article "Linguistics and poetics" (1949/1981, 751–756; 1981, 18–51; 1987, 61–94).

In 1949, Jakobson brought literary poetics together with the pancultural (and pansemiotic) process of uniting different arts into one whole process. He wrote:

> Arguments against such a claim must be thoroughly discussed. It is evident that many devices studied by poetics are not confined to verbal art. We can refer to the possibility of transposing *Wuthering Heights* into a motion picture, medieval legends into frescoes and miniatures, or *L'après-midi d'une faune* into music, ballet, and graphic art. However ludicrous may appear the idea of the *Iliad* and *Odyssey* in comics, certain structural features of their plot are preserved despite the disappearance of their verbal shape. The question whether Blake's illustrations to the *Divina Commedia* are or are not adequate is a proof that different arts are comparable. (Jakobson 1949/1981, 19; 1987, 63; Jakobson's emphasis)

Jakobson's explosive essay "On linguistic aspects of translation" (1959/1966) was a *coup d'état*, ready to overthrow the dynamic equivalence of mere sounds in poetry and literature to create real modern drama.

With his "transitional genres," Jakobson had at this point abandoned the static rules of Saussure's synchronic language (1959/1966, 81–100, 101–139) to build a contemporary base for literary poetics. It seemed at this politicized point in time (from 1950 to1960), after the horrors of World War II, that Jakobson's revolution in overturning diachronic linguistics (Saussure 1959/1966, 140–190) extended the consequence of linguistic signs, introducing the three types of translation—mainly the third type, the pancultural entrance of intersemiotic translation or *transmutation* (Jakobson 1959/1966, 233; Jakobson's emphasis). Jakobson actively sought to closely connect linguistic signs with non-linguistic vocalic signs in painting, music, theater and opera. He investigated the new category of artistic translation to actively promote the hypertranslation of the Cubist arts. Cubism divided reality into "cubes," or unstable fractures, juxtaposing fragments of the model with the geometry of colors, shapes and ideas. By transforming sentences and phrases into metaphors, Jakobson paid homage to Pablo Picasso's early fragments of visual representation, which transformed reality into fictional cubes or planes (Perl 2021). Now Jakobson re-imagined linguistic and vocal prose poems in a particularly poignant style to offer his new version of "poetics," lending a violent elegance to the incongruous combination of the linguistic word or sentence with the unexpected images of poetical language.

The general course Jakobson set in his linguistics was grounded on his early studies in Russia, where Ferdinand de Saussure's *Course in General Linguistics* (1959/1966, originally published in French in 1949) was the source of popular methodology for advancing a dyadic structure of linguistic signs (Sangster

1982, 3–7). Saussure advanced the formal phonetics of the (acoustic–visual) image (*signifier*) and concept (*signified*), uniting them to compose the concrete identity of the linguistic sign. Saussure's image and concept are "not abstractions but real objects; signs and their relations are what linguistics studies; they are the *concrete entities* of our science," so Saussure's visual principle made clear that

> [t]he linguistic entity exists only through the associating of the signifier with the signified [...]. Whenever only one element is retained, the entity vanishes; instead of a concrete object, we are faced with a mere abstraction. We constantly risk grasping only a part of the entity and thinking that we are embracing it in its totality; this would happen, for example, if we divided the spoken chain into syllables, for the syllable has no value except in phonology. A succession of sounds is linguistic only if it supports an idea. (Saussure 1959/1966, 102–103)

The image of the word is the sound-form of the *signifier*, but the idea of the word is the concept (*signified*). The *signified* can be

> considered independently, [so that] concepts like "house," "white," "see" etc. belong to psychology. They become linguistic entities only when associated with sound-images; in language, a concept is a quality of its phonic substance just as a particular slice of sound is a quality of the concept. (Saussure 1959/1966, 103)

Since the discipline of psychology was considered outside of the rationality of science studies in Saussure's time, psychology was pushed back into the "emotional" departments of religion, hypnosis, telepathy and spiritualism, which were popular at that time, to create the *signifier* with the *signified*. At the time of Sigmund Freud's attempts to decrypt the new science in *The Interpretation of Dreams* and *Psychopathology of Everyday Life* (published in German c. 1900), psychology (including Freud's psychoanalysis) was still regarded by many scholars as the spiritual dialogue of bad logic, generally looked upon as being far removed from science. The defective observation of the patient guided the psychoanalyst into a form of psychoanalysis, and even occultism. Psychology was seen as a vague and unconscious drive to discharge and channel the patient's instinctual repression, which is far removed from what Saussure, as a rational thinker in his research of the work-tool of linguistics, hoped to formalize in his mechanical representation of language in the scientific tradition. Since Freud's conception of psychoanalysis was continually revised, modified and expanded from 1900 to the 1930s. However, the "skeptics" were unwilling to forge a new paraculture that devoted attention to translating signs of pathology, exotism, morality and gender, only acknowledging Freud's psychoanalysis for treating the dark human psyche (Hall 1954/1982, 116–122) as a New Age science (Hess 1993).

Saussurean human intercourse was based on the static rules of linguistics, meaning the correct organization of the synchronic determination of signifier and signified (1959/1966, 101–139). Saussure used French examples without integrating the significant confusion of meaning into the diachronic reality of the activity of other languages (1959/1966, 140–190). For Saussure, translation signified reaching the intercultural and psychological diversity of Babylon's forked tongues, at least for those "nations that have reached a certain stage of civilization" (Saussure 1959/1966, 196). From the mythological legend of Babylon, Saussure derived the opinion that science today follows the geometrical chaos of including many official languages; he accepted local dialects but did not follow this subject further; perhaps they were not "civilized" enough? Translational scholars could discuss the causes, complications and breadth of the geographical diversity of languages and dialects (Saussure 1959/1966, 191–212), but it seemed that, in Saussure's method, some languages can have a common origin and possess some evidence of change to be researched in the similarities of their sound patterns. For Saussure, real translation remained in the static method of linguistics as a paradoxical activity.

Saussure compared the fixed entity of language with the chemical compound of water (1959/1966, 103); he separated the waves of dialects from the "ordinary" flood of language. Saussure set himself the task of describing the phonological characteristics of linguistic waves, yet in chemistry, water is made up of a compound consisting of the elements hydrogen and oxygen, so waves are composed of dihydrogen oxide compounds held together by electrostatic force. For Saussure, the "chemistry" of linguistic waves gives rise to "the indefinite plane of jumbled ideas" and the "vague plane of sounds" (Saussure 1959/1966, 112). Saussure transformed the understanding of the sound system away from a concept of official language into one of observing the "innovating waves" of the "undulating flood" of dialects and other speech idioms (1959/1966, 206; see 202–205).

Saussure read Johannes Schmidt's *Die Verwandtschaftsverhältnisse der indogermanischen Sprachen* (1872, Saussure 1959/1966, 209–211). After reading Schmidt's new wave theory, Saussure agreed that there was a continuity of social, historical and political waves in different speech forms, but he disagreed with the idea proposed by the migratory theory that negative discontinuity transformed modifications into language and dialects. Saussure held the principle that language has a basic solidarity of continuity and isolation, while subdialects form a "distinct branch, detached from the trunk"

(1959/1966, 211). Saussure's vision of the tree of languages was one in which language started to strictly order words in the field of grammatical rules, while dialects and idioms were considered marginal forms of brain waves.

The brainstorming wave theory is further discussed in the next chapter in the context of the experimental fiction of Virginia Woolf. Modern culture increased the dialectal tension between Saussurean rules and structural or formal translation, integrating other metalanguages, such as Jakobson's dialects of poetry and music. These foreign interactions were for Saussure a logical impossibility; his future was formal linguistics or mathematical logic. From a fresh angle, Jakobson gave translation an open texture, integrating the linguistic game of performative arts into the aesthetic, or even mythical, movement of transduction, as in gestures, dance and music. However, transduction plays freely with all signifiers, exploiting sound patterns and rhythmic codes and making Jakobson's method a poetical form of language. This revolutionary movement was followed by Virginia Woolf, who wrote her fiction with the same "dialectal" practice of rhythm and speech in her "wavy" forms of literature (Bunn 2002). After Woolf's death (1941), modernist literature reacted strongly to the "chemical" analysis of linguistic units to englobe the interdisciplinary fields of information theory or communication theory (Cherry 1957/1966). Research into the technology of vocal sound in its creation of meaning in language branched out into new directions, examining the alternative meanings of language (Jakobson 1961/1971a).

While Jakobson lived in the United States, his inspiration shifted away from Saussure's emphasis on vocal strategy in the direction of his own concept of poetical language. Jakobson disconnected poetical language from the formality of phonetic understanding to highlight the free beauty of poetical language. Against the background of Saussure's formal correspondence of signifier and signified, Jakobson interrelated literature with linguistics to balance the revolutionary signified in the thought and feeling of the sign-maker (agent). In order to reconcile the distinct branches of signifier and signified with variant shades of reading of one sign, Jakobson englobed the poeticized (that is, ethical and aesthetical) content of language as closely connected to fine arts. Jakobson's poetic language elevated Saussure's dyadic method into metaphor and metonymy (Shipley 1968/1972, 268–269, 271), thereby dealing partly with the metrical parallelism of rhyme and the phonic equivalence of words and sentences (Jakobson and Halle 1956/1971, 69–96). Saussure's signifiers were now viewed as insufficient to structure phonic elements in an understanding of linguistics.

After Jakobson's exile to the United States, when he read Peirce's fragmentary essays, edited and published by Harvard University Press (1931–1966), he positioned the narrative thought of literature, mainly verse, as a "wavy" variation on Saussure's signifier to be transformed into the sensory, emotional, but abstract signifieds of Peirce's interpretant-sign. By disregarding the semiotic methodology of Saussure's semiology to touch on some aspects of Peirce's semiotics, Jakobson regenerated Saussure's double sign composed of signifier and signified in Peirce's triadic system, which deals with the semiosis of language in terms of the categories of firstness, secondness and thirdness to give many invariants of meaning. The triadic structure of signs compliments the firstness of the mere sign (word) with the secondness of the object (sentence) to add (contrary to Saussure) the thirdness of Peirce's interpretant. Attempting to include the interpretant, which is a sign itself in the interpretant-sign, Jakobson perceived the sign with richer meanings. Jakobson's typology of signs utilized Peirce's dynamic vision of language to dramatize the role of the aesthetic and ethic functions of the sign, and he explained the meanings of literature differently. Although the development of the dyadic into the triadic notions for seeing the world gave Jakobson a wider insight, his lack of comprehension of Peirce's complex methodology caused him to make some errors in judging rhetorical inversions.

Jakobson's first mention of writing about Peirce was in his plenary lecture at the Conference of Anthropologists and Linguistics at Indiana University in Bloomington, Indiana (1952). He wrote:

> In the impending task of analyzing and comparing the various semiotic systems, we must remember not only the slogan of F. de Saussure that linguistics is part of the science of signs, but, first and foremost, the life-work of his no less eminent contemporary, and one of the greatest pioneers of structural linguistic analysis, Charles Sanders Peirce. Peirce not only stated the need for a semiotic but drafted, moreover, its basic lines. His fundamental ideas and devices in the theory of symbols, and particularly of linguistic symbols, when carefully studied, will be of substantial support for the investigation of language in its relation to other systems of signs. (Jakobson 1971a, 555–556)

Jakobson attempted to convert Saussure's informative system into Peirce's communicative interaction between agent and receiver to give various functions of meaning to poetic style. Jakobson's contribution resulted in the creation of a form of bilingualism and code-switching from linguistic signs to non-linguistic signs. Jakobson's new concept of sign requires not only the "two participants of the given speech event" but moreover an "interpretant" (1971a, 565) from the sign-receiver (reader, audience). However, he pointed out that the interpretant can be "performed by another sign or set of signs that occur together with the given sign, or might occur instead" (1971a,

565–566). Peirce's interpretant was not really defined, but in the lecture of 1952, Jakobson stressed the fact that "all these cases [in which] we substitute signs" must, in the case of literary translation, relate the "sign and thing" to the interlingual, intralingual and intersemiotic interpretants (1971a, 566; see 1959, 233).

In a brief remark (1952), Jakobson acknowledged "Charles S. Peirce, the founder of modern semiotics" (1971, 463 fn. 12). But in 1954, Jakobson seemed to return to the fact that language has two logical aspects of Saussure's *Cours*. He wrote:

> The addressee perceives that the given utterance is a *combination* of constituent parts (sentences, words, phonemes, etc.) *selected* from the repository of all possible constituent parts (the code). The constituents of a context are in a state of *contiguity*, while in a substitution set signs are linked by various degrees of *similarity* which fluctuate between the equivalence of synonyms and the common core of antonyms. (Jakobson 1971, 243–244; 1987, 99; Jakobson's emphasis)

Jakobson attempted to compare Saussure to Peirce. In the article of 1959 "On linguistic aspects of translation," Jakobson explicitly stated, "For us, both as linguists and as ordinary word-users, the meaning of any linguistic sign is its translation into some further, alternative sign, in which it is more fully developed," contrary to what Peirce, the deepest inquirer into the essence of signs, insistently stated (Jakobson 1959, 232–233, reprinted in 1971, 260). Jakobson did not cite Peirce himself, but an article written by Peirce's ex-student, John Dewey (1946).

However, in 1971, Jakobson reconciled Saussure's dyadic operation with Peirce's triadic device, mixing the two. For Jakobson, these "two operations" seem to

> […] provide each linguistic sign with two sets of *interpretants* [… and] utilize the effective concept introduced by Charles Sanders Peirce: there are two references which serve to interpret the sign—one to the code, and the other to the context, whether coded or free, and in each of these ways the sign is related to another set of linguistic signs, through an *alternation* in the former case and through an *alignment* in the latter. A given significative unit may be replaced by other, more explicit signs of the same code, whereby its general meaning is revealed, while its contextual meaning is revealed, while its contextual meaning is determined by its connection with other signs within the same sequence. (1971, 244; 1987, 99–100; Jakobson's emphasis)

Jakobsen had chosen Peirce's controversial "interpretant" in his plenary lecture at the First International Congress of Semiotics (1974). In "A glance at the development of semiotics" (reprinted in 1987, 436–454), Jakobson explained how the dialogue of signifier and signified in Saussure's sign concept was solved (meaning deciphered) by the triadic effect of Peirce's interpretants (1987, 443–444). This means that in translation, the interpretant does not stand for the signified but for the code of the received sign. This code does not have one meaning, as it seems in Saussure's vision, but stands for the Peircean context of interactive meanings. This form of meaning is not just drawing a circle but extends into the various shapes of ellipsis, hyperbole and parabole. Jakobson thereby liberated the sign from Saussure's fixed codes of grammar to reveal the dynamic codes of Peirce's three interpretants.

Charles Morris, a follower of Peirce's doctrine of semiotic signs, gave Peirce's emotional, energetic and logical interpretant-signs (also called immediate, dynamical and final interpretants) the label of "reactor signs," produced by examining the behavioral trend of the received source sign to respond with the target sign (Rossi-Landi 1992, 111–129). The task of the new interpreter (agent, reader, speaker, translator) is to redefine the meaning of the sign into the notion of Peirce's interpretant. The stimulus of the interpretant has no close synonyms to the original, but the extensional equivalences of creative metaphors generate a new emotional and energetic interpretation. If the interpreter understands the sign and the object, this knowledge activates the interpreter's power to mediate the ideas, opinion and judgment into the immediate and dynamical interpretants of the translation, but the final or logical interpretant of the translation is almost an illusion.

The interpretants interrelate with three interactive codes of reasoning, moving from illogical to logical categories. The "inner" code (emotional, energetic and logical interpretants) indicates the psychological efforts of the interpreter or translator of the agent's sign. Peirce's emotional interpretant is a muscular or quasi-mental effort in the energetic interpretant acting as a habit change or modification in the interpreter's tendencies to act in response to the mental action in the logical interpretant. The three categories embody in the translation the meaning of the target text. The "outer" code (immediate, dynamical and final interpretants) shows the successive stages in the interpretive process of translation. The first effect is produced by the received sign upon the interpreter or translator, which is the immediate interpretant; now the effect is direct and unanalyzed and calculated to produce upon the translator's mind the dynamical interpretant. The total effect that is produced by a sign at a virtual level is Peirce's final interpretant.

All these distinctions show unmistakably the very complex character of Peirce's interpretant, which is defined as the quasi-semiosis of linguistic words and sentences to embrace the logical evolution into semiosis. Peirce's continuity interacted with the three-way codes decoding the code rules in order to alter one language into another, but in the great majority of cases, the translation does not reach the translator's final interpretant. The maximally efficient or practical message achieves the lexical action, perhaps becoming the final interpretant, but often without reaching the ultimate goal. "Incomplete" translation Jakobson calls restricted "transcription," which is both the analyzed and unanalyzed replacement of the elements of the source language (in this case, Jakobson's native Russian) provided with unambiguous varieties of cultural meanings (in English) or *vice versa* (Jakobson and Waugh 1979, 27–28).

By discovering and exploring Peirce's interpretant, Jakobson's "poetics" of literary translation changed Saussure's extreme formality of phonetic spelling into the creative invariants of "poetic" differences to suit the rhetorical codes of poetry (Gorlée 2008a). The Jakobson–Peircean model combined with the categories of poetic signs ascribed to the transparency of literary (that is, quasi-semiosic) thought-signs consists of the combinations of firstness and secondness with thirdness. The Jakobsonian model pushes forward from Peirce's cultural tone, token and type to the equivalence of Jakobson's categories of sign types to end in Peirce's name, proposition and logic (Peirce 1976b, 21–24; CP: 4.538). The combined model of the code-channels (fragmented in Cubism's cubes and planes) gives the poetical semiosis from Peirce to Jakobson through Saussure, as illustrated in Figure 1.4.

The shared project was to embed the cultural analysis of linguistic units with Peirce's interactive categories, starting from firstness (icon, tone), moving to secondness (index, token) and advancing to final thirdness (symbol, type). Jakobson pursued the background of the artistic acts in the foreground of the poetical grounds of literature, theater and opera to make possible the dramatic processes of hypertranslation. Jakobson's ideas of emotive and expressive functions (addresser) refer to the metalingual, conative and appellative values (addressee) as the dominant cultural codes applied to making (or remaking) his linguistic and vocal methods of "poetics." The codes and subcodes are

tone	↔	addresser emotive	↔	channel referential	↔	context phatic	↔	(sub)code metalingual	↔	name
↕		↕		↕		↕		↕		↕
token	↔	message poetic	↔	context referential	↔	(sub)code metalingual	↔	channel phatic	↔	proposition
↕		↕		↕		↕		↕		↕
type	↔	addressee conative	↔	(sub)code metalingual	↔	channel phatic	↔	context referential	↔	logic

Figure 1.4 Poetical semiosis from Peirce to Jakobson through Saussure. Source: (modif. from Gorlée 2008a: 359).

present in the arts of vocal technique and interaction on stage to decipher the cultural stories of the novel, opera and other theatrical performance.

Firstness (icon, tone) becomes central in the poetic modalities of the personal mood of the interpreter (writer) in telling the narrated myth to the reader or listener, while secondness (index, token) is the ornamental device to create a functional, but radical, element for the novel, theater play or opera in telling the dramatic reality of fiction. Firstness and secondness are the basic frameworks of Jakobson's works. Firstness and secondness could possibly relapse into the "logical" pseudo-effect of arts in Peirce's intellectual thirdness, but the argumentative development of musical or operative translationese does not offer a dramatic translation into the logical ideas of other arts (Gorlée 1997, 244–248).

Jakobson generalized Peirce's natural languages in the terminology and vocabulary of his semiotic background, Saussurean poetical language. In his explanations of Peirce's works, he used speech sounds as a communicative bridge between the formality of phonetic understanding and the meaning. Opening his visionary mind to Peirce's terminology, Jakobson's freeplay of poetic signs can ground literary hypertranslation to create the same contexts in the figures of speech of other "sign languages" (Jakobson and Waugh 1979). Jakobson seemed to decode Peirce's patterns of speech to heighten the sense of the linguistic words and sentences in special rhymes, puns, wordplay, grammatical slips and all kinds of intertextual linkages, quotations and other cross-fertilizations that invite the radical transformation of the text into more than literary, poetic hypertranslations.

From Translation to Transduction

After the multilingual confusion of Babel, the world of languages, dialects and idioms regarded signs as vital systems with "organized sounds" (Raffel 1971, 154). These special "sounds" range from what Sebeok called linguistic writing and non-linguistic speech to the style of narrative conversation. Literary or artistic translation is mentioned in Raffel's later book *The Art of Translation Poetry* (1988). He looked upon syntax and semantics not in themselves, but as artistic forms of the target language (Raffel's native language). For Raffel, the translator has a vital role that is full of constraints, since translators are by nature specialists but also academics:

> Their training, their life's work as scholars, and their work as teachers all tend to reinforce specialization. But translation is by its very nature an interdisciplinary subject, whether one is practicing, theorizing about, or evaluating it. […] the translator is (or should be) a literary person in

the old-fashioned sense. The translator of poetry *must* be himself a poet, and the translator of literary prose is best able to do his job properly if he is himself a writer of literary (as opposed to scholarly or critical) prose. But the translator must also be something of a scholar. He must know more than simply the language with which he works. He must be aware of literary and cultural history both in that language and his own language. [...] He should also think about the act of translation, both practically and from some theoretical point of view. (Raffel 1988: vii–viii. Raffel's emphasis)

Jakobson's lifelong work focused on the transfer of ambiguous meanings into contemporary poetry and verse, pointing to a different path in a new paraculture (Gorlée 1997, 244–248). Poetry is a channel of wave crests moving with a different velocity than ordinary words. The translator's poetic task is to hypertranslate into artistic language. The literary translator needs to transcend the linguistic forms of standard language to embrace the pseudolanguage of linguistic and non-linguistic means in the special variations of Jakobson's poetic sense of translation, thus remaking the translator's cultural (that is, intuitively and ritually marked) choices of artistic quasi-speech to similarly mark the target text. The gestures of human speech, such as laughing, whistling, talking, singing and other pseudo-literary activities (Ostwald 1973; Attili 1977/1985) can equally articulate poetic speech in dance, music, painting and sculpture as the play of human senses (Sebeok 1974/1977/1985, 297; see 1976a, 1976b). But the artistic forms of the source text require an inventive knowledge of cultural and aesthetic signs to idealize new meanings outside ordinary language in a novel form.

The poetic laboratory of literary translation was envisioned in theory and practice by Jakobson to foreground his poetic field of specialization. This is also referred to in different words and terminology in James Holmes's work on poetic translation. Holmes mentions the acoustic and rhythmic tones of Jakobson's stylized poem in making his own recreative metapoem (Holmes 1988, 35–44). In Holmes' edited book *The Nature of Translation* (1970), he highlights the poetic play of translation theoreticians of Eastern Europe. Anton Popoviç's works further articulate this new direction in translation criticism (1975, see Holmes 1970, 78–87). Holmes experimented with the knowledge of literary translation in his own "laboratory" of research and experiments with metapoems (Weissbort 1989).

In Western Europe, George Steiner's *After Babel* (1967/1985, 414–470) anticipated the innovation of literary translation by extending linguistic signs into cultural, even musical, restatements, further inspiring Jakobson's work in its transferal to other arts. In his later work, Steiner (1990) narrated how Homer's spirit was "mirrored" in the prophetic illumination of Virgil's work, one of the poetic examples used in this book. In South America, the Brazilian linguist and semiotician Julio Plaza published the article "Reflection of and on theories of translation" (1981) followed by his PhD dissertation *Sobre traduçâo inter-semiótica* at the Catholic University of ã Paulo (1985, published in 1987) to set the first tone of translation's transition into transduction.

Claus Clüver's article "On Intersemiotic Translation" (1989) introduced the modern *ekphrasis* of playing the artistic game with sounds and letters in quasi-literature. Clüver engaged with the concrete poetry of the Brazilian poets Haroldo and Augusto de Campos and Décio Pignatari to create labyrinthine paths and casual associations in various arts. Clüver's interarts studies (2009) enabled him, as an artisan, to reconstruct through human memory the interarts studies of literary, musical and electronic compositions (see Glaser 2009) as poetry. Umberto Eco offered a variety of divisions with radical and dramatic relevance to negotiate the semi-meaning not between words but between general cultures. Eco captured these wave forms in *Experiences in Translation* (2000) and *Mouse or Rat* (2003). Jakobson's interlingual, intralingual and intersemiotic theory tell the wave story of the activities of rewording, amplifying, paraphrasing, condensing, parodying and commenting on the visual varieties of self-translation.

Not only may translation literally exemplify the exchange of ordinary linguistics units, but it also provides metaphoric expressions for the accepted codes of semiotranslation with foreign, even radical, meanings. The transferal of material between media can falsify the technical reading into a misreading, offering the phonetic, historical, social and dialectal transcription of the activity of retranslation and self-translation. But the translator can willingly play the "free" game of transductor to re-echo the cultural resonances of translation and give a new semiotic metalanguage to translation (Rey-Debove 1986; for the prefix *meta-*, see Hubig 1986). Metalanguage signifies concentration on the poetic, musical, sculptural or other artistic modification of translation in recreating the target metamessage from the original source message. This metamessage is a musical, choreographical, architectural or other poeticized design, freely borrowed from the multimedia labyrinth of science-with-art. Metalanguage describes the curiosity, policy and experience of the translator's quasi-mind as it enters into a different retelling of the old story. Literary translators can transform from being artists into artisans to produce the "transduction" of double or triple meaning, as argued in Jakobson's concept of poetry.

Transduction stands for the broad movement of the historical vanguardism of the arts in influencing the artists and developing the radical terminology of the continuity of translation in other forms of translation. Transduction processes structural vocabulary into other arts. While semiotics is about the mimesis of all semiotic signs of all kinds, Erich Auerbach's literary criticism provides vital insights in *Mimesis: The Representation of Reality in Western Literature* (1953/1957). Auerbach offers a comprehensive portrayal of real authors in transforming signs of literary art into a mimetic guide to the "representation of reality." Auerbach produced his criticism of literary signs, re-forming them into working metasigns. These metasigns work from the fabric of Homer and Virgil to Schiller to shape Auerbach's double vision of the literary criticism of language and rhetoric in *Mimesis*.

In literary translation, the two kinds of language show how the interaction between two languages can generate new metasigns, which are part of any coded language but signify an artistic shift in variations offering total metamorphosis into some other form of signs outside of standard language. Morris, a disciple of Peirce, wrote that:

> [...] in this usage the terms do not refer to two kinds of language but to a relation between two languages in a given investigation. So if we talked about French in English, French would be the object language and English the metalanguage. Now the distinction itself, as often interpreted, has certain defects. The first of these, the restriction to language, can easily be avoided by recognizing that there may be *metasigns* (signs-about-signs) which denote *object signs* which are not language signs. [...] the second defect is more serious, and springs not from the distinction itself but from the almost universal neglect of the great varieties of types of discourse: it is uncritically assumed that a metalanguage is either scientific discourse or logico-mathematical discourse. A metalanguage, however, might be of any type of discourse and its object language of any type of discourse: there can be poetic discourse about poetic discourse, scientific discourse about poetic discourse, legal discourse about poetic discourse, logico-mathematical discourse about scientific discourse, and so on. (1946, 179–180, reprinted in 1971, 256–257, Morris's emphasis).

Morris viewed translation firstly as a wide wave of syntactic and semantic facts that form the sign-family of metascience (1946, 20–21, 251 fn. J; 1971, 96, 108 fn. J). The second metalanguage is the metamessage in a further art designed to deconstruct the flexible metasigns. The translation shortens the order into the disorder of the translator's meta-vocabulary providing another collection of metasigns.

Morris did not use Peirce's emotional, energetic and logical interpretant-signs, nor the immediate, dynamical and final interpretants (Fiordo 1977, 47–48, 52–53). Instead, he reorganized human responses into special signs to judge the reaction to them. Signs serve as a stimulus to react in a certain way to the interpreters. Morris defined the new pragmatics as the disposition to react in a certain kind of way to produce the "analytical" interpretants (1946, 165; 1971, 244), which is different from Peirce's categories. The analytical interpretants neglect the complexity of vague signals in quasi-semiosis to achieve the semiosis of final symbols. Morris introduced the "weak" signals of fictive, legal, cosmological, mythological, poetic, moral, critical, technological, political, religious, propagandistic discourses as examples (Morris 1946, 123–152, reprinted in 1971, 203–232). He observed the non-linguistic signs (here, vocal signs) as coextensive signs with degenerate linguistic signs, denoting them as Peirce's iconic and indexical (meaning emotional/immediate and energetic/dynamical) signals on the way to logical thirdness (Morris 1946, 190–198; 1971, 271–279).

Jakobson's poetic discourse was not about the development of Morris's formal relations of "realistic" signs organized in grammatical and rhetorical types of language (1946, 136–138, reprinted in 1971, 214–217). Following the formal relations of interlingual and intralingual translation, Jakobson specialized language into the informal types of the third category: intersemiotic translation (1959). Literary speech materialized the abstract likeness of meaning of signs as Peircean "interpretants" of complexes of signs, while the degree of likeness came from the design of the interpreter (translator). Contrary to Jakobson, Morris thought of himself primarily as a pragmatic scholar of concrete behavioral content and what he could achieve for literary life, but he defined the genre of literature as a cultural quasi-language that styles the behavioral act of making "good" or "bad" interpretant-translations. Literature specifically denotes poetic translation, and Morris defined poetic content and uses as the "poetic and fictive primarily, perhaps mythical" subcategory of literary texts (1946, 266; 1971, 232).

Firstly, Morris defines *poetic discourse* as referring to the "finer" sense of poetry and prose (1946, 136–138; 1971, 214–217). The "appraisive-valuative" text describes the expressive and emotional signs of the sign by uncovering the varieties of metaphorical style in literature as well as the perception of emotional style, expressing the preferential status of poetic language for the agent (interpreter, translator). The use of the characteristics of the target message can be judged as "good" or "bad" signs by the readers of the received signs (interpretants). Morris stressed the novelty of poetic discourse when he wrote:

> The great significance of poetic discourse lies in the vivid and direct way that it records and sustains achieved valuations, and explores and strengthens novel valuations. In poetry the object signified is turned, as it were, before our eyes with symbolic fingers, and as we look at the object described and exemplified by the poet we come in varying degrees and for a longer or shorter time to take the valuative perspective of the poet in terms of which the object signified has the apprehended significance. The interpreter will naturally seek and prefer those poems most in accord with his own valuative attitudes, but even in them his own impulses will be somewhat modified and somewhat differently organized; and insofar as other poems can gain his attention, he will vicariously try out new valuations for familiar objects and familiar valuations on unfamiliar objects. In this process the valuative attitudes evoked by the poems will be intensified, modified, reorganized in various ways. (Morris 1946, 138; 1971, 216)

Secondly, while "poetry at its best is a symbolic antenna of human behavior at the immediate frontier of its valuational creativity" (Morris 1946, 138; 1971, 216), it can also be seen as *fictive discourse* (Morris 1946, 128–130; 1971, 208–209). Fictive discourse can happen in the inner emotional presentation of the discourse in the poetic message to create another fiction, different from reality. Fictive literature is the belief (or unbelief) in the artistic value of the poem, novel or theater play compared to the importation of a different worldview. Fictive literature wants to understand the

> [u]topias [which] are projected by persons interested in a world different from the one they inhabit, but a world different only in certain respects, namely, in those respects which would provide a more congenial environment for their actual needs. (Morris 1946, 130; 1971, 209)

The reader performs the meaning of the fictive text according to their own values and choices to provide an actual presentation of the "hidden" text in the

> signs of imagined environments. It permits the interpreter not only to delight in the way the story is told and indulge symbolically his actual preferences, but to get material to test, to reconstruct, and to form his preferences. The liberating quality of fictive discourse lies in the

exploration which it permits of how life might be lived in various ways in various environments. (Morris 1946, 130; 1971, 209)

Thirdly, poetic signs could be regarded as *mythical discourse* (Morris 1946, 134–135; 1971, 213–214). Myth gives the appraisive-informative sense of literary discourse to inform the readers with trivial and crucial details about the protagonists. Mythical discourse lets the readers believe in the deeper meaning of myth. Myth is larger than the etymological fragment of rhetorical speech, yet myth is a human discourse, not a theoretical system. Myth is encoded with social and psychological signs to be decoded and deciphered and wants to be interpreted by readers. Myths can be demythologized to observe the standards of cultural behavior. In the time of Morris and Jakobson, the word "myth," borrowed from ancient Greek and Roman mythologies, was a sophisticated fashionable word used in epical "poetics." Mythical research was far removed from what it was when Claude Lévi-Strauss made his cultural entrance into the structural study of myth (see Lévi-Strauss 1955). In Morris' technical view:

> The general significance of mythical discourse lies in the fact that it informs the interpreter in a vivid manner of the modes of action approved and disapproved by some group (or in the extreme case, by some individual). It thus makes available to the interpreter information concerning an important body of appraisals which he may utilize in his behavior, whether by way of agreement or disagreement. (1946, 135; 1971, 214)

Myth entered the circuitous descent into cultural labyrinths of deeper meaning to judge human behavior, enabling the interpreter to take up the active tasks of the cultural writer, either agreeing or disagreeing today with the classical and contemporary models of cultural myths.

Thomas A. Sebeok (1921–2001) was a disciple of Morris and Jakobson, but as a generalist thinker, he was hugely respected for the immense range and diversity of his fields of research, including linguistics, literature, anthropology and biology. Sebeok's scientific genius led him to break through into new interfields from a semiotic perspective, developing anthroposemiotics, zoosemiotics and phytosemiotics, which he named biosemiotics. Morris's *cosmological discourse* (1946, 132–134; 1971, 211–213) was a pivotal evolution for Sebeok's new sciences. Sebeok pointed beyond the interpretations of poetic, fictive and mythological discourses to the metascience of the biological laws of nature-and-culture. The cosmological type of discourse was Morris's category of designative-systemic discourse, which he separated from the description of the qualities of the object or situation in order to reflect the direct causal effects of nature. Morris followed Peirce's speculative hypothesis of semiotics, but also gave the non-standard key of evolutionary cosmology a place (Turley 1977, 84–88), which Sebeok developed further in his later work (from 1980).

Sebeok was the champion of anthroposemiotic semiotics, where semiosis and human, animal and cellular life converge in nature-and-culture. He invented the movement of "global semiotics" bringing together the entire range of scientific and cultural domains between philosophy and the natural sciences (including physics, physiology and the psychology of human sensation, between aesthetic and scientific) in the living (in his words, "vital") energy of semiotic theory. Since semiosis and life converge to form an evolutionary cosmology, any language or quasi-language can describe the process of translation as composed of expressive and emotional signs achieving semiosis in the professional activity of life. Sebeok's global approach to the life of signs presupposes the critique of anthropocentrism and glottocentrism. His global semiotics is open to his term zoosemiotics; indeed, even more broadly, Sebeok's biosemiotics extends the human gaze to full semiosis, where the whole living universe includes the realms of macro- and micro-organisms of cellular life. In Sebeok's conception, sign science is not only the study of communication in human culture, but indeed the study of communicative behavior across the whole biosemiotic perspective of human, animal and cellular ways of life.

Against the hierarchical content of Saussure's general discipline, Sebeok unfolded Peirce's complexity of signs-about-signs to demonstrate Morris's cosmological project transferred into bifurcated signs. Jakobson rethought metalanguage in the lyrical signification of expressive and emotive meanings, as seen in the *Princeton Encyclopedia of Poetry and Poetics* (Preminger 1965/1974, 460–470), but Sebeok went further, to the origins of language. In the article "Zoosemiotic Components of Human Communication" (1974/1977/1985, 296), Sebeok agreed with Hjelmslev, who saw language as a semiotic unit "into which all other semiotics may be translated" (taken from Hjelmslev 1953: 109) but disagreed with Saussure's notion of intranslatability, calling translation "intersemiotic transmutability" (Sebeok 1974/ 1977/1985, 296). Sebeok even framed an anthroposemiotic hypothesis to explain the origin of all the laws of the universe, and the methodical task of the new science of linguistics and non-linguistics explained the evolution of Peirce's quasi-semiosis of firstness and secondness to the third universe, corresponding to the semiosis of thirdness.

The existential universe of language and non-linguistic speech consists of various systems of human intercommunication which are capable of being translated into each other, although they embody in figurative language the scientific and cultural metaphor beating against the system of established procedures of language. Saussure's conclusion concerning translatability was that when the scientific and cultural metaphors were swept away, the translation would turn into a dispirited, irresolute and hopeless sea of waves. For Jakobson, however, literary translation was not a technical calculation with testable vital consequences but echoed the inner translation of the cultural and artistic spirit of hypertranslation, involving the artistic performance from inner to outer forms of art.

Sebeok identified translation as standing for the cultural habit of language englobing the explanatory power of personal and collective forces that come together in the collective life of culture. Culture combines energy and emotion to create figurative language, becoming new patterns of lingüiculture (Gorlée 2021). Translation is perfectly able to disencode linguistic habits to create intercommunication through language among poetry, music, dance, calligraphy and other arts. For Sebeok, the next step leads the way toward the critical point of transduction.

Sebeok's Transduction

To transform translation into "transduction," Thomas A. Sebeok revised and expanded his article "Zoosemiotic Components of Human Communication" (1974/1977/1985, 297, 303) to provide new terminology. The translation is a transfer from source to target languages which "transforms derivatives and substitutes" of different languages or dialects, but "there are those macrostructures that are based, in the final analysis, on a natural language, the 'primary system' on which culture is superimposed" (Sebeok 1974/1977/1985: 297). The speech surrogates are half non-linguistic and half-linguistic modalities, introducing not only gestural (that is, drum and whistle) pseudo-languages against standard language (Sebeok and Umiker-Sebeok 1976; Sebeok 1976), but also mediating the broad range of modalities by replacing linguistic signs with "mute communication systems [of speech] preserved in certain monasteries"; secondly, pseudo-languages figure in "aboriginal sign languages used among the peoples of the Americas and Australia"; thirdly, "complex (viz., nonisomorphic) transductions" came from "parasitic or restricted formations, like script or other optical displays of the chain of speech signs (Morse code, or any of the several acoustic alphabets designed to aid the blind, or sound spectrograms), optionally imposed upon chronologically prior acoustic patterns"; fourthly, one can add the "more or less context-free artificial constructs developed for various scientific or technical purposes" to transform other artificial languages into the artistic mimesis of transduction (Sebeok 1974/1977/1985, 297).

Sebeok's "transduction" has transformed "derivatives and substitutes of linguistic units" into "those macrostructures" of other signs used "independently of any linguistic infrastructure (although, of course, unavoidably intertwined with verbal effects)," but Sebeok closes with musical signs, which are a "species-specific, but not species-consistent form of behavior" of performative arts (1974/1977/1985, 298). The relationship between linguistic and musical signs is investigated as the opportunity to see the history of the anthroposemiotic noises of animal signs, which in this book, *From Mimetic Translation to Artistic Transduction*, are transformed into the fine arts of the musical terminology of transduction, involving the linguistic and musical signs of songs, opera and operetta (see Sebeok's note on Woody Allen 1974/1977/1985, 294).

Sebeok is short in the introduction of transduction. In semiotics, Saussure outlined that linguistic science is like "a chemical compound" (Saussure's analogy is water), so that the linguistic sign is the "total determination by the double relationship, consisting of the union of signified and signifier" (McCannell and McCannell 1982, 101). Image and concept, sound and idea relate to each other as sound-image and concept to form the mimetic term "transduction." Sebeok employed the physiology of human language and literature to explain the geometrical variations and invariations of the electromagnetic and chemical magnetic capacity of the human mind to intertwine the energies of source signs with the target signs, involving terms from the different arts. The term "transduction" was originally a technical term referring to the physical oceanography of waveforms (see James H. Bunn's *Wave Forms: A Natural Syntax for Rhythmic Languages*, 2002). Waves are described as the change of "one form of energy into another, such as the migration of electrical energy to acoustic energy and vice versa" (Sheriff 1984/1991, 82, 255). The energy of electromagnetic dynamics can be measured in the regular pattern of acoustic, visual or sensory transducers, as happens in light bulbs, radio, microphones, X-ray photography and other technical devices.

These technological forms of energy are based on the conservation of energy from source to target in the first law of thermodynamics. Energy creates order, but transposed to arts, the transduction "may be changed from one form to another but is neither created nor destroyed" (Arnheim 1971, 8). Mimesis from technology to arts happens in the sphere of the opera "heavy with leitmotifs and ornate with a vocal virtuosity [...] of serious drama" (Kerman 1956/1989, xii). The level of energy stays the same, but contrary to the existing order, life in the theater will create dramatic orders and disorders, as in the electromagnetic interactions of complex experiments that lead to a variety of meanings in the artistic function of an opera that is provided with the balletic movements of spirit, heart and body in painting, music and dance.

Following the history of the second law of thermodynamics, a revolution takes place (Bunn 1981, 160–182). The qualities of translation have been transformed into the activity of retranslation and self-translation. Now, the natural equilibrium is based on the uncertain steps of the source message in producing the mental process of transduction, which has transformed itself into the informative forms of ellipsis, parabole and hyperbole. This uncertainty of the human mind wants to build up a new theory of certainty with the uncertainty of transduction in arts. The abundant disorder of the target message creates traces of ambiguity in an isolated system hardly understood as standing for elementary words with a broad range of linguistic possibilities. Transduction takes from the environment the physical and chemical traces of gaslight, thunder, smoke and storm, which serve as the information of uncertainty, to redevelop the human mind in order to give new mental phantasms of dramatic uncertainty (Wolff 2021).

The newly formulated reduction of entropy (Rifkin 1980/1981) has the thermoelectrical power to energize colder bodies into hotter bodies (that is to say, from symmetrical into antisymmetrical and asymmetrical metaphors). Thermodynamics has changed the epicenter of the source–target circle of translation into creating from identical synonymy the complexification of the cryptic clues of nature (see the physics underlying the granular dynamics of the chemical reactions in tsunami waves and volcanic explosions). The triadic method of Peirce's language presents the agency, grammar and cultural context to respond to the dramatic and controversial power of asymmetry to qualify the action of mimesis in the environment. The response can be real or fictive (that is, true or untrue), so that the future of nature can be transformed into the uncertainty of the imaginary dialogue mode of arts (Flannery 2020; Kockelman 2007, 375–401).

The cosmological paradigm presents an infinite universe of energetic particles which can spontaneously recreate itself from a featureless uniformity to become disordered, both backward and forward. The different arts can manage the disorder by creating dance and drama, as well as sculpture, film, theater and opera (Arnheim 1971, 8–12, 363–370) as represented in these arts. The obscurities and clearnesses of the progressive breaks in historical fragments (tokens) can be retraced from the ancient "footprints on sand, photographs, fossil bones" or even "written records" (Smart 1967, 131–132) to recreate from old history the order of natural disorder. The particular tokens disentangle the statistical and probabilistic continuum of time and space providing evidence of perpetual motion in the statistical thermodynamics of nature-and-culture (Crossland 2012, 30–135). The hyperreality of choosing from the various branches of research does not present the original circular forms but the ahistorical shapes of arts in the asymmetrical figures of ellipsis and other clues (Panofsky 1954, 25). This was semioticized in the anthropocentric nature of Sebeok's term "transduction." His mimesis energized the classical laws of thermodynamics to obey the scientific and biological energy of the vital "signs of life," dramatizing all human arts and non-arts (Sebeok 1984a).

The name "transduction," invented by Thomas A. Sebeok in his later years, was a step forward from translation as a "prefigurement of art" (Sebeok 1981). In his official report *Communication Measures to Bridge Ten Millennia*, prepared for the Office of Nuclear Waste Isolation of the USA Government, Sebeok explained the "filter" of semiotics as

> [...] the discipline which brackets the conjoint scientific study of both verbal and averbal systems of communication. It is thus relevant to the problem of human interference and message exchanges involving long periods of time, [...] making it necessary to utilize a perspective that goes well beyond linguistics (the formal study of verbal messages), which traditionally (mainly in the 19th century), has dealt with the relatively brief diachronic past, or (mainly in the 20th century) the synchronic present. (Sebeok 1984, 1–2)

The "transmutation from this unconscious parallel processing" is called "crucial <u>transduction</u> [which] is called <u>encoding</u>" (Sebeok 1984, 8, Sebeok's emphasis). The encoding happens in the "intermediate chemical steps from one state to another," which Sebeok explained as

> [a] message [which] is said to be "coded" when the source and the destination are "in agreement" on a set of transformation rules used in the exchange. Because of entropy (a measure of disorder) in the system [...], the message-as-encoded can never be identical with the message formulated and launched by the source. (Sebeok 1984, 8)

Transduction can happen from the neurophysiological input of energy offering the multiplicity of output. In human science, this transmutation happens through the impulses of electrical energy adding to the acoustical universe of the human brain, thereby increasing the certainty that the input will generate an electric current in the output (Sheriff 1984/1991, 79, 180, 255). For Sebeok, transduction transpired through semiotic terminology

> at the interface between internal and external message systems, which, in a broad sense, stand in a specular relationship, in a homology of spatial and temporal transition probabilities. When the destination

receives the encoded messages another transduction, followed by a series of further transformations, must be affected before this message can be interpreted; the pivotal reconversion is called <u>decoding</u>. (Sebeok 1984, 8, Sebeok's emphasis)

In general terms, Sebeok represents how the encoding of semiotic signs can be retraced from the disorder and transformed into another sign to be decoded with the order of a different code, thus producing a multiplicity of meanings. Sebeok defined human interpretation as "an electrochemical post-coding process assumed to occur in a vertebrate's central nervous system after the recording of the message as received" (1984, 29). In transduction, the genetic code and the metabolic code of sign processes transform the electrochemical codes into the uncoded dimensions of quasi-language, which is removed from language to another place as cultural paraphrase of speech surrogates. The restricted "kind of code selected by the source depends crucially on the total sensory equipment at its disposal" (Sebeok 1984, 8). Human interpreters can reinterpretate (that is, encode) the evolutionary cosmology into other crafts and arts to work upon the thermodynamical energy of transduction. Sebeok briefly defined transduction in the *Glossary of Technical Terms*: "TRANSDUCTION: transformation from one form of energy into another" (1984, 30).

Sebeok "greatly expanded, brought up to date, and refocused" (Sebeok 1974/1977/1985, 294) the article "Zoosemiotic Components of Human Communication" several times. Starting as a plenary lecture at the *First Congress of the International Association for Semiotic Studies* in 1974 (re-edited 1977, reprinted in 1985), Sebeok's article was rich in new theoretical paradigms about promoting linguistics through the filter of other sciences and arts. Now that "transduction" was transformed from the origin myth of the Tower of Babel into the technical-physical non-equilibrium of dynamical energy, the electrical voltage of a certain message could be converted into dynamic energy to transfer the electrical voltage of one message into that of another uncertainty (Anderson et al. 1984, 26–33; see 1984, 17–22, 33–35). Sebeok replaced the half-linguistic or even non-linguistic "speech surrogates" with "complex (viz., nonisomorphic) transductions into parasitic or restricted formations, like script or other optical displays of the chain of speech signs […] optionally imposed upon chronologically prior acoustic patterns" (Sebeok 1974/1977/1985, 297). The term transduction broadened the conservative habits-of-speech reactions into non-conservative habits of transferring energy into different arts (Gorlée 2015, 2020).

Black's Medical Dictionary (1987, 232–235) proposes that electrical forms of energy exist in the human pain of headache, neuralgia, the rheumatic condition with spasmodic cramps or even paralysis of bodily members. Electromagnetics is also the basis for human vision, the sense of which depends on chemical reactions promoted by light. The lens receives the light image, but the reverse image is transformed by the retina to vary the focus, adjusting the light-sensitive image to control the left and right hemispheres of the human brain. There exists in the human brain a regular change in electric potential to work with vision, due to the rhythmic discharge of energies by nerve cells. These electrical changes can be recorded graphically as electro-encephalograms (EEG). Certain brainwaves with small electric current can be transformed into the inflammatory interaction of uncertain brainwaves, thereby modulating the human brain into the "disordered" forms of transduction actively involved in electromagnetics and chemical magnetics.

Whereas the brainwaves encode the original code rules of translation, the coercive powers of the magnetic energy of the human brainwaves bring source and target texts together into radical transduction. The encoding activity of language has reactive rules but could decode into a wide curve of mostly free landscape, allowing a sensitive amount of twist to change in the environment of the signs. The encoded messages of transduction are not identical with the curve of the original source of the translation but are regarded by Jakobson as poetic displacement into another art. With the forces of transduction, there is no coherent rule between the intensity of the source and target texts, so that the target form of transduction is not a photographical image with a fixed object and a coherent reference beam. The acoustic, visual, sensory play of the two-dimensional game of transduction can magnetize nature with arts to form a double clue. The intensity of the magnetization is the electrical force emitted by the sign-receiver (reader, agent, translator) to provoke disorder in the creativity of transduction from the original order, moving from the "rigid circle" of linguistics to the "gentle flexibility" of ellipsis, parabole and hyperbole in the different arts (Arnheim 1954, 429; 1971).

Sebeok transformed the "field of transducer physiology" (1974/1977/1985, 303) into the semiotic bifurcation of sociobiology. The reconversion of cognitive signs into their emotional input reconsidered "the relative or absolute contrasts between the pathways of information outside the body and the pathways deep inside it" (Sebeok 1974/1977/1985, 303). Transduction was observed by Sebeok as a "transducer physiology" for studying the conversion of "outer" signs in order to refer to the initial "inner" input (1974/1977/1985, 303). He referred to psychiatrist Harvey Shands's mythological story of Narcissus, in which Narcissus reflected his person in the "discovery of *reflection*" (1970, 274, Shands's emphasis) by falling madly in love with the reflected mirror image of himself. Self-analysis and self-love are "the human problem of the greatest moment [...] of so relating the outer to the inner that the minimal information derivable from inner sources comes to be a reliable index of the external situation" (Sebeok 1976, 303). Sebeok stated that Shands's "bifurcation must eventually be dealt with in semiotic terms in a new science" in order for Narcissus to lose his balance and disappear. He agreed with Shand's use of the myth of Narcissus in order to "demonstrate the unconscious human understanding of the human unconscious long before it becomes possible to describe the unconscious in conscious terms!" (Shands 1970, 275–276). The remedy was for Narcissus to become involved with others at an early stage of the human psychological process in order to move with the other waves of human intelligence.

Returning to translation, the inner and outer waves are the retrospection and transcription coming from the translator's mind, which actually or potentially interpret and reinterpret the source sign to measure new knowledge-making from source sign to target sign. The translator's quasi-mind influences the feelings, beliefs and persuasions to produce Peirce's interpretants of the message in transduction (Gorlée 2004, 147–150). In electromagnetics, for example, the translator is a transistor of the interaction between source and target. The translator reads the source to control the sensitivity and resolution of the receiver in one direction, the target text (Sheriff 1984/1991, 198, 255). The sign-receiver seems to work as a "waveform generator" to receive a signal and give a new signal (Sheriff 1984/1991, 273). The interrogating signal (Peirce's interpretant) stands for a new voltage which over time changes the current flow between the two terminals of source and target.

The reactive speed of the voltage is the reactivity of the signal to transduction, which is amplified with the alternating flow of electrons to refresh the "sonar waves" (Sheriff 1984/1991, 255–256 see 217, 208) into a novelty. Electrons are tinier particles than atoms, so the stream of electrons in the human brain works like waves in magnetic conduction (Sheriff 1984/1991, 3940, 81). The translator becomes an electronic "conductor" for finding the electric current from the simple readability of language to emotional sensitivity in order to transfigure the new codes in transduction. The circuit of metaphors distances itself from the circle to displace the electric current of artistic meaning, thus recreating itself as figures of ellipsis, parabole and hyperbole. Finally, the definitive stage of transduction infuses the human brain with the patterns of the new metalanguages of art (as exemplified in the following chapters). Transduction blows the inner fire of the translator's electrical voltage to experiment with the freedom of acoustic energy, and vice versa. The electromagnetic field is similar to Peirce's interpretant-sign: both signs conduct electricity from the sender to a different magnetic field in order to search for coherency in the target arts. Transduction is made by an artist transformed into an artisan.

This reformulation of the inner speech of the translator on the path from metaphorical conductor to metalinguistic transductor is detailed here in the examples of this book, *From Mimetic Translation to Artistic Transduction: A Semiotic Perspective on Virginia Woolf, Hector Berlioz, and Bertolt Brecht*. The mimicry illustrated in the varieties of examples intensifies the conventional message of linguistic translation to produce, through the thought sequences of the human brain, the alternative power of conduction and transduction, implying different variations and invariants of the human mind in arts. James H. Bunn's dimensionality of electrical signs from the book *The Dimensionality of Signs, Tools, and Models* (1981, 160–182) is used to provide the analogy with temporal phases of history. Bunn's analogy starts "in the spinning jenny, the flywheel, [and] the dynamo" (1981, 162) to show the "semiotic acceleration" (Scheffler 1997: 1) of the electrified velocity of tempo and rhythm in literary translation. Starting with the electrical current of conduction that shifts language into quasi-languages, semiotic transduction expands the human brain to acknowledge the mimicry of variants and invariants. Analysis of the interruptions, incoherence and surprises of other arts forms a mixture of verbal and averbal components of language, allowing the readers to imagine a new wave train of thought (Scheffler 1997, 2 ill.).

Chapter 2

WAVE AFTER WAVE: WAGNER'S WAVES ECLIPSED BY VIRGINIA WOOLF

Play Within Play

The double replacement of Wagner's linguistic-and-musical songs with the equivalent linguistic words of Woolf's novel is mingled together in Jakobson's interlingual translation and intralingual translation. Jakobson and Waugh (1979) paved the way for the pseudo-critical line of thought as lived through the sound shape of language. The transduction of vocal songs and their meaning can be defined as the retranslation of singable and performable words from old to new code languages (dialects, idioms or jargons), while the music remains unchanged and untranslated. Vocal or operatic translation seeks to transform lyrical works into the new setting of a different language. The double replacement of sound is made by a specialized translator working in the mixed area of literature and musicology, which also involves knowledge of theater studies. The hypertranslation made by the musical-and-literary translator becomes a co-authoring of the source translation brought to another language or pseudo-language, meaning that the translator's role is upgraded from that of secondary interpreter of the source text to that of a primary target interpreter.

Transduction works independently on the translational work through the translator co-interpreting the thematic, space-time and conceptual qualities of the source text. These revolutionary construction methods are inspired by the brain processes of the translator. The translator changes the elastic wave of conduction into the energy wave of transduction. The speed of the waves travels from the gravity surface of water into the higher graphical waves of the ellipsis, parabole and hyperbole (Shipley 1968/1972, 270–275). These waves are layered with the private "differences" in personal and cultural choice that make the "variations" and "invariations" of the source text, reshaping the target text away from the source text. The vocal translator is in the mixed position of doing more than intellectually retranslating the verbal text into another language without touching the musical values of the text.

The operatic singers reinterpret and transpose the sounds into a different key—the perfect wave to perform the song or aria as a medium between artist and listeners. However, the emotionality of the primary author is experienced by the vocal translator within their own psychological structure in the process of transduction, which enables them to produce the singable words and sentences for the listeners to understand in terms of *"what* is said and *how* it is said"* (Dewey 1934, 106). In this way, following Jakobson's thought, new poetic language is built from ordinary language, creating a new style.

In the close encounter with the vocal music of opera, logocentrism defends the general dominance of the linguistic word through the aphorism *prima la parole e poi la musica*—but the imaginative dilemma is not solved by taking the opposite, wordless approach of musicocentrism, *prima la musica e poi le parole* (Gorlée 1997, 237, 2005: 8–10; Apter and Herman 2016: 6–10). Instead of following the formal intent of singing a song, translation finds new words for unchanged music; the vocal translator may re-imagine him/herself to become a poet or novelist who under- and overplays the words and sentences (Apter and Herman 2000). The competing forces of mixing and transplanting reassert the personal linguistic translation as cultural transduction (Gorlée 2015). The "simple" model of translation (firstness and secondness) adopts an artful style (thirdness) to complexify the sound particles into the ambiguous parallax of the source text. Operatic translation is the translator's *tour de force*; the translator tries to create the target text but never detours from the source reality. The different variants and invariants, and even desvariants, settle in the theatrical effect of the poetic versions. The target text shifts from normal translation into rhythmic and poetic waveforms involving personal and cultural forms of translation as creative translation.

The first terms of vocal translation include "two equivalent messages in two different codes" (Jakobson 1959/1966, 233). Wagner's force of operatic translation is illustrated in the codes and subcodes of his opera *The Rhinegold* (*Das Rheingold*, composed 1853–1854, first performed in Munich in 1869). This opera was translated into English verse, with the music left untouched (Gorlée 1997, 248–264). The first vocal (singable and non-singable) English translation was composed by Andrew Porter in 1976 for the English National Opera and Royal Opera in London (Wagner 1985, 43–92). Porter's static translation with unrhymed verse and contemporary English stress, meter and prosody is the mirror image of the Wagner source. After other singable translations, the most recent English translation was made by the American team of librettists Mark Herman and Ronnie Apter (Wagner 1983; see Gorlée 1997, 248; Wilson-de Roze 2018, 55–56). They took the radical liberty of producing their grittier singable and performable translation of *Das Rheingold* (as seen in the following examples).

The secondary step for shifting translation to transduction is taken in not confining the poeticized fairy tale to verbal structure but by establishing a kind of traffic between the language and other arts to create what Jakobson calls the "poetic" environment. Operatic translation features the independence of the final hypertranslation by translating the "poetic" versification into "beauty," to use Jakobson's terminology, as the very essence of sound-music. Hypertranslation develops the dramatic imagination further by moving away from transduction into the real codes and subcodes of arts. The example here shows how the English vocal translation of Wagner's Prelude to *Das Rheingold* retraces the paths of Virginia Woolf's transduction in the process of writing (not translating!) her novel *The Waves* (published in 1932, written from 1929 to 1931). Woolf had a copy of Wagner's opera cycle *Das Rheingold* (Wagner 1873/1913[?]) in her library, and she could easily read the popular opera guide *Kobbé's Complete Opera Book* (Harewood 1922/1961, 232–245), which was updated yearly for English operagoers (King and Miletic-Vejzovic 2003).

Virginia Woolf could familiarize herself with the intricacies of Wagner's source text in order to plan a different target text with an "equivalent" function of mind and heart. However, despite having the intellect to be able to translate German into English, Woolf had the strength of imagination for more: she was beyond being a strict translator, but as an art lover she transmuted herself into a conductor to become a transducer. She invested herself both psychically and spiritually in the composition of her own music drama. The transplantation from translation to transduction guided Woolf into her distinctive art of vocal translation. While translation draws a circle from one language to another to effect one-for-the-other equivalence, transduction replaces the oneness of the versification of language by throwing light on otherness—the subcodes moved away from Wagner's musical language into the strange territory of creating Woolf's new art form. As the transducer, Woolf felt free of the tyranny of the source text to undercut Wagner's anatomic waves and transmute the content and substance of Wagner's story into the wave-motion of water molecules, shaping them into meaningful particles of art (Jourdain 1997, 8–9, 23). This was the physical design of Virginia Woolf's pioneering study, which she demonstrated by balancing the sound strategy of Wagner's poetry with the wave particles of her novelistic transduction (Crossland 2018).

Transduction means effecting the artistic simultaneity of one art as another art, meaning that one form of play is juxtaposed with a different form of play (Scheffler 1997, 97–109). The game of play-reacting is not a matter of copying another source writer and retranslating the source into another language. It provides the translator with a crucial transposition, highlighting the transducer's artistic self in creating a new *objet d'art* with a different meaning. Woolf internalized the waves of the source text, prioritizing the different— but paradoxically equivalent—radiant energy to displace the whole target text with a strange likeness. Woolf remodeled (that is, overplayed) the undulating form of the sound waves of Wagner's articulatory model of operatic waves into another perfect waveform. The textual (musical, sculptural and dramatic) sense of transduction is not a perfect game in terms of reproducing the same linguistic translation, but it stages the twists and turns of the story to generate the new plot.

Woolf's transduction projected her into an imaginary scene that renewed and refreshed her previous emotions and the events of Wagner's opera, giving her the opportunity to reflect on her artistic trends that suggested the future of literature. While ordinary translation can transfer a special sound effect from one language into another, the dynamic effect of transduction can lead the transductor away into designing any other artistic performance, such as dance, sculpture, film or opera, thus creating what Jakobson described as the poetry of forms and shapes. Transduction recreates the mixed sense of the art object by emerging with new technologies to perform a new art object in a new time and place. The futuristic lesson of transduction can be judged as pro-art or even anti-art that generates novelty (Gorlée 2015).

In the case of Richard Wagner's masterpiece *The Ring of the Nibelung* (*Der Ring des Nibelungen*), the Prelude (*Vorspiel*) of the verbo-musical opera was *The Rhinegold* (*Das Rheingold*), which was first performed in 1869 (Harewood 1922/1961, 232–245). The "Preliminary Evening" of *The Ring of the Nibelungen* was, at a later date, analyzed and refashioned by Virginia Woolf into a transduction that transformed it from an operatic performance into the "open texture" (Scheffler 1997, 18–21) of the subcodes of the novel's literary paragraphs or fragments. This interconnection across time and place was suggested by DiGaetani (1978, 109–129) and explored by Marder (2001), McGregor (2009, 152–190) and Sutton (2013, 137–153), but perhaps the analysis may now (after Makiko-Pinkney 1987, Miller 2015, 232–263, O'Hara 2015, 67–82), and Kirsch 2023 require more details and nuances to suggest the ways in which *The Rhinegold* can be regarded specifically as the source text which half a century later serves as the model of Woolf's target novel *The Waves* (1931).

Virginia Woolf was invigorated by her knowledge of German, which allowed her to be able to read German newspapers featuring images of Nazi groups in Germany. For her, the activity of retranslating Wagner's lyrics was strongly impacted by the political inconvenience and troublesome international climate caused by rising Fascism in Germany. In her experimental novel *The Waves*, Woolf created her own symphonic and emotional metapoem on the political situation (McNichol 1990; see Holmes 1988). This literary work is not merely Woolf's translation of Wagner's first scene but reflects how she struggled against the political culture of Nazism. Her endeavor over- and underplays Wagner's musical features to capture them differently in the cultural playpoem of her modern novel (O'Hara 2015: 71). In her mind, Woolf electrified the novel in her own rhythmical voice, not against Wagner's mythical story. She focused on the social and political "worksong" to under- and overplay English right-wing politics as oriented to the Left. She even regularized her own bodily activity and physical movements to coordinate with the emotional tensions and frustrations she suffered during the lyrical writing of her revolutionary novel *The Waves*.

As a modern minstrel, Woolf vividly remembers her own wild enthusiasm as a young girl for Wagner's operas, when she and her sister Vanessa paid an idyllic visit to Bayreuth (1909) (Levy 2017, 61). In the later period of writing *The Waves*, international relations had turned uneasy, since European politics was restricted to secret diplomacy, and international news in the press analyzed the political structure of the messages alone, without being influenced by sociological, cultural and historical considerations. In Woolf's time, there was no modern communication theory available as there is today. International politics was diplomacy, but international news was uncertain. Technology was limited to the telegraph, which reduced words and phrases to a vocal ambiguity hard to recompose into normal speech. The "talking machine" the telephone was there, but its tones were artificial (Cherry 1957/1966, 45–46, 109, 120–123). Indeed, there was no real quantity of correct information in view of the high chance of error, confusion and ambiguity in understanding political events abroad, as they were mainly reported in foreign languages. English newspaper headlines published alarming pictures of Nazi guards patrolling the streets of German cities. Woolf viewed these pictures nervously as the "skeptical wolf in sheep's clothing" (Dretske 1981/1982, 125). Indeed, she feared that this news would bring a flow of failure and disgrace to world politics.

In this troublesome situation, Woolf's political position switched to the reverse: her radioactive mind squarely faced the crisis of political exile. Her reaction was to compose an ironic fiction of Wagner's ideology of Germanic culture in the Modernist novel *The Waves*. Woolf did not retranslate or self-translate Wagner's first scene of *The Rhinegold*, but perhaps used the old epic of the *Nibelungenlied* as a toxic tradition to understand the political-ideological taste of the intellectual audience in the 1930s. Her goal was to fight against the rise of Nazism in Germany (1965/1969, 354–357; see Auerbach 1953/1957, 96–97). In the duplicity of writing the political parallax, Woolf's dramatic parody was an electrical effort to transrupt translation from the exact dynamism of transduction. The fixed meaning of the strict rule of ordinary translation emerged with the continuous revolution of underplaying and overplaying waveforms seen in Woolf's conversations on her novel *The Waves*.

In the musicality of her English prose, Woolf's poetic wordplay echoed the rhythmic sound patterns of Wagner's music-and-verse to enable her to disinfect the political thought of Wagner's Germany. The evolutionary circuits of the imagination and reasoning of Wagner's protagonists influenced Woolf's dramatic re-expressions to tell her the life-dramas of Germanic heroes and heroines (O'Hara 2015: 72). Woolf characterized the group of friends in the novel *The Waves* not as real speaking persons with a political identity, but as glimpses of dreamy characters living in their own Utopia. Their personal and individual endeavor is a deeply dialectical conflict explaining the spiritual firmness of their personality (Peirce's oneness-and-twoness) so as not to take the political programs of the 1930s seriously (thirdness).

Despite the role that Wagner's work played in her writing of *The Waves* (1929–1931), Woolf was no fan of Wagner. However, the political tensions of Nazi Germany gave her a sense of cultural freedom (Perl 2020), allowing her to take arms against the growing social disorder of Nazi ideology in Germany to reach the critical point of Leftist politics. Woolf's key point as an author was not to draw the "normal" circle of synonyms from Wagner, as in translation, but to bridge the gulf between the serious affair of the political situation in Germany and her emotional reaction. Woolf created her vision to reorient the result in the opposite direction: the elliptical half-circle. Her ellipsis had no fixed artistic line and took a longer route than that of Wagner's source opera, using a metaphor from the political Left shared by the intellectual circle of her friends in the Bloomsbury group. Her political ellipsis created distance to Wagner's ellipsis: she replaced the German ideology with an opposing one, indirectly tracing the changes by under- and overemphasizing Wagner as her secret source (Goodman 1976/1985, 81–82; see Nida and Taber 1969/1982, 202). Woolf encapsulated her mystical vision in Wagner's work. Whereas Wagner had been received with political ambiguity in the early twentieth century, Woolf's metaphorical structures with language created a complex waves of sameness and difference.

Woolf was an English woman who, as a modern diplomat, abandoned the troubled waters of British politics to explain the new idiomatic grammar in her clever combination of poetry and prose. Her robust voice, "rising and falling in a symmetrical way" (Ostwald 1973, 106–107) exhibits the "asymmetrical" poetry of the twentieth century, briskly announcing the innovative ideas of modern fiction. The English literature of the Edwardian age, taken from 1890 to the First World War, could be traced back to old-style Victorian writing, but the anti-Victorian novelist Virginia Woolf called the old-fashioned arrangements into serious question. Conservative and unadventurous neo-classical art had turned away from continental art and stayed with the old-fashioned movement. British culture even ignored French *art nouveau*, the decorative *Jugendstil* of the German school and the *Secession* movement in Vienna. The medieval romances of the Pre-Raphaelite Brotherhood were mediated by the arts and crafts of the Middle Ages and the Renaissance. The patriotic splendor of the British army and navy was tarnished by the calamities of World War I. What the spirit of the Edwardian era needed was visionary designers such as novelist Virginia Woolf, who attempted to escape from the symbolic overtones of realism to saturate her political program with modern fictionality.

In Modernism, literary arts needed to take *avant-garde* steps to close the conventional traditions of eighteenth-century Britain. Woolf's postmodern process emerged strongly from Charles Dickens' realist and social novels, reviving the old role of the individual to explain the true-to-life world of the social sciences after the horrors of World War I. Woolf's literary criticism emphasized the individualism of the audience, modernizing and adopting the exploration of future thoughts, feelings and fears leading secretly to World War II (Garner 1974, 6–14, 28–33). Modernism led Edwardian modernity to Woolf's experimental forms of prose poems embellished with new structures to reflect cultural civilization of her day. She engaged with Modernism by embracing abstract art in her literary experiments, moving away from real narratives to writing literary-critical episodes and events that operated with the new stylistics, keeping her deep sense of independence in writing narratives moving to the future.

Returning to Virginia Woolf's younger years in London, the summer season of 1909 was a crucial time for her cultural vision. She was 27 years old and was able to travel abroad. She immensely enjoyed the performances of Wagner's operas at the Bayreuth opera house (*Festhaus*) in Bavaria, Germany. Following a special visit to this celebration of the epic heroes of German mythology, Woolf became fascinated by the dramatic performances of Wagner's *Ring, Parsifal* and *Lohengrin*. As a young musical critic, Woolf displayed great personal intimacy when she authored the discerning little essay "Impressions at Bayreuth," published by the *London Times* (Woolf 1909/1976). She was not a *faux naïf* "amateur," but was, in her own words, in the "ambiguous state of musical criticism," since for her "the lack of tradition is of course the freest and happiest state that a critic can wish for" (Woolf 1909/1976, 22). Modern journalism was, in Woolf's early literary canon, the innovative medium for announcing the signpost of modern times.

In her lyrical language, she painted the scene of Wagner's operas as the dramatic festival of pilgrims many of them from distant lands, [who] attend with all their power. As the lights sink, they rule into their seats and scarcely stir till the last wave of sound has ceased; when a stick falls there is a nervous shudder, like a cripple in the water, through the entire house. During the intervals between the acts, when they come out into the sun, they seem oppressed with a desire to disburden themselves somehow of the impression which they have received. (Woolf 1909/1976, 22)

For Woolf, the sensuous, almost religious, "waves of sound" drifted over to the stream of "pilgrims" waiting to experience together the mythical performance of Wagner's *Gesamtkunstwerk*. Woolf's early article conveys a journalistic sense rather than being a review of the operas. For her, music and poetry were the vocalized verbal influences of the dramas that Wagnerian operas contain, expressed by pitch, duration, loudness and timbre to spread the new dynamism of cultural art more widely. But the musical world of play included theatrical elements in the elaborate setting and staging to fabricate Wagner's theatrical operatic event. The costumes, make-up, props and lighting intensified the elaborate action on stage to create Wagner's objective: the audience's spiritual revelation, awakening their own genius. Woolf's article took the operagoers out of the bourgeois mindset they lived in and initiated them into her *coup de théatre* of sensuous, even sexual, pleasure.

Virginia Woolf was in her younger years a Wagnerian *aficionada*. The revolutionary writer of the twentieth century was deeply influenced by the romantic spirit of Wagner's operas. The poet-musician Wagner was Woolf's old favorite, inspiring personal excitement in her ideals as a young woman, but he was not the fictional inspiration of her literary work. To set a new trend in literary studies, she explored the mediation with Wagner's musico-verbal work to carry this culture further and rewrite it in the fashion of the contemporary novel. The opposition between fictitiousness and criticism (which meant, for her, irreality and non-reality) signified Woolf's debate of what "modern fiction" was painted as:

not a series of gig-lamps symmetrically arranged; life is a luminous halo, a semitransparent envelope surrounding us from the beginning of consciousness to the end. Is it not the task of the novelist to convey this varying, this unknown and uncircumscribed spirit, whatever aberration or complexity it may display, with as little mixture of the alien and external as possible? We are not pleading merely for courage and sincerity; we are suggesting that the proper stuff of fiction is a little other than custom would have us believe it. (Woolf 1925/1933, 189)

The period of modernity in which Woolf lived was characterized by the "current alienated sense of the literary [history] as structured, fictional discourse bidding for an interpretative history" (Chambers 1984: 26). Chambers warned that polysemy "requires careful control" to ensure that the sense of "entropy, of slippage, or of drift is carefully balanced by a negentropic appeal to the act of reading as an ordering, fixing, or channeling phenomenon" (1984: 26). Woolf's "modern fiction" stirred the political wave which projected the contemporary reader into her artistic and fictional text. Woolf gave her literature a political "reading situation that is uniquely the right one for that particular piece of discourse" (Chambers 1984: 27). As the author of experimental novels, Woolf granted a good example of "I am art" or "I am fiction" to specify generally to her readers that art is a thrilling adventure:

> "Read me as this type of art (fiction), not that"—romance, not realism; philosophical, not psychological; social comedy, not metaphysical drama, et cetera. Consequently, the self-referential text inescapably forecloses itself in the very act of opening itself to ongoing meaningfulness. (Chambers 1984: 27; see Winterson 1996)

Advocating the importance of women's liberation, Woolf wanted through her literary work to gain the vote and voice of women, defying the eternal dominion of masculine reluctance to take the women's vote seriously. The Victorians thought that women were physically and intellectually inferior to men. As an Edwardian *suffragette*, Woolf objected to male political dominance and depicted women's experience in order to seriously set in motion the meaningful wave of feminine voices. As a novelist, Woolf used her literary voice to defend the equality of women with men in modern society. After the Victorian era, the nature of man's superego was disfragmented from old fiction to emerge in the Edwardian age with new conventions, changing old traditions. Woolf excavated the traditional conventions of male otherness in her personal career of feminism, which was for her and her readers a literary and political signal characteristic of the social changes signifying the twentieth century (Minow-Pinkney 1987).

Virginia Woolf was brought up as a lady in a respectable, bourgeois, British upper-middle-class family at 22 Hyde Park Gate in Kensington and was therefore excluded from attending university. Instead, she largely educated herself through her father, Lesley Stephen, who had an intellectual library. She taught herself German and took classes at the Ladies Department of King's College in Kensington. When she joined the Bloomsbury group, which included her sister Vanessa Bell, Roger Fry, Lytton Strachey, Leonard Woolf, E. N. Foster and John Maynard Strachey, her artistic goal and mission drastically departed from the old materialistic work of Victorian reality to Abstract Expressionism (Levy 2017). Virginia avoided writing "of unimportant things" but flourished with the tentative success of her intellectual "life or spirit" of offering the "truth or reality" of the political Left (Woolf 1925/1933, 187–188). At a later date, with her growing concern about the political rise of Nazism, Woolf's enthusiasm for German operas left her spiritually and critically unsettled concerning the unpolitical nature of her earlier writing about the authoritarian spirit of Wagner (Bostridge 2018, 16–17; Marder 2001, 172–179, 260–266).

Frightened, Woolf re-enacted her sentimental celebration in the rupture of her psychic identity. She toned down the "old" debate on Wagner's operas and changed her poetic taste to the trend of Modernist arts. As an innovative writer, Woolf moved away from the old fictional fantasy of German literature to shelter from its ideological bias, far away from the "waves of murder" of Nazism (Steiner 1967/1985, 172). As a last residue of it, Woolf seemed to keep the immersion of Wagner's fiction unbroken in her writing, as the literary deconstruction of her political reconstruction broke her spirit (Wilson-de Roze 2018). Wagner's operas were constructed throughout the earlier rehearsals of Woolf's work but were in later years reconstructed to withhold the polemic nature of Nazism and generate an entirely other ideology in Modernist literature.

Woolf in her lifetime served as a "double agent" of old and new literature. She knew that Wagner had upgraded the heroic Nordic sagas and German nationalism as the essential mythology of contemporary culture in Germany. But instead of writing journal articles about "translating" Wagner's operatic performances in English, she retreated from public view to retranslate in solitude her modern fiction to approximate the perfect waves of modern speech (Cherry 1957/1966, 77–87). Modern speech had radically changed in the language of daily newspapers and periodical journals. Woolf contrasted herself as a novelist against the images of Wagner the composer. She repeated the leitmotif technique (German *Leitmotiv*) by further restructuring the separate scenes into the melodic music of her lyrical art (Antović 2016: 107, 116–117, 120–126, 131). In *Der Ring des Nibelungen*, Wagner put forward the leitmotifs of the Ring, the Contract, Valhalla, and the Sword. While Wagner associated the musical motif with the extramusical reference, which he drew from German and Nordic mythology, Woolf saw the metaphorical application of politics in Wagner's use of leitmotifs in his lyrical verses. The dogmatic value of each scene was given a special determinate meaning (Kerman 1956/1989, 173–175; Ehrenzweig 1967/1968, 54–55, 95–97; see Langer 1941/1948, 182), but Woolf's novelistic writing was more flexible and polemic.

In the process of shifting from conduction to transduction, Woolf expressed the leitmotifs in the wavy language of sound-signs inspired by the high voltage of the linguistic speech of the speaking artist as represented in the characters of her novel *The Waves*. Woolf's narrative symbolized acoustic modernity in her "journalistic" fiction. Culturally struggling with Wagner's basic "unending melodies" (Perl 2020), she distanced her literary work from his to play the eternal metaphors of the human mind, developing in her transduction the modern meaning of her emotional life. She waged against hypocritical behavior and the unfair treatment of women as represented by Wagner. The old waves of Wagner's expressive music were transfigured into Woolf's "lighthouse," which served as a modern metaphor to illuminate further paths in the epic tradition, making her work into far more than a novel, indeed into a narrative poem (Auerbach 1953/1957, 463–488).

In the novel *The Waves*, Woolf's wavy "signposts" of artworks (1925/1933, 191) enwreathed Wagner's archaic legends with a novel framework fighting against old mythology to highlight the modern pre-war discourse of abstract art. The *avant-garde* movements of Dadaism, Cubism, and Constructivism were favored as popular orientations in modern art (Jakobson 1921/1987, 1961/1971, 3–4). They had emerged on the European continent but were hardly acknowledged in England (Brendel 2016: 23) and flowed out from Cubism into Dadaism, de Stijl, and ultimately, the Bauhaus and Abstract Art. Jakobson and Woolf were in part contemporaries of the revolutionary approach, which moved away from the so-called "realistic" trend of the conventional one-point perspective, metonymically digressing from the plot to unite linguistics with music, and *vice versa*. The "old" painters and other artists

> introduced the "pointillist" technique, relying upon the capacity of the visual apparatus to fuse dots of color physically separate on the canvas, they exemplified but did not originate an organic activity that transforms physical existence into a perceived object. It is not just the visual apparatus but the whole organism that interacts with the environment in all but routine action. (Dewey 1934, 122)

This new approach implies the presence of cultural points of view with a total focus on the pancultural unity of all arts. Since Jakobson and Woolf lived in different political worlds, each of them challenged the futuristic analysis of their time against the bourgeois art of the early twentieth-century arts. The metaphoric and metonymical waves of Cubism, as proposed by Jakobson, are transformed "into a set of synecdoches" and "the surrealist painters responded with a patently metaphorical attitude" of "synecdochic 'close-ups' and metonymic 'set-ups'" to reveal the "metaphoric 'montage'" (Jakobson and Halle 1956/1971, 92; see Kostelanetz 1993, 50–51).

Speaking from Eastern Europe, literary scholar Jakobson, influenced by the Modernist revolution in the arts, created his own futurist poetry and poetic translations. As an *avant-garde* scholar, Jakobson was stimulated to introduce new meaning to literary and theatrical works by constructing a single framework for narrative theory. This new framework connecting poetic language with verbal and non-verbal arts he called "poetics." The combination of linguistics and literature in one field had parallels to Woolf's revolution in modern literature. Woolf integrated the multiplicity of emotional and cognitive senses and uses of language as poetical actuality, social propaganda and political satire, using Western modes of thought to transform the structure of Cubism into a new interpretation of perspectives of focus or filmic "shots." Modern critics introduced the epic novelty of abstract art into literature, music, painting and sculpture as a perspective symbolizing the "reversed" world of a novel transformed into epic poetry.

Virginia Woolf found a revolutionary form for her own fiction. In the early years of her career, the emotional tone of her prose fiction was unclear. The sounds of the sea incorporated gesture into the rhythmical colors and the textures of the waves as a common element in Woolf's *The Waves* (as shall be argued here). If the first scene of *The Rhinegold* was the base of the lyrical narrative of *The Waves*, Woolf's inner and outer process of transduction was her goal. Indeed, transduction can be argued as the proper type of her spiritual artwork. Since Woolf studied the old convention of Wagner's musicopoetical waves, she passed through various phases or steps in her literary career, moving from one step to the next to try to remodel and redevelop her novelistic work away from the model of Wagner's opera into modern arts. She interdepended the complex representations of the rhythmic symbols of Wagner's waves in the heartbeat of transduction to dynamize her own stream-of-consciousness. A fresh stream of sensory, acoustic and visual waves marked Woolf's psychologizing intelligence as a modern novelist. To symbolize her freedom, she claimed the energy of Wagner's old waves to build the swirling waves of her special fiction. If Wagner and Woolf are connected in translation and retranslation on the way to transduction, their mystical unconsciousness is established by Woolf's waves with twisting surprises.

Three Waves

The *Oxford English Dictionary* defines the noun "wave" as a "movement in the sea or other collection of water, by which a portion of the water rises above the normal level and then subsides, at the same time travelling a greater or smaller distance over the surface; a moving ridge or swell of water [...]; one of the long ridges or rollers which, in the shallower parts of the sea, follow each other at regular intervals, assuming an arched form, and successively break on the shore" (OED 1989, 20: 1).

The wave has *three* types: the *first* step is to receive the wave as an outside atmospheric impression of an "undulatory movement, or one of an intermittent series of movements, of something passing over or on a surface or through the air" (OED 1989, Vol. 20: 1). The body wave can also spread forward to express, as the *second* step, human emotionality, coloring the sea with riddles of waves streaked with color, zigzag patterns and circling sounds. The symbolic garb of the "swelling, onward movement and subsidence" can pass beyond the poetic delight of first and second waves to appear as the *third* step in the collective "movement" of waves "sweeping over a community, and not easily resisted" (OED 1989, Vol. 20: 1). The intoxication produced by the wavy forms in *The Waves* does not just evoke the imbalance of sea waves but also gives Woolf's novelistic work a scientific and technical hallucination and creates a complex text rewritten in prosaic poetry. The vivid sense of the "pluripotentiality" of the moving waves symbolizes the total "diabolism" of science, music and literature, suggesting a literary totality of waves (Wilshire 2016: 221).

In geophysical science, the waves of the sea come in *three* forms: surface, interface and long waves (Sheriff 1984/1991, 270–275). The wave can fall rapidly with the "surface wave," while the "interface wave" separates different waves of close contact, and the "long wave" reaches the speed of the waves moving from the surface toward the depth (Sheriff 1984/1991, 129, 145, 239). In other words, the longitudinal wave is the *first* wave on the surface, suggesting the first tone of energy, with the vibration in the middle of the wave modifying the movement from blank silence into the energetic successive of waves. *Secondly*, the transverse wave softly propagates the central vibration at the left and right angles of the wave train, so that the sounds of music move as the deep tonality of rich waves. *Thirdly*, the hydrodynamic nature of the torsional waves stands for the pulsing flux of energy rotating back and forth. The waves are the synthetic drama of three undulating waveforms distinguishing the reductive or diminutive ways of listening to the volume and sounds of the ocean's tide to make a sense of what the subjectless "words" of the waves can possibly signify.

In science and arts, linguistics agrees on the natural and artificial ecosystem of *three* waves to define the linguistic units: real, referential and metaphorical waves. Real waves correspond to translation, while referential waves are the formal and informal units between translation, retranslation and self-translation. The process of transduction includes the middle waves of conduction, while metaphorical waves work in themselves as transductive steps. Waves interconnect with linguistic-and-musical waves in the libretto of singing operas. The musical sound of the waves is transplanted into linguistic words, while the linguistic speech points to the ebb and flow of *three* syntactic types: the longitudinal wave *firstly* concentrates on the regular action of translation, moving the units of language into the same natural direction. The *second* wave indicates the asymmetrical wave of the special energy to resist translation in retranslation or self-translation, while the *third* wave epitomizes the flow of the electric brain in displacing the natural waveforms into the symbolic syntax of drawing, music and poetry (see James H. Bunn's book *Wave Forms: A Natural Syntax for Rhythmic Languages*, 2002, 192–193).

Electromagnetic transduction moves away from regular waves in order to find the structural harmony (or even disharmony) of different waveforms. It adjusts to and unites with the structure of the transducer's (that is, the translator's) brain waves in listening to the pitch, loudness, tone, stress and tempo of the musical and acoustic sounds. The wave has the magnetic and electrochemical resistance of the transducer's brain as the working energy of light and sound to "electrify" the current into other sciences and arts without any barrier.

At the beginning of the twentieth century, general linguistics consisted of the logical branches of phonology, general syntax, dialectology, rhetoric and other subjects, but the experimental arts of translation and the rational development into conduction and transduction were regarded in arts as Surrealist word puzzles without meaningful clues. John Dewey's *Art as Experience* discussed the innovative sense of waves in art to describe the rhythmic shocks of modern art and accept the freedom to play the games of poetry, music, sculpture, architecture and dance as the total explosion of "mixed" arts (Dewey 1934, 214–244). As a modern *litterateuse*, Woolf found that word-clues give a real meaning, as she streamlined the writing of *The Waves* (1931). Her endeavor produced a literary explosion of sounds and words. In the period when Woolf was writing this novel, Bloomfield's seminal work *Language* (1933/1967; see Beaugrande 1991, 58–87) heralded the emergence of modern linguistics. In his general approach to language, Bloomfield describes the function of "sound waves" passing through the air between speakers in order for them to hear a (correct or incorrect) speech message (1933/1967, 25–26).

Bloomfield's wave theory makes a *three*-stage distinction, dividing the speech sounds into discontinuous, discrete and cumulative sequences. *Firstly*, Bloomfield acknowledges that it is thanks to the "sciences of physiology and physics" that linguists know enough about speech-events to be able to study them and conclude that they consist of three parts. The "speaker, move[s] her vocal cords […], her lower jaw, her tongue, and so on, in a way which force[s] the air into the form of sound-waves"; *secondly*, the "sound-waves in the air in [the speaker's] mouth set the surrounding air into a similar wave-motion"; and finally, "these sound-waves in the air [strike the hearer's] eardrums [with the effect that the hearer] *hear*[*s*] the speech" and responds to the "*substitute* stimuli" of the speech sounds uttered by the speaker serving in place of the *practical* stimuli that the speaker experienced (Bloomfield 1933/1967, 25, Bloomfield's emphasis). In Bloomfield's view, the speaker experiences a practical stimulus (either bodily or mentally) and instead of responding to it directly, the speaker uses speech to indirectly convey the need to satisfy it to a hearer in their environment. The vocal noises of natural language function to stimulate a speechless reaction in the hearer, who provides a practical response. Bloomfield argues that scientifically and psychologically, the "*speech* stimulus" in the human brain can be regarded as a waveform in which humans consciously (and unconsciously) think in order to produce one of the three speech-events (Bloomfield 1933/1967, 25; see Cherry 1957/1966).

The energy of the speaker and hearer working together seems to be Bloomfield's structuralist event of communication, but generally nonhuman speech communication is subject to "uncertainty and variation," since "*The gap between the bodies of the speaker and the hearer—the discontinuity of the two nervous systems—is bridged by* [*comprehending*] *the sound-waves*" (Bloomfield 1933/1967, 25–26, Bloomfield's emphasis). Linguistics focuses *firstly* on the biological waves of sound waves, concentrating on the phonetic and phonological script of oral speech. Then, *secondly*, the linguist abandons the acoustic forms to focus comparatively on how structural sound waves create speech oppositions. Intermediate dialects use an idiom that conveys the "natural" but informal, art of spoken language. The *third* wave maintains formal contact with social language. "Grammatical doctrine" was not accepted by Bloomfield as the social norm in his perspective of verbal communication from speaker to hearer. The grammatical framework of "artificial" wave-sounds merely serves as an ideal. In Bloomfield's view, the traditional presentation of language remained "uneconomic and confusing" (1933/1967, 506), making it difficult to employ in real speech situations.

Jakobson wrote that the composer Wagner attempted to coordinate linguistic-and-musical signs to create the mystical significance he needed for his operas (Jakobson 1932/1971a, 553). But the general trend in linguistics was to take a more traditional outlook: music was seen as a phonological system of sounds that reflected the reality of the world in sound figures. Jakobson's "poetics" included musical dialect, which was taken up by the linguist and anthropologist Kenneth L. Pike. As a Christian missionary, Pike learned the Mexican dialects of the Native Americans to communicate and translate the biblical scriptures for the local populations. Language and music started for him as two separate things, but the otherness of music and language could be brought together by learning the phonetic sounds of the foreign language of the Mexican dialects to form one whole totality.

For Jakobson and Pike, the variety of "outer" features of language find a niche in the "inner" approach of Ferdinand de Saussure's acoustic waves of sound (Pike 1948, 34–36). For Jakobson, in poetical language, analytical figures of speech are united through metaphor in the metrical parallelism of rhyme and the phonic equivalence of rhyming words and sentences. Jakobson included grammatical length (verse), different from the "ordinary" form of literary prose, but not "exotic" sound structures that required interpretation by the reader or listener in order for them to understand the meaning of the metaphor and metonymy (Shipley 1968/1972, 268–269, 271; see Jakobson and Halle 1956/1971, 90–96). Jakobson followed the Sapir-Whorf hypothesis in his poetical method (Gorlée 2021, 530–536). Claiming that foreign dialects and slangs depended on the culture of the individual and affected their linguistic responses and perceptions changed the understanding of natural language as being merely behaviorally reproduced "grammatical" units. Language is viewed as consisting of "musical" speech-events adorned with human emotionality, giving both an individual meaning.

The origins of language were first designated as the "scenic pantomimes" of "primitive" man, which "still adhere to the ordinary speech of civilized man by motions of the face, hands, head, and body" (Mallery 1972, 271). Sebeok called the bodily gestures of sign language technically "quasi-language," involving the individual performance of quasi-speech from translation to transduction. This evolution meant that song may occur with or without lyrics or substitute forms of quasi-language—as in gestures, child language, drumming and whistles—that are considered as preverbal speech forms situated halfway between music and speech but having a linguistic character (Umiker 1974; Sebeok and Umiker-Sebeok 1976).

In contrast to Bloomfield, Sebeok proposed the alternative "speech surrogate" as a linguistic gesture of verbo-musical activity that expresses tone, melody, harmony and rhythm of language to be performed publicly as human, even native, forms of speech. It regulates the "feedback" language, activating the "feedforward" process of a sound-making speech-utterance and creating the "feed within" mechanism of transduction (Sebeok 1984a, 29). Quasi-language in Sebeok's terminology was the half-linguistic message imitating the vocal movements of harmony, sounds, rhythms and colors characteristic of musical speech. Thanks to this kind of quasi-signal, social communication, according to Sebeok, transforms the statistical translation of two languages into the mental process of transduction, re-forming the focus on rigidly reasoned general grammar as unconventional speech in artful transduction.

Changing the statistical language of translation into quasi-language and further into the dynamic transduction of quasi-speech once again classifies the continuous units of language as *three* concepts: "item," "process" and "arrangement" changed into "static," "dynamic" and "functional" concepts to focus on the meaning of the linguistic-and-musical sounds of wave theory. The phonetic units changed first into provisional units of sound, stress and tone to intersect at the articulatory classification of sentences (vocabulary) and fragmentary sections (grammar). After Bloomfield's classification of verbal units, Pike's functional phonetics (Beaugrande 1991, 88–121) operates on the contradictory but new complementary functions of "particles," "waves" and "field" to identify vocal language.

The contrastive analytical approach to linguistics that prevailed at the end of nineteenth century led from the hierarchical framework of geographical linguistics to the wave theory derived by the German physiologist Johannes Schmidt. In Schmidt's book *Die Verwandschaftsverhältnisse der indogermanischen Sprachen* (1872, reprint), the old geographical separations mediating between the frontiers of Indo-Germanic dialects were modernized from examining different phonological criteria to functioning as pancultural (that is, biological, economical or even mythological) interactions between Germanic languages. Schmidt's concept of dialects led to the scientific novelty of his wave theory, since he expanded separate dialects into "brain waves," interplaying human speech in innovating waves of thoughts and ideas. Schmidt's analogy showed how waves can be extended and outlined to organize the world from the atomic level upward, even to understanding linguistic dialects as meaningful units that seem to coincide and overlap in a wave-like process in one geographical zone.

Schmidt's wave function was taken over in the fixed ideas of Saussure, who saw synchronic language in the "floating realm of thought [...] as a series of contiguous subdivisions marked off on both the indefinite plane of jumbled ideas (A)" together with the "equally vague plane of sounds (B)" (1959/1966, 112, see 203, 209, 224, Saussure's original 1949, 156, see 277–278, 307). This is depicted in Saussure's model (see Figure 4) (Saussure 1949, 156; see 1959/1966, 112).

Saussure remarked in his *Course in General Linguistics* that Schmidt's *Wellentheorie* addressed the problem faced in the following way:

Thought, chaotic by nature, has to become ordered in the process of its decomposition. Neither are thoughts given material form nor are sounds transformed into mental entities; the somewhat mysterious fact is rather that "thought-sound" implies division, and that language works out its units while taking shape between two shapeless masses (Saussure 1959/1966, 112).

Schmidt's *Wellentheorie* articulated a new organism for visualizing the "chaos" of sound varieties in languages and dialects. Saussure metaphorically observed how linguistic details or elements are like a surface of water subjected to changes in "atmospheric pressure" resulting in "waves," which resemble the union of thought with phonic sounds (Saussure 1959/1966, 112).

Schmidt's wave theory was also read by Jakobson, who reformulated the waves in the poetic waves of literary retranslation (1960/1971a, 402; 1960/1964). Schmidt's theory of waves enabled Jakobson to develop his concept of "poetic" hypertranslation consisting of the harmonious interaction of intralingual, interlingual and mainly intersemiotic forms of translation (1959). Language was for Jakobson an "electro-chemical precoding process assumed to occur in a vertebrate's central nervous system prior to the recoding of a message in an externally communicable representation" (Sebeok 1984a: 29).

The three-way quasi-system of "sound waves" (Pike 1967, 317–320) changed the linguistic focus on interlinguistic waves of the brain, moving it away from logical linguistics toward less logical, even fictional, literature, as intended by Jakobson with what he termed as intersemiotic translation or *mediation* (1959, 233, Jakobson's emphasis). In Virginia Woolf's time, however, literary critics turned away from centering human language on the social (economic, political and ideological) toward believing in the more critically challenging "higher" atomism of the physical and chemical sciences that form the actual basis of human language. The critics subjected the properties of force, gravity, velocity, elasticity and speed to reading-and-writing the refreshed structure of linguistic units. Linguistic words conjure up sensations of the movement, weight, speed, stretch and timbre of waveforms with the characteristics of the thermoelectrical waveforms of word molecules lending a special, even mythical, structure to artistic speech (Jakobson 1961/1971, 4; see Cherry [1957]1966, 80; Cassirer [1957]1966, 439–440).

In Pike's "Language as Particle, Wave and Field" (1959/1972, 129–143, ills. from Jakobson 1960/1964, 363), the wave theory covered the "particles" of words functioning as discrete and static units with some boundaries between them (Nida and Taber 1982, 204). Particles were defined as single words in a vocabulary with clear-cut and well-defined sounds, but language is not regarded as a "political" program of uniform rules for word-particles but instead consists in the undercurrent of mechanical "molecules" that conjure up the complexity of the grammar of "brain waves." To build literary waves, the continuous flow of waves forms meaningful word-clues on which the continuous flows of three waves represent the magnetic and electrical lines of the evolution of first, second and third waves. The physical process consists of the waves spreading out from center to edges, changing from right to left and moving with increasing frequency, surface and depth. The waves are more compact in the first zero-wave but, as this wave passes, the second waves stretch apart into a variety of wavelets moving as third waves from center to depth.

The wave-like particles of Schmidt's wave function are complexified into the compound network of word molecules connecting units of ordinary language as transformed into their literary function, cultivating "poetic" communication in the play of words (see Casti 1994, 209, 264–266). Waves are the stylistic device of aesthetics in language. In Pike's approach, the basic element of the "field" of language is the functional process of the capacity of language to make the particles (or words) ready to be articulated as words to form sentences (Pike 1943, 1947). Phonemics was the cultural counterpart to the phonetic sounds of language, which Pike extended to the sounds of the English language, encompassing the vocalic differences, but without obscuring the varieties of the English language (1959/1972, 85–99; see Malmberg 1954/1963). Because Pike worked as a Christian missionary, his work had a practical aim. In his work, he was familiar with foreign languages and applying their mode of expressing functional units and using speech (Malmberg 1954/1963, 91–98).

According to Pike's "Grammar as Wave" (1967/1972, 231–241), the "field" is the systematic or functional model for describing the "interwaves" of human speech. "Field" was for him the phonetic grammar of language, but Pike mainly brought together the particles of words, waves and field in the quasi-structure of *three* distinct meanings: "particles" were words, but the "waves" allowed for movement of the overall theory of "field," making the verbal units fuse together in a wave experience. The sound waves are set in motion by a source of vibration of the air to form the wave-like grammar of acoustic and articulatory language (Pike 1967, 545–564; see Malmberg 1954/1963, 53–55). The linguist Pike stated that beyond learning foreign languages, as a missionary he had singing classes to learn the tone of church hymns (Pike 1943, 17–18). In Pike's singing instruction, he learned the flow of the tone for connecting the separate words in a continuous, meaningful wave, preparing the congregation for worship (Gorlée 2005a).

M. A. K. Halliday's functional linguistics flows into Pike's *three* lines of language to create textual, experiential and interpersonal grammar, reflecting the geometrical anatomy of human language (Beaugrande 1991, 237, 241, see 223–264). Starting out in the study of intonation like Bloomfield and Pike, Halliday presented in his acoustic grammar the rhythmic sequence of simple words articulated into tone groups, but he divided the complex expressions according to socially acceptable standards of pitch, duration and intensity (Halliday 1967). Bloomfield's "sketches of speech" were considered by Halliday as textual sound waves transferring the phonetic aspects of individual discourse to reflect the linguistic level of social grammar. Complex speech has a variety of meanings, making it possible to understand the generalized context of culture (Nida and Taber 1982, 199). Halliday's paradigms have multidimensional meanings to be reinterpreted and complemented to make the communication systems workable in collective speech. Halliday wrote that textual meaning was the "wave-like pattern of periodicity that is set up by peaks of prominence and boundary markers," confirming that "interpersonal meanings are expressed by the intonation contour" (1967: 169). Since the social "pattern here is prosodic, that is 'field'-like rather than wave-like" (Halliday 1967: 169), Halliday followed Pike in arguing that "wave" is the same as "field," that is, the structure of grammar in different fields.

For example, the formal analysis of the particle "wave" (as argued by Bloomfield, Pike and Halliday) was transcribed phonetically as [wāv] with lax vowels. Thus, the lack of vibration in the vocal cords produces the unvoiced [a] and mute [e]. Yet the timbre of the German nouns "*Welle*" [velə] and "*Woge*" [vogə] articulate a combination of tension in semivowels. After the bilabial fricative [v], the voiced vowels [a] and [o], produced with a round, open mouth, generate sharp vibrations, but followed by the final soft [ə]. Returning to the story of Woolf transcribing Wagner, Wagner's vocal harmony in *Stabreim* used the "rhyming" words "*Welle*" and "*Woge*" in the versetones of German pronunciation. Woolf's novel needed to re-articulate the sound structure elsewhere in her transduction of *The Waves*. She re-used the wavy elements of English meter and rhyme to form sound figures of poetic speech, while leaving the meaning to be discovered.

Woolf's passion for thermodynamic literature was recently discussed as working in the cellular processes of life on chemical and physical systems (Crossland 2018, 131–134). She prioritized the fictional discourse of Wagner's wave-like chemical patterns to form a bridge between formal and less formal phonemics. In the strategy of planning the novel *The Waves*, the organism of Woolf's novel was compared to a continual flow of waves in the sea of literary poetry bridging between poetry and prose. She considered the wave theory as coordinating the phonetic and phonemic wholeness of words and sentences arising from the particular individuality of sounds in order to produce the end product of a dramatic recitative in writing (Crossland 2018, 56–59).

Prior to *The Waves*, Woolf had been inspired by Wagner's fragmentation of *Stabreim* into fixed leitmotifs to transform his "frozen" poetry into the poetic romances of her previous novels. However, the recitative waves of Wagner's "unending melody" expressed the musical-and-verbal meanings which Woolf needed to emphasize her literary point. She rewrote, reinterpreted and reoriented the spoken dialogues of the novel *The Waves* into abstract art with different meanings. She radiated the continuous stream of phonemic sounds to stress the vital energy (German: *Lebenskraft*) of certain words in the sentence, suggesting with each syllable a degree of cultural emphasis (Ehrenzweig 1967/1968, 96–101). Woolf's rule of concept, system and method of vocabulary and grammar had to be unformalized, moving away from Wagner's fragmentation of sectional waves to be recovered and refictionalized in the free cooperation of swirling waves. Woolf created a cultural-political trend in this communicative method of poetic speech, avoiding the ambiguous, even contradictory, character of Wagner's prose-and-poetry to create the modern recitative of *The Waves* (Miller 2015).

Woolf's mimicry for reinterpreting Wagner's discourse (1929–1931) found an alternative in Freud's *Civilization and its Discontents* (1930/1979), written in 1929. Freud discusses the mastery of speech as a feeling of immortality created through the speaker identifying themselves with the "grammar" of their cultural group (Shands 1970, 350–355). The human ego was able to overcome the politically troublesome years of rising Fascism, returning from the trauma of poverty and economic inflation in Vienna to the proper "self." Freud's wavy self-analysis of the human psyche disrupted the intoxication of the rising "dream of a Germanic world-dominion [that] called for anti-Semitism" and avoiding the contemporary dangerous body of thought presented by the "communist civilization in Russia [...] in persecution of the bourgeois" (Freud [1930] 1979, 52). Freud himself criticized how his new psychoanalytical therapy was misused by artists as a self-help remedy (Freud 1930/1979, 15).

By observing the novelty of the curved mechanism of the ocean waves as a new object of psychology (Shands 1970, 350–355), the artist's unconscious self can blend with the natural phenomena of waves to reach the conscious feelings of Freud's "oceanic" experience and color in abstract art (Kramer 1980). The therapeutic imagination of the emotional feeling of oneness (Freud 1930/1979, 13–26) stands for the personal wavelets of self-translation. But the translational waves with their emotional moods expend enough energy to reflect the otherness of transduction in other arts. Following the subtle deep and formless feelings of the oceanic waves, the *three* stimuli of the "outer" phenomena of waves can re-form the translator's "inner" emotions to reveal the mystic oceanic feeling of transduction. As formulated by Kramer,

> [t]he first of these [waves] is simply a moment of recognition, in which the ocean's sublimity makes its demand on consciousness. There follows a phase of anxiety and self-questioning, in which the mind momentarily

yields to that demand and allows the imaginative self to die away. This reduction of the self, from an independent subjective presence to a vehicle for disclosing the sublimity of the world, corresponds to Freud's "oceanic feeling": a loss of the self in the great whole. (Kramer 1980: 212)

The oceanic feeling of waves breaks into new creative work, bypassing the self-interpretation of translation to move into the experimental flow and channel the libido of the self into dynamic transduction.

In watching and listening to the mighty flood of water, the translator is invaded by the waves of transduction. Moving away from Wagner's source text, Woolf felt adrift—her mind was not "normally" anchored in stylized translation, and she began to operate in dangerous waters, fabricating the "three phases of creativity" (Ehrenzweig 1967/1968, 95–109), which Woolf perceived as three waves. In the first wave, she experienced a "schizoid" stage of creatively "projecting fragmented parts of the self into the work"; in the second "manic" wave, the "oceanic limit where all differentiation ceases" attempted to bind "the single elements together," resolving the fragmentation "between ego and superego" to reach an unconscious space; while in the third wave, "the chaos of undifferentiation" was pushed into Woolf's consciousness on a "higher level," at which she gradually elaborated the designs of the novel with "severe anxiety" (Ehrenzweig 1967/1968, 102–103). The three waves are discussed in the examples from *The Waves* as the fragmented vision of Woolf's wave of ellipsis.

Wagner's Water Music

The lengthy opera *The Rhinegold* is divided into a web of leitmotifs giving a special meaning to the introductory passages of the first scene—Wagner's Prelude—to introduce the opera. The intensification of rhythm and sound articulate the subjectless meaning of different waves in order to receive in Woolf's elliptical version the sensitive and emotional feelings of the musical motifs (Meyer 1956/1970, 56, 260). Wagner's *The Rhinegold* was structured as a progressive network of waves that turned the low waves of the arias into the swelling of crescendo tones to create the magic of his opera. This technique helped him to harmonize the high token of waves into the totality of leitmotifs. Wagner introduced these instrumental motifs to remodel the musical-and-textual waves into the whole meaning of his Ring cycle (Abbato 1991, 202; Rosen 1996, 469–470). In contrast to Wagner's sound waves, Woolf's emotional mimicry was more meaningful than the fragmentation into *staccato* and *crescendo* waves: Woolf's undulating waves textualized the special structure of the narrative of the novel. She reconfigured the fluid and solid mass of verbal waves in the different textures of the verse-tone of the dramatic action, reflecting the musical sound and rhythm of the meanings of the whole novel. The title of the novel *The Waves* reconstructs the formal relations of Woolf's sound motif, but she divided Wagner's figurative scenes into her novelistic plot, allowing the rhythmic stream to flow into poetic waves to model the meaning of the novel.

The original waves determine the narrative scenes recounting the actions of Wagner's dramatic scenario onstage, but Woolf reorganized Wagner's literary world into the subtler rhythms of single words, creating wave-like sentences to flow like the sounds of the waves. In terms of the figurative and functional "grammar" of Woolf's novel, reading her novel has the same wavelength of time as listening to the beginning of *The Rhinegold*, but the change in process from fixed to dynamic waves produces a different spherical strength of character (Lakoff and Johnson 1980, 165). Wagner's "cosmic theater" guides the listeners "with a bittersweet authority" through the drama to "the ultimate fate that lies ahead" (Rifkin 1980/1981, 251), but the energy (high entropy) of this opera decreases into nothing (low entropy). Woolf's experimental mimicry of sound forms and the phonetic rhythm of her sound waves made her prose version into a poetical ellipsis, transfiguring the hearers from their passive role into an active one of giving diverse meanings to the lyrical verse. Listening to the pronunciation of Wagner's sung verses transports the listeners away from hearing the meaning of the operatic pronunciation, but reading Woolf's prose poetry with its diversified meter and rhyme allows them to discover a variety of meanings.

The *three* phases of understanding Woolf's waves enable the readers to climb an ascending scale. Woolf re-imitated her waves in order to characterize and identify what Jakobson described as the poetic metalanguage. Wagner's poetry-with-music was retranslated into the quasi-language of speaking-and-singing to become in total the oceanic waves of transduction. The longitudinal waves of acoustic speech include the transverse melody of the musical tones, in which the torsional waves of human emotion break Wagner's waves of interaction of poetry-with-music into Woolf's metalanguage (Bloomfield 1933/1967, 97, 120–126, 375; see Crystal 1987, 173; Pike 1967, 94). Woolf incorporated rhymed verse into the structural sections of the waves in order to construct the solid base of the discourse building her novel, but she moved away from Wagner's method of *Stabreim*. Thereby, she destroyed Wagner's *Gesamtkunstwerk*, described by him as the whole and perfect drama (*das vollendete Drama*) and explained in his theoretical book *Opera und Drama* (*Opera und Drama* 1900/1995) (Gorlée 1997, 248–252). Wagner's grand opera was redefined mimetically into Woolf's personal retranslation from German into English, but her psychological mimesis was located in the meaning of the sound theory.

Wagner's large-scale vocal cycle of *Der Ring des Nibelungen* was composed in the post-Romantic theory of *Opera und Drama*, published in 1852, just before he composed the libretto of *The Rhinegold* in 1853–1854. He applied the simple "Melody" (first and second waves) to the grand "Harmony" (third wave). In his own words, Wagner felt submerged in "a huge expanse of waters" and he "swam aimlessly and restless to and fro, until [...] he saw nothing but an endless surge of possibilities" with "no definite purpose" but "merely a floating sentiment" (1900/ 1995, 288). Wagner's temptation was to return to the quiet inlets of his homeland, "where the water flowed restfully between its narrow shores, and always in one definite tide" (Wagner 1900/1995: 289). But the turning point was to mount "from the depths to the surface of the sea of Harmony" to follow the "wave-borne mirror-image" of melody (Wagner 1900/1995, 280). Wagner emphasized the Harmony of collective feeling, integrating the song-and-words into the "Tone-melody" with his "Word-verse," thus creating the "waves of Harmony" (1900/1995: 306). For many theatergoers, probably including Virginia Woolf, Wagner's wavy poetics had "crippled" his poetic harmony, creating a disharmony between music and words (Raffel 1971, 157).

Following the early operas *Tannhäuser* and *Lohengrin*, the new style featured in *The Rhinegold* was an expressive break from Wagner's previous operas. *The Rheingold* binds together the rhyme technique of Wagner's *Stabreim* (1900/1995, 227–229, 276, 286, 291–293), which stands for the musical movement of the tonal waves of the scenes. The repeated leitmotifs bind the operatic scenes of the tonal waves together in one drama. In keeping with the features of *Stabreim*, Wagner adopted the use of words featuring the same initial letter, as was usual in the ancient Anglo-Saxon chronicles of *Beowulf* and the Icelandic *Edda* sagas. He also blended medieval ideas from the folk mythology of Norwegian sagas and the Germanic epic of the *Nibelungenlied* as part of his operatic scenario. Wagner even seemed to draw on the German fairy tales of the Brothers Grimm. His "modern" versification of *Stabreim* served as a mythological imitation to reinterpret the phonetic clues of medieval poetry. He transformed his verse into the coded recitation of prayers or even mantras in order to guide the audience around the magical waves surrounded by infinite melodies. The ritual of Wagner's operas repeats the synthesis of waves by retelling the rise and fall of life, with the repetition of the waves constituting the full force of the sea (like the waves of entropy).

As explained in *Opera und Drama*, Wagner uses the highly alliterative verse form of *Stabreim*, which is provided with assonant and consonant root syllables. The internal rhyme predominates this verse form, but with irregular forms of end-rhythm. Wagner introduced the ancient method of *Stabreim* as a new meter in German versification, but the rhymed consonants and vowels were stressed with unstressed syllables. These syllables were a puzzle in deciphering the alliteration and assonance of Wagner's writing, but when sung, the lyrics sounded out slowly as wholly understandable code-words. Imagine Wagner's juxtaposed senses of love ("*Liebe*") in "*Lust and Leid*" and "*Wohl und Weh*" conveying to the operagoers the mixed emotions of love.

The musical modulation of the German consonants [*l*] and [*b*] in the single verse "*die Liebe bringt Lust und Leid*" is transformed into the triple rhyme "*Die Liebe bringt Lust und Leid, / doch in ihr Weh auch webt sie Wonnen*" (Wagner 1900/1995, 291–292). The triads *Liebe–Lust–Leid* and *Weh–webt–Wonnen* make the verbal composition of the word an invention of Wagner's finished craftsmanship as a genuine poet of German verse. Another example of verbal-musical assimilation is the irreversible binomial in German of "*Aug' und Ohr*" ("eye and ear") (1900/1995, 276), in which the long assonance of the German vowels [*au*] and [*o:*] articulates the internal rhyme of the human senses. Regardless of the beauty (or ugliness) of Wagner's literary meaning, both separate words are compared musically to have a common meaning. Wagner's repetition of speech sounds was the free and forced device of alliteration in singing, which interconnects the rhyme scheme of the words in the organic parts of the verse.

Wagner stressed in his book *Opera und Drama* that the verse line consists of two halves to be sung in half-verse. The two halves are separated by a *caesura* (or break) to interlace the emotional wave and relax the singer's vocal cords to continue singing. The expressional intervals are meaningful overlaps, since the singer produces the strength and power of words-with-music by introducing a pause when interpreting the song (Wilson-de Rose 2020, 254–259). The accent of German words, which are often polysyllabic words, has the upbeat of stressed syllables alternating with the downbeat of unstressed syllables to follow the inhalation and exhalation of the singer's breath. The lungs need to be filled with air to lyrically synthesize the verses into verse-and-music in order to create Wagner's "waves of Harmony" (1900/1995, 314). Wagner claimed that the verse-melody (*Versmelodie*) lies in the folkloric root of *Stabreim*, which stressed the word to prepare the verse-tone for singing (1900/1995, 252, 313), but translating this root from German into other languages was an almost impossible task. After Wagner's time, the poetic technique of *Stabreim* was not generally appreciated, since it sounded like artificial waves stereotyping the near-rhyme of stressed syllables. The focus on the stressed syllable with similar rhyme was regarded as a metrical function, not a poetic style, since it lacked lyrical emphasis on the emotional poetry (Jakobson 1960/1964, 358–360).

Wagner's Prelude starts with the waves of Scene I, in which the opening measures are followed by *three* episodes of waves moving up and down from sunrise to sunset. Human life is also lyricized in the triple cycle of events happening in the sound movement of the waves of the river Rhine (McGregor 2009, 163–197). To illustrate the picturesque events of the first scene, he depicts the sunrise in the morning. Wagner's sequence of musical waves reflects the waves of the Rhine water as they stream into the movement of the river; the three Rhine daughters swim in the water. During the dramatic actions involving the Rhine daughters, the Rhine motif becomes entangled with the Nibelungen motif as the gold treasure of the Rhinegold leitmotif, where the fear of the unknown is entangled in the darkened waves of the river. Woolf seems to have enjoyed Wagner's first scene depicting the Rhine, prompting her to use it as the model for her novel *The Waves*.

Wagner's legend of *Das Rheingold* (meaning the Gold of the Rhine) revolves around the movement of the waves of the Rhine as dramatized in the non-orchestral staging of the opening measures (Scene I, Wagner 1873/1913[?], 5–63). The first act depicts the dark depths at the bottom of the river as a silence without orchestral music (Kirsch 2023: 19). At the beginning of the first act, the stage directions indicate the silence of the river Rhine, the noiselessness provoking a vacuum of emptiness on stage and in the audience. This nothingness is Wagner's magical dissonance of music and speech. The silence represents the darkness of the Rhine, creating the allegorical symbolism hiding in the prophetic depths of the river. Wagner's absolute silence is the shadow of non-verbal communication without musical sounds (Kurzon 1998, 5–19). This "soundlessness" seems to ground the "auditory system in repose" (Jourdain 1997, 1). The entropy (Sheriff 1984/1991, 82) of Wagner's silence stands for the "unproductive" zero tone, which must be carried over into the productive token of Wagner's information to flow into the typical magic of his fairy-tale operas.

The silence of the Prelude stands for the unexpected deprivation of power for music and speech; the composer-and-poet Wagner listens to the "many-voiced sea" without hearing the "water music" of the orchestral sound waves (Mlinko 2020, 41). The quasi-speech of the Rhine River guards the "prophetic" treasure more deeply than the flat surface of impersonal water (Attila 1977/1985, 11–12). The music waits for its turn to pulse rhythmic wavelets from the nether regions of the river to the upper speech of music. The waveforms (token) are the vast and dangerous territory of Wagner's work, changing the theatrical play into cultural and political narratives (the quasi-type of tone and token) (Cherry 1957/1966, 196–201). The vibration of Wagner's waves seems to come from the hiding place of the Rhinegold treasure, which lies deep beneath the surface of the river but remains hidden from the audience.

After the absence of melody, the emptiness is broken by the wavy *arpeggios* intoned by Wagner's alphorns. The broken-chord patterns are not prefabricated, but the sound is played successively or in isolation with extended notes to add a new tempo and rhythm to the opera. Wagner introduces the rustic Alpine horn to the operatic orchestra so that the *diminuendo* sound effect of the double bases are the first "primitive" waves audible as the hidden wavelets of the river Rhine. The alphorn is a pastoral instrument used by Alpine herders to signal to each other across the meadows and mountains (Gorlée 2005a, 81; Voigt 2015, 186–190). The low resonant tones of the wooden trumpet, which measures from four to twelve feet long, play horizontal and vertical melodies, halfway between E flat and B flat. Wagner's alphorns intone the leitmotif of the hidden secrets of the river Rhine (Nettl 1965/1973, 79; Kruse 2011, 50–51; Leach and Fried 1972/1984, 40). Traditionally, the alphorns are also used in folk music to signal the waves of sunrise. The pastoral sounds (*Hirtenlieder*) of Wagner's alphorns seem to parody the folk style (*Volkston*), transforming Wagner's typical tonality of "high" opera (*Hochkunst*) into a repertoire of folk songs (Schwab 1965, 131; Chambers 2010).

After the silent Prelude, when the curtain rises for Scene I (Wagner 1873/1913[?], 8), the audience sees the waves of the Rhine in full flood, with the stage of the theater transformed into a swimming pool. In the *first* wave, the three Rhinemaidens, named Woglinde, Wellgunde and Flosshilde, swim around in a balletic performance to and from the artificial waterfall of the river Rhine. They circle around the middle reef, vocalizing in lighthearted fun to each other as they swim in the waves of the river. The water nymphs in their high sopranos intone the natural wave of the river when they start singing in loud cries:

Wei - - a! Wa - - ga!
Woge, du Welle!
Walle zur Wie - - ge!
Wagalaweia! Wallala weiala wei - - - -

(Wagner 1873/1913[?], 9–10, 43)

Woglinde's soft-voiced waves on the initial consonant "w" [v] glide into the soprano voices of Wellgunde and Flosshilde. Translator Andrew Porter (1985) rendered this passage as "Weia! Waga! Wandering waters, lulling our cradle! Wagalaweia! Wallala weiala weia!" (Wagner 1985, 45). Mark Herman and Ronnie Apter (1983) translated this into the free variations of "Lula leia, billowing water, swirling in waves of shimmering wonder, lulalo, lalalo leia!" (Wagner 1983, 1) (Gorlée 1997, 254). Porter's vocalizations (Gorlée 2015a) blindly follow a literal translation of Wagner's versification. The translation of the cry is hardly a real translation, but the wordplay follows the Rhine waves. Jakobson's term "jocular song" (Jakobson and Waugh 1979, 8) describes the emotional double waves of Wagner's passage. However, Herman and Apter composed a decisive departure from Wagner's *Stabreim*. The musical voice of the waves is musicoverbal quasi-speech provided with the "quasi-natural" sound of metrical tones and rhythmical pauses stressed by the breath to be sung as the harmonic artwork (for details, see Gorlée 1997, 254–255).

The Rhine daughters sing together as a playful trio of high sopranos. Their word games in natural *Sprechgesang* (recitative song) are responded to by the emotional salvos of Alberich. In the *second* wave, Alberich's erotic attraction to the laughing water-maidens is articulated physically in his leaps from rock to rock to embrace their fine bodies. The swimming Rhine daughters sing with loud laughter "*Ha ha ha ha ha ha!*" (Wagner 1873/1913[?], 19, 29, 57) (Hahahahaha, transl. Porter [1976] [Wagner 1985, 19]; Ha ha ha ha ha ha!, transl. Herman and Apter [Wagner 1983, 2–3]). In the phonetic alphabet of "sporadic doublets" (Jakobson and Waugh 1979, 8–9), the hard and unvoiced throat sound [*hä*] stands for the monosyllabic, but asymmetrical, "*Ach-Laut*" (Malmberg 1954/1963, 50). The German fricative sounds pass through the narrow space between the back of the tongue of the singer to be constrained in the singing. The front–back opposite is translated naturally by Herman and Apter, who add an intermediate stop between "*Ha ha!*" to provide the human throat with an intermediate pause in order to sing the final stress of the following "*ha!*"

Trying to escape the twisting motions of Alberich's body through the water as he attempts to catch one of them, the Rhinemaidens swim quickly upward in the Rhine's waves. They laugh their way out of the eager grip of his hands, singing

> *Walla-la! Walha-la! La-la-lei - - a! Lei-a-la-lei!*
> *Hei - - a! Hei-a! Ha ha!*
>
> (Wagner 1873/1913[?], 31–33, 47–48, 53–55)

Porter (1976) translated the alliteration into the same motif in "Wallala! Lalaleia! Leialalei! Heia! Heia! Haha!" (Wagner 1985, 50), while Herman and Apter translated freely in their version "Fa la la! Fa la la! La la leia, leia la lei! Heia, heia, ha ha!" (Wagner 1983, 4). Herman and Apter transform the initial tones from the fricative sound [*v*] to [*f*], that is from the flat and open friction to the strong and narrowing friction of the mouth. The quick pulsations of rhythmic intertonations that continue in the Rhinemaidens' cries of "Hahahahahaha" (Wagner 1985, 50) are translated by Porter with the same sounds of "Hahahahahaha" (Wagner 1985, 50), while Herman and Apter included Alberich's spasmodic articulation to give space to the hard thrill of the singer's voice. The causal sequence of "Ha ha ha ha ha ha ha!" (Wagner

1983, 4) associates the literary signs with each other in a discernible non-literary pattern for singing.

In the transverse wave of the *second* wave, the increase in tempo produces the *crescendo* story crucial to Wagner's *Rheingold*. Woglinde, Wellgunde and Flosshilde are the guardians of the Rhinegold treasure, which is secretly kept in the river. The golden radiance comes as a total surprise. The gold glitters splendidly and the Rhinemaidens intensify the melody in the verse-tone:

Hei - - - a ja - hei - - - - - - a!
Hei - - - a ja - - hei - - - - - a!
Wal - - - la – la la la la lei - - - lei - - - a ja - - - hei!
Rhein - - - - - gold!
Rhein - - - - - gold! (...)
Hei - - a ja heia!
Hei - - ja - hei! (Wagner 1873/1913[?], 40–43)

Porter literally translated the surrogate speech of the Rhinemaidens when they catch sight of the golden treasure as "Heiajaheia! Heiajaheia! Wallalallalala leijahei! Rhinegold! Rhinegold! Heiajaheia! Heijaheia" (Wagner 1985, 51–54). Herman and Apter translated this singing episode as a jubilant cry between the free sound particles in their version "Heia la heia! Heia la heia! Fa la la la la la leia la lei! Rhinegold! Rhinegold! Heia la heia! Heia la heia!" (Wagner 1983, 4–5).

Finally, the erotic wildness of Alberich's voice reaches the summit with a final leap. The *third* wave comes close to the golden treasure, which is plunged down into the secret depths of the river. Wagner instructed that the Rhine waters sink to the bed of the river, while the rocks disappear in thick darkness, spreading forward to fill the whole stage with black waves. Alberich is out of control and the treasure is shrouded from the public eye in a gray mist. The Rhinemaidens abandon their fanciful exclamations to sing with loud voice the final cries "*Hülfe! Hülfe!*" followed by a soft "*Weh! Weh!*" (Wagner 1873/1913 [?], 59–60; see Poizat 1992, 91). Porter's *forte* translation was "Help us! Help us!" while Herman and Apter focused on the transformation of Alberich's sexual lust into greed, rendering the translation as "Stop him! Stop him!" Porter's troubled "Woe! Woe!" [*wō*] was rendered by Herman and Apter as the emotional plea "Help! Help!" (Wagner 1985, 54; 1983, 4). Alberich's role changes as he goes from being the mocked magic lover to becoming the dramatic chief villain of the piece, while the loss of sexual lust transforms the Rhinegold treasure into the richest fortune lost in the river Rhine.

The first scene of *The Rhinegold* is the model for Woolf's novel *The Waves*. The speed of Wagner's waves is shortened into a ballettic performance of the

Rhinemaidens in order for them to survive the strong waves of anxiety. The passionate and sexual response of the sopranos provides the physical exclamations of the *first* wave, but the opera is associated with the development of the *second* waves, which manifest in low to high notes. The *third* wave is Wagner's top note *di bravura* raising the pitch to the great waves of the repertoire of the opera *Das Rheingold*. The Prelude seems to arrive with soft waves until heavier and louder waves announce the twilight of the gods, who actively intervene in the story. In Wagner's *The Ring of the Nibelung*, the succession of waves seems to articulate the mood and tempo of the union of musical tone with tune (Kruse 2011). Wagner's operatic performance delivers musicocentrist and logocentrist brain waves as the foundation of Woolf's episodes (her variety of leitmotifs) (Antoniç 2016, 107, 111, 115–117–122, 131).

Virginia Woolf's Brain Waves

Woolf's plot is different from the romantic and picaresque images of Wagner's swimming Rhinemaidens singing together as they greet the treasure of gold. Hers is a novelesque sound drama expressing in poetic prose how a group of male and female friends get together near the sea to discuss their hopes and emotions. Woolf creates a basic unity in their narratives by not mentioning Wagner as her source, but by linking her words through psychological and logical ellipsis, presenting the sound, rhythm and meter in alliteration, assonance and consonance to create the poetic language (McGregor 1977, 328–333). Woolf retranslated Wagner into an experiential and psychological novel.

Wagner was essentially a musicocentrist composer. While fabricating the musical composition of words-with-music, he employed the tone-words of *Stabreim*, enclosing the semantic verse in imaginary and ambiguous arias and ensembles of rhyming words. The syntactic forms of singing delineate a protected, almost private seclusion. According to Georg Steiner, Wagner's verse is not the "authority of rational statement, of designation through governed structure, which are its proper genius," but stands for his specialty at reaching out in words "into the twilight zone to enclose the word in its own comprehensive syntax" (1967/1985, 63). Indeed, the rhetoric of *prima la musica e poi le parole* led Wagner to state that music must be the "master of the bargain" of words-with-music (Steiner 1967/1985, 63). Doubling the two modes, the Wagnerian opera creates the first waves in the rhythmic tonality of the *Gesamtkunstwerk*, but the lyrics of the operatic libretto work as the poetic quasi-language. The lyrical words serve as a secondary gesture to enclose the first gesture, the music.

In contrast to Wagner's musicocentrism, Virginia Woolf defended the logocentrism of her own fictional ellipsis, which embodied her bodily lived experience of writing literature to express her art of vocal wordplay. Woolf greatly favored the sounds of words and sentences (Bloom 2002, 328). Woolf's word game was to activate the vocal voices in retranslation to recreate in her innovative novel *The Waves* the ideological sounds and cultural feeling of a literary singsong. Her principal endeavor was to liberate the lyrics from Wagner's music and shift the prosaic text away from it. Woolf borrowed the poetic and rhythmic undertones of Wagner's words to create a reliteration of musical verse in the ellipsis of her prosaic versification. Woolf gave a false appearance to Wagner's verse in her art of verbal sounds. Her primary frontier was *prima la parole e poi la musica*. Woolf's logocentrism was expressed in the sound metapoem of *The Waves*, in which she lets go of the material exercise of Wagner in retranslating the periodic waves; indeed, she created the literary moments in disharmony outside of Wagnerian harmony in order to offer her political vision of life. Woolf distanced herself from Wagner to delve into her own cosmological discourse of transduction (Bloom 2002, 327–332).

Virginia Woolf's stream-of-consciousness seemed to imitate Wagner's strict pattern of operatic sound movements in the long, mediate and energetic waves of her work. In the transition to retranslation and quasi-speech, and further to transduction, the pseudo-translation of Wagner's opera transduced into Woolf's novel with sufficient time and energy for the readers to listen to and read the verse-tone of Woolf's *three* waves differently. In Woolf's sea, the problems cause the waves to bubble and boil, and Woolf determines the conversations of her speakers situated on the seashore, that is, left between life and death. In the italicized beginning of *The Waves*, Woolf notes that she had to find a parallel for the "rhythm of the waves [which] must be kept going all the time" to move her novel forward (Woolf 1976, 749; Sutton 2013, 142–143). She found her own wave rhymes in the moving evolutionary process of describing the sounds, the poetic and novelistic waves of the vocal interaction of words and sentences. Woolf's wave occurs in one direction (that is, reacting to Wagner), but the art of Woolf's musical rhythms must stand out as a meaningful sign structuring the prosaic waves of the novel. While Woolf's waves transduce Jakobson's rhetoric into the outside sound shapes of *The Waves*, inside she patterns the poetic meaning of her phonological method (Jakobson and Waugh 1979; Culler 1982, 12–19).

Woolf's first wave before sunrise is a non-wave, following Wagner's non-melody in the Prelude, in which the zero hour of flat waves symbolizes non-language in silence (Jakobson 1939–1940/1971, 211–223; Kurzon 1998, 8, 131; McGregor 1997, 329). The literary emptiness of sea and sky is expressed in Woolf's first vision: "*The sun had not yet risen. The sea was indistinguishable from the sky, except that the sea was slightly creased as if a cloth had wrinkles in it*" (Woolf 1931/2000, 3, Woolf's italics). The assonantal effect of the rhyming series "sun," "sky" and "sea" depends on Wagner's *Stabreim* but is articulated in the initial consonant [s] followed by various vocals. On contact with this voiceless fricative [s], the vibratory thrill of the articulation of those words brings no sense of synonymy (as in Wagner's *Stabreim*) but alliterates the doublets into strong or weak waves with different rhythms and rhymes (Jakobson 1979, 8–9). Sound experiments show that vocal [s] narrows the air in the flat-shaped consonant, but the breath is modified by the movement of the tongue and varied into the half-voiced sound. In phonetic script, the stream of air from the fricative closure of initial [s] produces the articulation of the semivowels [sēn] and [sī]. This produces a soft friction, but the palatal semiconsonant [ski] brings a hard friction (Culler 1982, 14). The stream of air gives the singer a limited or restricted breath of air, but Woolf's tone of reading starts with soft wavelets growing into harder waves.

At the beginning of *The Rhinegold*, Wagner's sound material arranged in *Stabreim* weaves the words of human voices into *three* waves. Woolf amplifies Wagner's source model by adding the words of vocal and italicized sentences as separate waves. The verse-tones of the speakers follow the discourse of the speakers in monologue and dialogue, but in her writing of the novel, Woolf gave emphasis to each of the word waves and its word elements. As a poet, Woolf pieced together the literary unity stylized in an almost biblical style: "*As they neared the shore each bar arose, heaped itself, broke and swept a thin veil of white water across the sand. The wave paused, and then drew out again, sighing like a sleeper whose breath comes and goes unconsciously*" (Woolf 1931/2000, 3, Woolf's italics). "On the *first* day, God created the earth as an empty waste. But on the *second* day, He separated the sea waters from the sky waters to make dry land and make the evening and the morning" (Gen. 1: 2–10). In the book of Genesis, the frontier between mortal and immortal waves is that of Woolf's unknown period of "*dark line*" (1931/2000, 3). Was this Wagner's silence as the sign of his privacy? The verse language "musicalized" the zero words into *three* singable waves, but as the *first* and *second* waves are moving out, God's plan is to reach the *third* wave when the largest wave secretly transpires. Woolf's strategy seems to follow Jakobson's literary version of "poetics."

The chaos and multiplicity of *three* waves sound like an illustration of the rebirth of speech from the beginning through the rising of the sea waves to the descent of the sea waves. In Woolf's literary text, after the blank silence of the *first* wave, the *second* wave is the sensual motion of sounds disturbing the horizontal surface of the wave with the vertical curves of the centrical wavefront. Woolf wrote that she observed in the waves the "*thick strokes moving, one after another, beneath the surface, following each other, pursuing each other, perpetually*" (1931/2000, 3, Woolf's italics). The progressive vision of the imperfect word energizes the movement of the waves flowing from the first particles of words into the continuous flux of sea waves.

Woolf's experimental project benefits the broad scope of the physical body of waves according to the volume, shape and size of the atoms (particles) of words (Crossland 2018, 19–69). The sound mechanism of the waves is considered a quasi-language between translation and transduction. In Woolf's writing, a close reading of Wagner's verse structure is used in metaphorical symbols to transpose his poetry into prose. Wagner's stilted transcription (Jakobson and Halle 1979, 27–28) of *Stabreim* is transformed into Woolf's wordplay of rhythms to form a sound harmony. The mechanical stress of sounds is transformed by an electric shock from Wagner's fixed *Stabreim* into Woolf's sound images, creating meaningful word-clues.

From the *first* sound wave, the voiceless constriction of the initial sounds [*th*] and [*s*] becomes, with pauses between words, the voiced cluster of hard consonants "*thick strokes*" [*thik strōks*], from vocal [*i*] to [*ō*]. The alliteration of the repeated [*p*] in "*pursuing each other, perpetually*" provides an accentuated image, giving time and space to the growing waves (and the tempo of the readers). The triple alliteration of [*p*] lends an electrical sense of energy, activating the advent of the waves in the mind of the reader. The emblem of the sunrise shapes the greater stream of tempo and velocity, dominating the *second* and later the *third* waves. At the seaside in Woolf's novel, the "*white*" wave turns into the *second* wave, changing from a colorless tone into an impressive spectrum of colors. The "*white*" surface may become "*green, and yellow*" flames of fire. The *third* wave becomes the "*broad flame*" surrounded by "*an arc of fire burnt on the rim of the horizon, and all round it the sea blazed gold*" (Woolf 1931/2000, 3, Woolf's italics). Woolf follows Wagner in referring to the waves' colors constantly (Riley II 1995). The sustained foggy mist of sea and sky starts as the *first andante* wave accelerating into the entire spectrum of *più crescendo* and *molto vivace* waves to depict the ravaging sea waves.

The sea waves are colored by the conversations spoken by the chorus leaders of the group of friends: Susan, Jinny, Rhoda, Neville, Louis and Bernard. They talk on everyday topics as their *first* topic, but this then leads into Woolf's *second* passage (Deleuze and Guattari 1987, 252). Beyond the interventions of the six talking characters, Woolf gives echo to the silent figure, Percival (Winterson 1996, 86–87). As in Wagner's *unendliche Melodie*, the fluid streams of operatic speech have no form of discussion but are redefined in Woolf's personal waves to sketch the characters of the speaking friends. While their voices explain their impression of the paradoxical worlds of English society, Percival remains the *incommunicado* outsider, absent in the conversation, but present as "unsung" hero (Abbate 1991, 29, 131, 155; Cherry 1957/1966, 80–81). Percival's voice works as the ground wave effecting the deeper voice to govern the group conversation. Despite his bodily absence from the scenario, Percival seems to be the emotional hero orchestrating Woolf's pattern in *The Waves* (Greimas and Cortés 1982, 1, 242–243; Deleuze and Guattari 1987, 340–343; Sheriff 1984/1991, 283–284).

In Woolf's literary experimentation with the prose poem *The Waves*, the continuous stream-of-consciousness pronounced by the speakers changes Percival's silent voice, allowing the reader to see "further" than information about the day-to-day lives of the characters (Kurzon 1998, 74–75). In the dramatic *coup de théâtre* of Wagner's opera, Percival seems to speak for the omniscient voice of creator God. The image of Percival transforms itself into the *third* wave, in which he addresses the other characters directly and indirectly. In his invisible performance, Percival translates the *first* monologue of the separate speakers into the transduction of the *second* duologue. In *The Waves*, through Percival's life and death his voice gives God's divine truth to the circle of friends.

Woolf seems to expand Wagner's operatic Rhine waves into the vocal speech of her novel. She disguises the flux of first and second quasi-speech in the *third* wave, which is the moral lesson. Opposing Percival's silent voice, the alternative voices of the figures speak in stylized musical "arias," but pronounced in recitatives (*parlando*) in the half-speaking, half-singing waves of Wagner's ensembles in *Sprechgesang* (Gorlée 2008a, 122–123). The six speakers speak their "elevated" bourgeois speech (German *Sprechstimme*) as the *second* waves, but they comment on a daily piece of journalistic news in the circle of friends. Woolf also seems to remodel the figures of Wagner's other operas— including the crazy caricatures of Wagner's *The Mastersingers of Nuremberg* (*Die Meistersinger von Nürnberg*, written in 1862–1867; Gorlée 2008a). Despite this content, the psychological effect of Woolf's writing transduces the non-referential messages into a well-structured and referential hypothesis, but without any "laws" of fixed information (McGregor 1997, 329). *The Waves* works as a circular gameplay probing the depth of the characters' souls and offering something of a conversational plot to guide the vague recitative of the speakers. Woolf's speaking-and-singing metapoem overflows from Wagner's sexual ballet of *Das Rheingold* into the dark undertones of *Parsifal* and *Die Meistersinger*, bringing death to the victims (McGregor 2009, 152–158).

It seems that the name Percival was chosen by Woolf as an English "translation" from Wagner's opera *Parsifal* (written in 1877–1882), but the improvised metaphor acquires new forms and contexts (Weiss 1961, 164–165). Originally, Parsifal was one of King Arthur's knights engaged in the quest for the Holy Grail. The Celtic and Christian history of King Arthur's romance resounds in the melodic repetition of Wagner's trombones, pseudo-imitating the mellow tone of the alphorns, to give the message of the Holy Spear to the sacramental brotherhood. *Parsifal* was Wagner's mystery or miracle drama in which the character represents the figure of Jesus as a prophet triumphing over the erotic love of Amfortas and Kundry (Adam and Eve). Through Parsifal's shame and his feeling of guilt, Wagner was able to conjure the mystical vision of pure love, but Woolf's symbolism is similar to that of Wagner in terms of the leitmotif representing the symbolic vision of *three* waves. It seems that the hero passively shares the adventures of the other speakers to propagate the truth as their perfect knight.

Wagner's first waves of the Rhine are vocalized as the speech action expressed in the high sopranos of the three Rhinemaidens carrying on their flirtation, but Alberich's heroic tenor symbolizes the emotions of love and hatred (Donington 1963/1976, 45–65). In Woolf's *The Waves*, the six speakers form a chorus of voices and have serious intentions. The intertextual orchestration and the sound phonetics of the mixed chorus are reflected in the poetic soliloquies spoken by Bernard, Susan, Rhoda, Neville, Jinny and Louis, as well as in the silent voice of Percival. These voices recite the emotional recitative (*Sprechstimme*) in natural *parlante* to themselves, in contrast with Wagner's waves of chorus leaders speaking in dramatic *parlante* in separate arias and ensembles as the musical scenery of the opera (Kerman 1956/1989, 114–117, 182). Woolf gestures the chorus to speak in short wavelets that foreshadow the "structure and decoration, abstraction and figuration, figure and ground" (Norris and Benjamin 1988, 27) of the following wave.

When the sun rises over the sea, Woolf theatrically depicts the waves to tell the stories that make the fabric of the friends' lives (Miller 2015). The friends feel both alone and together, making Woolf "musicalize" their words in a wavy pattern to set the climatic scenes of their lives in their human words (Jakobson 1956/1964, 363–364). In their emotional voices, the protagonists of *The Waves* look for new waves to possibly share their own "word stress in polysyllabic words from downbeat to the upbeat" helped by the "reversed feet" (Jakobson 1960/1964, 363) of the phrases, meters and pauses of the group of friends. The collective "speech about speech, a message about a message" produces a "'relayed' or 'displaced'" form of vague response (Jakobson 1956/1971a, 130). Direct discourse is turned into a theatrical recitative in order to tell and retell some stories without a consensus, merely gesturing or displacing what the other characters were attempting to say.

Woolf's soliloquies reflect how real communication brings what Jakobson termed as "shifters" to color the poetic speech. This dual sign, including Saussure's message and code, is a waveform fluctuating between the referential context of the addresser and the message of the event to establish contact between addresser and addressee (Jakobson 1960/1964, 353). This verbal material of Saussure's binary opposition is contrasted, even opposed, by Jakobson's poetical words, moving away from standard and formal linguistics into the "intrinsic values of a literary work by a subjective, censorious verdict" of informal beliefs and sentiments (Jakobson 1960/1964, 352). Is Jakobson's shifter the equivalent of Peirce's interpretant as a psychological reaction to the received sign? When Woolf's clueless characters only speak to themselves, the social routine of "conversational repair" needs Woolf's formal speech to "mitigate and patch up the consequences of failure to communicate" with each other (Wardhaugh 1985, 214). Woolf provides the remedy for the "misunderstanding" between linguistics and poetry, repairing what is "unfortunately a fact of life, understanding and cooperation" between speech and poetry (Wardhaugh 1985, 214). In the overstatements of those personal opinions, Woolf understates "the very cement of society" (Wardhaugh 1985, 214) to overcome personal opinions with a final interpretant. Conversations about anxieties and other life matters give the personal interpretants sensitive emotions, including the understatement of sacrifice and suffering (O'Hara 2015). Woolf's monologue and dialogue game-played not one meaning to living their lives, but a wide range of meanings moving away from "theatrical" waves to produce the artistic wholeness of life and death balanced by Woolf's particle-like wave theory (Crossland 2018, 19–20).

Wagner, as a political "insider," originated the image of waves from Germanic folk culture as the stylized symbol of the rising sun in the new time (Elliott 1959/1980, 56–57, 60, 64). The sun was described in runic inscriptions in the Nazi metaphors of the tree of life, love and fertility (van Heemskerk Düker and van Houten 1941, 13–24). Woolf was the "outsider" of Wagner's ideological performance; she epitomized how her storylines seem to camouflage the rise of Nazi folk symbols (Wilson-de Roze 2018). She unbalanced the audience with a smokescreen (*Vernebelung*) to give a new meaning (*Umdeutung*) to news and visual information. In her elliptical parallax, she wavered Wagner's exalted waves into the emotional waves of her own rhythmic fiction. Her exercise in transduction renewed the political meanings for the future (Woolf 1931/2000, 4–14).

Turning away from Wagner's compromised ideology, Woolf created a novelistic storyline or poetic plot, but she crossed Wagner's lines of political thought with her own lyrical words and sentences to give the truth. Asking a number of pseudo-questions (Cherry 1957/1966, 246–247), Woolf addresses the thoughts, feelings and fears of the speakers to reveal that the "closed balanced series of weights and measures and proportions that agree with one another and that agree as a whole" are unnecessary (Winterson 1996, 93). Woolf created a new horizon to the political landscape. For example, in *The Waves*, the protagonist Bernard sees the sea waves swelling in the Wagnerian "ring [...] hanging over me," while Rhoda hears the "sound [...] cheep, chirp; cheep, chirp; going up and down," cutting Wagner's versification of sound down to Woolf's size (as Jakobson turned phonology into poetics). Neville sees the wave of the sun as a spherical "globe" in the air, and Jinny sees the heraldic sign of "crimson tassel" ensigned "with gold threads" of the bourgeoisie. Louis seems to hear the waves of the sea as the "great beast's foot [which is] chained" and "stamps, and stamps, and stamps" (Woolf 1931/2000, 4). The waves are three. The journey of the sea is like the mighty "elephant with its foot chained" (Woolf 1931/2000, 5). Sailing out on the sea seems to be Woolf's desire to be engulfed in the diving waves and perhaps be frozen to death.

The metaphorical speech forms are creative waves distributed as dialogues from hearer to speaker, yet their speech is not a real question but simply a rhetorical answer (Carlson 1983/1985, 118–119, 104–105). Although they each address something to the other speakers, their self-answering speech does not evoke a reply but keeps the final dream hidden. The alternative voices display Woolf's dialogue game in which she abandons Wagner's source waves and moves away from his unended arias and ensembles; Woolf wanted to re-form the character types as social and political mimicry. As a novelist, she kept in tune with Wagner's forms of versification, kinds of diction and conventional style in the melodramatic passages of *The Waves*, but Woolf's phonetic quasi-language shortened and diminished Wagner's "artificial" waves of art song into "emotive" waves of political life, social poetry and egalitarian society. In the speech-form of metanarrative discourse, Woolf's irony turns the episodes of waves into the *first*, *second* and *third* waves, producing new political sounds to solve the problems of the world.

Woolf as a fictional adventurer freed herself from the traditional plot of Wagner's music-and-verse. To create the complex waves of life from separate sentences, she articulates one word to another, with one sound wave following after another, when Rhoda cries "cheep, chirp; cheep, chirp; going up and down" (Woolf 1931/2000, 4). In Woolf's process of transduction, this quasi-language sounds out like the cry of an animal which is imitated in a "song," informing of the event without lyrics. The nonspeech sounds of the "cheep" [$ch\bar{e}p$] half-rhyming with "chirp" [$ch\bar{\imath}rp$] produce an acoustic effect by strongly articulating the stressed and vibrant syllables in the voiced [ch] but neglecting the unstressed vowels of the voiceless and bilabial fricative [p]. This quasi-speech has the *"regressive undulatory curve"* (Jakobson 1960/1964, 362, Jakobson's emphasis; see ill. wave, 363) of speaking in rhythmic sound-signs to alarm the readers against what they wanted from life.

Another of Woolf's examples that includes the protagonist Rhoda's speech applies Wagner's old story of the Rhinemaidens "swimming from shore to shore" (1931/2000, 5). Woolf's "Rhine daughters" merrily chat to Bernard, who is perhaps playing the role of Wagner's Alberich. In telling the adventurous story of his life to the circle of friends, Bernard is Knight Parsifal

(Donington 1963/1976, 61–62). Woolf bases the characters of *The Waves* in the principle of free speech, but she transforms the oceanic waves of musical verse into acoustic rhymes. For example, when Rhoda says, "The birds sang in chorus first," but "Off they fly. Off they fly like a fling of seed" (Woolf 1931/2000, 5), the contrast between "first" and "now" indicates her plan to run "off" [ôf] and "off" to "fly" [fli:] with "fling" [fləŋ] to stress in the flying sounds of the strong fricative consonant [ʃ] flying away from her world into strange adventures.

The desire for adventure in life means throwing oneself into the fluctuating world of new waves to live the thrill of the *second* and *third* waves (Crossfield 2018, 19–20). But if one stays at home, there is no call from the waves to sail the seas: "Look at the tablecloth, flying white along the table" are Rhoda's words. "Now there are rounds of white china, and silver streaks beside each plate" (Woolf 1931/2000, 5). The experiment of "flying" is now colored down to the "white" wave of silence, depicting the *first* attempt at strictly maintaining a bourgeois household. A British lady could merely pronounce a pure vowel with her mouth to give her opinion. Her real voice comes from the back of her throat, relaxing the throat and giving her a sense of identity (Riley 1995, 275, 337). But genuine singing starts with the *second* wave, not simply "flying" but listening to the "first stroke of the church bell," after which "the others follow: one, two; one, two; one, two" (Woolf 1931/2000, 5).

Virginia Woolf's parallax form abandons the unmelodic sounds of Wagner's melodies and hears life as reflected in "church bells." The tones produce standard vibrations, but do not create pure colors, as demonstrated in the symbolic signs of her invention of the vocalic sound structure. The sound of the church bells instills warm emotions in the hearers, touching them with a mélange of warm and inviting tones, but can these tones "electrify" the human brain to feel spiritual conduction? It is true that church bells connect the vibrations of the air to give warmth to the human chest, throat and face, but their "story" is the transition of the *first* iconic wave to the *second* indexical waves to perform the emotionality of the listeners. However, as Sebeok and Umiker-Sebeok (1976, 192–198) state, the order and succession of the church tones stand for the quasi-linguistic waves of the "surrogates" of coded language. They show in the tonality, loudness and rhythm how a simple translation can travel from the single wave to the complex stimuli of fluctuating waveforms, transmitting the sacred tones to other hearers (Pike 1948).

In her writing, Woolf opposes the role assigned to women, who for her are not the "surrogates" of the coded language of men. She transforms the spontaneous soliloquies of the female friends in *The Waves* into a discussion of the political crisis of women struggling to assert their right to active participation in social and political matters. Women were condemned to barely exist as anonymous legal persons. The working-class population and bourgeois women were denied their rights, so women needed to reject this symbolic world of unreality and engage in "schizophrenic modernism," changing the social and political images of womanhood in order to create a new reality of womanhood (Minow-Pinkney 1987, 155). Woolf's *The Waves* symbolizes the identity and loss of the neutral existence of women, who were expected to stay at home, get married and govern the household. For Woolf, women needed to take hold of the active power of a thinking mind and dedicate themselves to work and suffrage.

Woolf's new vision affected herself and others (that is, both women and men) when she pitted herself against the patriarchal system of Great Britain, abandoning the vague uncertainty of the situation that women faced and demanding political certainty. The effort of the patriarchal system to constrain women to domestic household chores was not remedied by Woolf's translation of these tasks into ornamental words, for instance in her description of the rhythmic work of polishing "white china" with "silver streaks" (1931/2000, 5). Woolf was an extreme feminist and declared that women (and men) should demand the independence of women, as well as their full legal authority and equal educational and commercial opportunity, the right to practice any profession or trade and the right to vote.

As a novelist, Woolf committed herself to the strenuous chore of introducing Leftist feminism against the British authority of the Right. In the prologue of *Rheingold*, the scenic details of women's existence are sketched in "discrete clusters of words or isolated images which are not pigeon-holed in a syntactic hierarchy," but in the rest of the soliloquies in *The Waves*, Woolf works to unite her ideas and thought, moving from "narrative necessity" to "logical connections" (Minow-Pinkney 1987, 172, see 155–174). In semiotic terms, that moves practical Peircean oneness-and-twoness into intellectual thirdness. Traveling from "stroke" [$str\bar{o}k$] to "streaks" [$str\bar{e}ks$], Woolf abolished the losing streak of women, transforming it into a winning victory. She took a stand against bourgeois domesticity to advocate for a break from the traditional view that a woman's place was to guard the family and household goods, and she definitively broke the traditional rules in order to promote women's work rights. Woolf did not resign herself to having no political rights, but, as an intelligent woman, she believed in foregrounding the "wavy" movement of feminism (Tallman 2019; 2020, 10, 14). In her novel *The Waves*, she poetically transfers the acoustic timbre into what Jakobson calls the "poetics" of vocal sounds: she transports the closed vocal [$\bar{o}$] to [$\bar{e}$] and further to the open vocal [$\bar{\imath}$], seeing "white," "china" and "silver" as acoustically characteristic of the servant work of kitchen maids in contrast to the empty-handed existence of bourgeois ladies.

Wagner fragmented the rigidity of *Stabreim* to create an interplay of words in metaphorical sentences. Woolf's first project was to modernize Wagner's versification onward, rediscovering the power of the "musicalized" prose to hear and feel the emotional tone with the new rhythm of female action struggling against Wagnerian antifeminism. Her second project was to make a political statement against Wagner's fascist trend in thinking, as argued before. Woolf was a political thinker, actualizing her thoughts forward in ideological but experimental forms of writing. Her literary method did not follow the linear nature of translation to globalize Wagner's synonyms as parasynonyms; instead, she moved in the opposite direction. In her political ellipsis, she retranslated Wagner, shortening the political distance to pronounce herself at war with his versified leitmotifs. The difference with Wagner lies in Woolf's strength of emotion in investing these thoughts into her novel. Her goal was to restyle Wagner in her own symbols of sound, rhythm and imagery in her experiment of *The Waves*. To achieve this effect, she introduced *avant-garde* literary elements into her art to evince beauty and truth. Woolf's adventurous spirit paved the way from conduction to transduction.

At the end of *The Waves*, the fictional protagonists Rhoda and Bernard redefine Woolf's life. Their life stories suggest the way in which psychological waves react with violent waves, prompting the human minds of Edwardian society to engage in reason and thought. English culture needed to be reformed to stimulate equality of the sexes, but movements toward this were often controlled and disappeared in the subwaves of political affairs. Women were not welcome to participate in Parliament, nor in politics in general. Woolf's sensitivities are her political *tour de force* in radically advocating for women's rights. She wanted all women to have their own lives, to have freedom of speech and other liberties that were the privilege of the male domain. Women should not be constrained to the role of housewives but should take action for themselves. This is reflected in the monologues of the individuals in *The Waves*, in which the male and female voices in the chorus are assigned the same harmonic (and disharmonic) emotions. Woolf's discourse was her world image imagined from varying viewpoints. She read the English newspapers, but her close association with the Bloomsbury group made her attitude skeptical and tolerant; yet the second point that made her social attitude complete was the solitary experience of being female in a life with no votes for women.

At the beginning of *The Waves*, Woolf insists on symbolizing (or even mythologizing) the psychological journeys of the sea waves into despair (Kirsch 2023, 20). The adventure of going to the seaside was for the thrill of feeling the constant flux of the waves. To thrill the speakers, Bernard loses himself in the darkened waves of the ocean. He speculates to Susan about the adventure of exploring the sea and being "like swimmers" diving down into the waves and "sink[ing] through the green air of the leaves"; but he adds philosophically that "the waves close over us, the beech leaves meet above our heads" (Woolf 1931/2000, 8). Susan sees life more in terms of hereness and nowness, but Rhoda likes affirmative action. She has a metaphorical fleet of ships "swimming from shore to shore," but although the "waves rise" in the storm, her ship "mounts the waves and sweeps before the gale" to reach the shore (Woolf 1931/2000, 9).

For Virginia Woolf, waves can be zones of great danger. Rhoda is "sailing on the high waves," but has to "pull [herself] out of these waters" (Woolf 1931/2000, 14) to save her own life. The dangerous waves "heap themselves on me; they sweep me between their great shoulders," but she responds saying, "I am turned; I am tumbled; I am stretched; among these long lights, these long waves, these endless paths, with people pursuing, pursuing" (Woolf 1931/2000, 14). Rhoda's life crisis stands in contrast to Bernard's adventure. Rhoda's life is not in danger, but she demonstrates a dramatic change at the beginning of every sentence with her desperate cry "I am," using past participles to tell the others her fatal message, "I am lost." Then, more prosaically, the four alliterations of [p] return the end of the last scene to the beginning of *The Waves* (Woolf 1931/2000, 3). The final point of Woolf's personal yet graphic novel is Bernard's mortal "adventure," the recounting of the misadventure of his life. For him, the long waves of the sea have passed the point of no return. In the midst of sorrow, in writing the final conversation of *The Waves*, Woolf felt the angst of progressively stronger waves, which engulfed her in the rough sea. She suffered mood swings and terrible headaches and felt depressed, but in her emotional misery, she remained an intimate novelist and sociable friend (Rose 2022, 24–25), until, at the end of the emotional waves of her life, she finally succumbed to the temptation of death (Marder 2000, 346, Kirsch 2023).

Chapter 3

WAR AND LOVE: THE PARABOLIC RETRANSLATION IN BERLIOZ'S OPERA

Berlioz's Poetical Drama

The French composer Hector Berlioz (1803–1869) was born in La Côte-Saint-André in the department of Isère, which is located in the Rhône Valley, close to the Alps, halfway between Grenoble and Lyon. The Berlioz family had some distinction in the French region. Hector's father, Dr. Louis Berlioz, was a successful and prosperous physician in the region (see Berlioz's bibliography, Cairns 1989/1999: 3–5). He practiced healing through acupuncture to relieve chronic pain, thereby attempting to introduce this healing practice to the Western world. Acupuncture comes from Chinese medicine, originating two thousand years before the birth of Christianity, but in the Napoleonic era, acupuncture was regarded as an alternative, even occult, pseudoscience. Dr. Berlioz furthered Western medicine, helping take it from the simple observation of symptoms to the scientific reality of being able to heal patients as experienced today.

Louis Berlioz had an inquisitive mind with logical rigor, but for his children he was also interested in poetic literature, fine arts and music. His son Hector Berlioz was born in 1803. Hector turned against the financial chaos of the Old Regime. As a pioneer of the French Revolution, he seemed to mark a turning point in politics. As a result of his fascination with Napoleon's tumultuous, but short-lived, government, Hector Berlioz furnished Napoleonic ideas to the modern world. He advocated the revolutionary ideas of liberty, equality and fraternity to serve as a movement against the world of the privileged classes. Hector gained his initial education under his father's guidance. Under his father's tutelage, Hector engaged in scholarly pursuits that included the study of intellectual subjects such as Latin grammar, French literature, history and geography. In 1821, Hector passed his examinations in philosophy and rhetoric to enter the French *baccalauréat* in Grenoble. His Latin specialty was the ancient literature of Virgil's *Aeneid*, Horace and Cicero, which he had read and translated with his father (Cairns 1989/1999, 46–60). The two of them shared an enjoyment of Virgil's long poems in Latin, which Hector retranslated into French lyrics. In adapting this version, he found himself caught up in the difficulty of readapting Virgil's verse into French lyrics for the romantic opera, *The Trojans*.

In his youth, Hector had music lessons, so already as a young boy he was able to read music notation and play various instruments. He also learned to sing and played the flageolet (a descendant of the recorder), the flute and the guitar. He was one of the few composers of classical music who could not play the piano; instead, he was tuned toward other sounds, substituting piano fingerings with the vibrations of the metal strings of the woodwind instruments. He transformed other instruments by creating other harmonics not yet used in the orchestras of his time (Rosen 1996, 554–556). Berlioz resonated the melodies of the wind instruments against the sharp edge of other instruments (Berlioz 1844/2002, 137–146). Since he also played the guitar, a stringed instrument played by plucking the strings with the fingers of one hand while the other was arranged to form harmonic chords on rhythmic strings, he also integrated this instrument into the orchestral works he composed (Berlioz 1844/2002, 80–88).

This variety of old and new instruments inspired Berlioz in his technical mastery to invent modern instrumentations for the orchestra, forming unusual combinations. His theoretical work *Orchestration Treatise* (French original 1844; English translation and commentary by Hugh MacDonald [ed.] 2002) included new instruments like the saxophone, concertina and a battery of percussion instruments. In his scientific treatise on musicology, Berlioz as a virtuoso composer invented an alternative art of orchestration by modernizing the tonal and coloristic qualities of the symphony orchestra, thus creating the modern orchestra as we understand it today. He also included the voices of the principal and secondary singers, covering men, women and children (sopranos, contraltos, tenors and baritones) (Berlioz 1844/2002, 246–264), as musical instruments. In Berlioz's time, his music was considered to be extravagant and surreal, but today his music is seen as an expression of emotional and free melodies. Hector Berlioz's father, however, thought that music was merely a hobby to entertain his son in his leisure time, but Hector regarded his vocation to be a real composer as an opportunity to leave behind his provincial social *milieu*. In French society at that time, Hector's ambition to leave provincial society was a big step, and for him it meant seeking the adventures of the music halls, operettas and other light entertainment.

Dr. Berlioz wanted his son to enter the School of Medicine, but young Hector had already shown his genius for learning and composing his own symphony music. He rejected his father's bourgeois choice of vocation in life and desired to be a composer. Deciding between medicine and music was a crucial point for his future perspectives. Becoming a country doctor would be fitting for his social position, and he could follow in the footsteps of his father, but becoming a composer was Hector's picaresque adventure, allowing him to become a hero in the dramatic underworld of the music halls. After a heated family argument, Hector ignored his father's criticism and embraced the alternative career of becoming a music composer. In 1821, he left for the metropolis of Paris.

In the Parisian theater scene, Hector's extravagant behavior showed a shift from his former provincial attitude to the utterly alternative pose of "playing" different theatrical roles to express the scenes of his romantic life. Hector's passionate sensibility made him susceptible to his own melodramatic behavior, and he playacted with stage gestures to symbolize his feelings. His gestures inspired and influenced his irrational love affairs. The young Hector had read Jean-Jacques Rousseau's *Confessions* and Goethe's *Werther*, which had inspired him to make the striking change in his cultural environment and move from the provinces to the cosmopolitan city. Living in Paris, Hector identified himself wholly with the romantic *rêverie* of the dramatic *mal du siècle* plays of Romanticism and delighted in expressing the dramatic motivation of "spleen, ennui, nostalgia, alienation" (Cairns 1989/1999, 59). As a composer, he grew to become a great spirit of the nineteenth century, but psychologically he behaved as a self-actor, emphasizing his own physical relationship, exchanging his emotional identity to become a wild composer of highly dramatic works of art.

Berlioz was enslaved by his passion for romantic love (Spiegl 1997, 36–41, see Cairns 1989/1999, 1999). He gestured his inner feelings of love in his outer mannerisms when speaking about his emotions, but love never came his way. He was a *sui generis* person displaying his madness in combination with the romantic genre of an artistic life. He was strikingly different from others with his wildly undulating red hair, big nose and sharp eyes. He echoed the mood of the emotional young artists and the misery of forgotten loves in his theatrical attitude. His amorous disposition lent his music the special tone and eternal nostalgia of a fairy world. He had experienced his first love affair when he was just 12 years of age, when he met Estelle Duboeuf, who gave young Hector an "electric shock to his whole being" (Cairns 1989/1999, 61, see 61–65). The acute and painful ecstasy of Estelle remained a star undimmed all his life. The electrical conduction of this experience was later transposed into the dramatic end of Queen Dido, which builds up the opera *Les Troyens* to a climax of amorous transduction.

Berlioz's later love affairs were embodied in his uncontrollable passion for several women whom he venerated as female ideals and whom he gave heroic names taken from Shakespeare's comedies and tragedies. Berlioz overdramatized his lady friends Harriet Smithson, Camille Marie Moke and Marie Recio (a pseudonym for Marie-Geneviève Martin) by embodying them as his Ophelia, his Desdemona or his Juliet. In *Les Troyens*, Berlioz transformed his female ideals of eternal love into acrobatic sopranos (Aucoin 2019, Saules 1975). Acting as the dramatic poseur of eternal love, Berlioz thought of himself as hearing the temptations of erotic pleasure deep in his body, suffering in his appearance the emotional pain of the untraditional disharmonies of love and disfiguring the voice of his musical arias into tragedies. Like the figure of Hamlet, Berlioz seemed to alienate himself on the battlefield of love, identifying with the darkness of Shakespeare's graveyard in mourning the beloved. He did not look for emotional delight in love but met his misfortune with the female singers with a smile to keep the painful intensity of his melancholy and grief alive in his music (Spiegl 1997, 41; Jourdain 1997, 316).

While Berlioz was engaged in his love affairs, France was taking part in the European political rebellions of the 1830s. Berlioz composed his *Fantastic Symphony* in 1830 (Op. 14A), which was subtitled *Episode in the life of the Artist* (Cairns 1989/1999, 352–375). His creative mind was a whirlpool of personal ideas out of which he drew a nine-piece symphony, composed to convey the sense of the dark figure of French Emperor Napoleon, whom Berlioz simply adored. The titles were *Rêverie-Passions*, *A Ball*, *Scene in the Country*, *March to the Scaffold*, and a three-piece *Dream of a Sabbath Night*. Berlioz seemed to grieve for Napoleon's exile and death on the island of St. Helena, where he was imprisoned after his defeat at Waterloo (1815). Berlioz mourned for the last six years of his life.

As a young man, Berlioz also had major success with his scientific work in musicology. His *Orchestration Treatise* (1844/2002) highlighted the novelty of orchestral practice, including modern instrumentation employing the instruments of his time. Berlioz modernized the tonal and coloristic quality of orchestration with lasting influence. His first attempt at transduction was in replacing the old tradition of having two or more compound notes corresponding exactly to each other with eccentric tunes of dissonance that glided into consonance. From the old consonance of musical notes, he created a degree of dissonance with sometimes drastic or even fugitive notes. The audience was taken by surprise by the disharmonic sounds, which transported the emotional drama into the interesting poetry of music (Meyer 1956/1970, 229–232).

Turning to Hector Berlioz's theatrical productions, he composed the opera *Les Troyens* (*The Trojans*), a historical costume drama with a poetic libretto in French, between 1856 and 1859. This was a turning point in the genre of opera: Berlioz's vocal material transformed the long epic poem of Virgil (Publius Vergilius Maro 70–19 BC) into the relative brevity of the vocal opera. In his musical and textual variations, Berlioz tried firstly to capture the attention of the music-loving audience. Resonance became [Berlioz's] only goal; to his vision of opera, musical resonance was his goal. To achieve it, vocal *shading* was eliminated, as was the *mixed* voice, the *head* voice, the *lower notes* of the tessitura; tenors were given only high notes to sing, in the so-called *chest* with *chest* voice; basses became baritones […] the highest, shrillest female voices were clearly preferred over all others. Only those tenors, those baritones, those sopranos who could hurl out their voices at the top of their lungs received any applause. (Berlioz 1853/1971, 121, with Berlioz's emphasis; see Poizat 1992, 40–41)

Despite Berlioz's melodic and harmonic effort to produce a vivid movement away from the existing operas that were fashionable at that time, *Les Troyens* was and remained his almost neglected masterpiece, unloved and without public success. He published the vocal scores in 1863 and composed the full scores in 1869 (the music was performed in 1863 and the libretto was published in 1969, now reprinted in Berlioz 2013).

In terms of content, following the separate part of the Overture, Berlioz's masterpiece *Les Troyens* is divided into two parts consisting of frequent changes in military scene depicting the Greek and Trojan battles over the city of Troy. The story recounts that, after the Greek victory over the city of Troy in the Trojan Wars, Aeneas is a refugee who roams across the Mediterranean Sea only to be shipwrecked by storms off the coast of Carthage. There he falls in love with Queen Dido of Carthage. After his Odyssey on land and sea, Aeneas leaves his lover Dido and goes to Italy, where his descendants Romulus and Remus, would found the city of Rome, glorifying the victories of the military state of the Roman world.

The Trojans was Berlioz's romantic opera. He moved away from generating melodic symphonies to creating the romantic melodies of a real tragedy. He wanted to highlight Aeneas' adventures, and especially to hear the high notes of the Shakespearian soprano singers (Poizat 1992, 40–41). Designed for the audience's ear and the eye, Berlioz's new opera emphasized the acoustic pleasure of vocal and orchestral music, together with the lyrical arias, ensembles and choruses. The performance of verbal speech in the form of lyrical arias blended with the visual dramatization of movement in the operatic scenery, light, costume and other scenic effects happening onstage (Gorlée 1997, 236). The music was his own, composed without any formal model, but Berlioz transferred Virgil's setting to a memorable year of the Trojan War. The Trojans had lost in battle, Troy was totally destroyed, and the Trojans were either dead or enslaved. After a decade of warfare, evil words and deeds are abandoned and the deserted beach celebrates the unknown destiny of the city.

Berlioz's opera voices an abysmal failure in terms of the radical change in spirit in the first part of *The Trojans*. The Greek hero Aeneas, son of Venus, the goddess of love, wants to end the military destruction and the eternal battle of Troy. As a virtuous man, Aeneas leaves Troy with his father and son to return home. Contending with the storm and shipwreck on the wild sea, Aeneas symbolizes the birth of the new spirit. In the second part, Aeneas is stranded in the city of Carthage and falls in love. After Aeneas's amorous encounter with Dido, he leaves Carthage to go to Italy and found the city of Rome as its Roman patriarch. Berlioz loosely constructs continuity between the two opposed patterns of war and love, reproducing in the opera the emotional interactions between the verbal and musical arts, thus completing what Jakobson describes as the movement of "poeticalizing" language (1960/1964, 359). Berlioz rekindles the operatic elements of "spirit and sensitivity and beauty" interweaved into the dramatic content of the pseudo-translated opera (Kerman 1956/1989, 16).

Jakobson's "hypertranslation" (Hays 2017, 58) describes the upgrade of "ordinary" speech to the "poetic" function of translated verse. Jakobson stressed lyrical musical rhyme and rhythm to overemphasize "poetics" against normal speech. Berlioz's "transcription" from Latin to French (Jakobson and Waugh 1979, 27–28) focused his perspective especially on the music of the opera, with the functional modeling of the poetic modulations of lyrical words as a second perspective. Opera involves the meaningful function of literary music rearranged with verse to produce the lyrical beauty of opera. In Jakobson's understanding, the aim of "poetics" is to produce a high "figure of sound" (1960/1964, 367) in language, which can be contrary to the direction of the linguistic words.

For Berlioz, the musical notes of the opera in the series create a further level of retranslation beyond Virgil's ordinary translation. They express a poetical message consisting of musical sounds alluding to a wide range of related messages in lyrical literature. The elements of speech as understood by Jakobson include their own sound texture, metrical pattern, rhyme structure, alliteration, assonance and verbal phrasing to restructure the external elements into the "internal nexus between sound and meaning" (1960/1964, 373). Berlioz's intercode translation seems to neglect Virgil's Latin words, retranslating the words according to the music. His musical interpretation consisted in creating the lyrical meaning of music, while he underplayed the lyrical language as a second possibility (Gorlée 1997, 242, see 240–244).

Whereas the operatic music was the original opus of Berlioz's *The Trojans*, the poetic lyrics sung by the operatic singers and the chorus were readapted in Berlioz's standard style to accompany the previously composed music (Pavlovskis 1981). In his book *Translating Poetry: Seven Strategies and A Blueprint*

(1975), Lefevere describes the process of retranslation from ancient Latin as consisting of the three phases of textual, contextual and intertextual "variations" (1975, 16). In the first section, the first variation is about the textual variations of Latin language seen as a source medium. Latin "entails a number of limitations: there are certain things one cannot—because of the very nature of the language—say in Latin, as well as a number of opportunities" in other languages (Lefevere 1975, 16). The second section features stories about contextual variations where the ancient writer struggles to come to terms with the dimensions of the verse, since the ordinary recitation of Latin verse was different from the way in which operatic arias were sung in Berlioz's time (Lefevere 1975, 16–17), while in the third section, the variations are intertextual about the series of efforts to restructure modern literature out of ancient literature. The sensation of "the impulse to write can only come from previous contact with literature," but the impulse to write "an occasion, an experience, an event, may inspire the inspiration that 'crystallizes around the new event'" (Lefevere 1975, 17), surprising the audience.

This mediation is not the art of many text writers. Since Berlioz's intertextual creation primarily involved the musical side of the opera, he remade the lyrics by retranslating from Latin into French. Considering his deep knowledge of the Latin language, he needed no dictionary or other tools to recode and retranslate the Latin verses of Virgil's ancient epos the *Aeneid* (Raffel 1971, 114–115, 159–160; Holmes 1989). After composing the music for the opera, Berlioz completely redacted Virgil's *Aeneid* (reprinted in the classical Loeb edition 1916/1999), which he needed as the lyrical base text for opera *Les Troyens*. The *Aeneid* was the poet Virgil's gift to the Roman Emperor Caesar Augustus (63 BC–14 AD). With his poem the *Aeneid*, Virgil offered Augustus the necessary mythology rooted in the prehistory of Rome to sanctify his family roots and present him with a genealogy worthy of the imperial family (*gens Iulia*). For Virgil, Augustus's dynasty was rooted in the foundation of Rome by Romulus and Remus. In their imitation of this mythology, Berlioz's battles of hatred and love in *The Trojans* express the details of the drama for the enjoyment of the bourgeois audience of French operagoers (Raffel 1971, 114–115, 159–160).

Although the staging of the opera *Les Troyens* was a massive undertaking requiring a huge investment of time and money, the five-hour ancient historical drama was criticized in Berlioz's time as being "static and untheatrical" (Orrey 1972/1987, 153–154). Berlioz's over-the-top opera seemed impossible to produce in French theaters due to the limited finances of the French concert halls. Since Berlioz willfully adapted the opera in two parts, he succeeded in having the first two acts performed as *The Capture of Troy* (called *La Prise de Troie*) and *The Trojans in Carthage* (*Les Troyens à Carthage*) in 1863. However,

Berlioz's monumental drama was not crowned with any Olympic wreath of olive leaves—not for French opera and certainly not for Berlioz himself. Truly, *The Trojans* was Berlioz's transgression against French tradition, not understood by operatic critics. In his later years, long after composing *The Trojans*, Berlioz felt like a misunderstood composer, bitter and unacknowledged. The reason was that some parts of this opera were only produced in a brief and mutilated version—such as the excerpts played at the opera's première in *Théâtre-Lyrique* in Paris (1863)—but a complete single-performance staging of the opera did not take place until a century later, long after Berlioz's death.

The reason for the lack of interest in performing Berlioz's opera *The Trojans* was that in France there was little interest in "foreign" operas with non-French stories. Berlioz expected a stronger response to his work, as had the younger composers Charles Gounod (1818–1893) and Camille Saint-Saëns (1835–1921) to theirs. The international repertory, retranslated into English, Italian, Russian and other languages, had to deal with strong waves of French nationalism together with the French culture of operatic traditions, as well as with the mercenary finances of French theaters. However, in French society it seemed "that the opéra was an essentially bourgeois taste in the nineteenth century, and now neither the intelligentsia, nor the young people, nor the poor, are born opera-lovers," although it seemed that this situation somewhat improved in the postwar period in the twentieth century, when "the element of competition [was] helping to lift France out of her state of complacency" (Tubeuf 1962, 42).

This national attitude to French operas even aroused a dislike of receiving foreign artists, singers and musical conductors. In his time, Berlioz imagined himself to be an international artist. He enjoyed traveling abroad in Italy and Russia, where he was accepted as a specialist in modern music. At the high point of his life, he was invited to visit England to lead the Grand English Opera (1848–1849). The real reason he accepted was that he sought to escape from the rebellious years of the French Commune (Cairns 1999, 391–342). Berlioz was nevertheless invited to represent France on the international jury of the Great Exhibition in London (1851) and the Paris Exposition Universelle (1855). His innovative duties as juryman, composer and conductor in judging new music were widely reported in the French press. There seemed a real prospect that the operatic landscape would change, and it was thought that perhaps with Berlioz they were "witnessing the beginning of a new golden age" (Tubeuf 1962, 42). To be sure, French culture was extremely nationalistic and very removed from Berlioz's life.

Beyond the fact that Berlioz and Wagner were both revolutionary contemporaries working as musicians and librettists, their lives showed barely any parallels. Both worked on operas, but operas sung in different languages

(French and German). It seemed that after 1839, when the political disturbances in Prussia broke out, the German composer Wagner and the French composer Berlioz were both political rebels. Wagner sought asylum in Paris. He and Berlioz were seen as foreign rivals criticizing each other's works (Newman 1972, 97–101, first published in 1904). It was clear that Romanticism in German operas had more liveliness and invention than in the French tradition. *Sturm and Drang* enthusiasm was embodied by the contemporary music of both Wagner and Berlioz. In France, however, Romanticism was started at a later date by Berlioz (Longyear 1969, 59–129) and flourished after Berlioz's death. Wagner returned to Germany to direct the Dresden opera, while also composing the trilogy of *The Rhinegold*. When Wagner turned to the Germanic myths and legends, Berlioz took up the challenge by composing the opera *Les Troyens* from ancient mythology.

When in 1870 the war between France (now under the weak emperor Napoleon III) and Prussia broke out, Prussia's forces proved superior to the French army. After some weeks of bloody battle, France surrendered to the Prussian armies. As part of the final settlement with chancellor Bismarck, France lost Alsace and part of Lorraine. France felt a general misery and indignation about this loss, and the tense political situation erupted in a violent uprising in the Paris Commune, with calls for the establishment of a socialist Republic. Napoleon III feared that the monarchy might fall for the Republic. The year 1871 remains a landmark in European history. Europe had found some political stability with the unification of Germany, although Franco-German relations gave rise to the renaissance of instrumental diplomacy, with performances of German musical dramas taking place in Paris.

Wagner and Berlioz were both revolutionary musicians, but with opposingly different lives and lifestyles to each other. While Wagner postured as the great star of the operatic festivals, Berlioz struggled to overcome his romantic follies and hoped to be considered as the great musician of the future (Tiersot 1917). The lack of recognition of Berlioz's operatic style in his home country differed sharply from Wagner's dramatic successes in the "magic" universe of the playhouse in Bayreuth. Following *Tannhäuser* (1845), Wagner wrote the *Nibelungen* operas between 1853 and 1876. At the same time, Berlioz composed the opera *The Trojans*. Despite his noble efforts, Berlioz was no grand idol who ruled French opera, but a gifted and dedicated composer who struggled to make ends meet.

While Wagner produced theatrical festivals with success to celebrate the romantic cult of opera, Berlioz was a romantic composer struggling to earn a living, and not through the composition of his own music but through his work as a conductor. Further, Berlioz even earned his living through the chores of "musical journalism, arrangements of Weber's and Gluck's operas for performances in Paris, and poorly paying sinecure positions" (Longyear 1969, 94). In terms of prestige and income, the opera *The Trojans* brought no income and gained no popularity with the Parisian operagoers.

In the libretto of Berlioz's opera *The Trojans*, Berlioz seemed to "crystallize a shifting and drifting musical theme into artistic form" (Langer 1948/1980, 241). After the musical transduction of the theme into operatic music, Berlioz worked intensively to retranslate parts of the Latin verse into French words and sentences to be sung and recited in the French arias by ensembles and in mixed chorus. Yet the battles of the heroes in Wagner's German *Nibelungenlied* were seemingly more beloved by the French opera aficionados than was Berlioz's poetic retranslation of Virgil. The fact that *The Trojans* was played by transferring pseudo-Shakespearian romantic heroines into French arias did not help. It seemed that Berlioz's opera was a romantic drama with an unhappy ending which abandoned French operatic reality to symbolize Berlioz's new imaginative space of retranslating. Berlioz sketched the rebellious spirit of the individual hero (Aeneas) to recreate the strange universe of Virgil's account of his travels across the Mediterranean Sea, exploiting the empire's capital of Rome to honor the imperial period of the ancient emperor Caesar Augustus. This was Virgil's adroit propaganda to survive the troublesome years of Augustus' imperial reign (Holmes 1989, 67–68).

Berlioz's visionary project was to redesign Virgil's original poem in the form of an opera, but how did he proceed? One technical device he used was to transfigure Shakespeare's heroines as part of the opera. French audiences were not in tune with Berlioz's serious operas but enjoyed transduction into French. Berlioz reduced Virgil's ancient epic versification from Books I, II and IV into usable French romantic lines, but after this intellectual labor, he felt depressed and unhappy with the result. His individual genius as a romantic musician and librettist did not allow him to consider himself as creating musical melodies to be readapted using symbolic images and verbal metaphors. French audiences were not in tune with Berlioz's serious operas: instead, they enjoyed the sentimental *opéra comique,* such as the French operettas of Giacomo Meyerbeer (1791–1864) and Jacques Offenbach (1819–1880) (Longyear 1969, 84–86). These light operettas were adorned with popular dance-like interludes, with love romances, dance tunes, cheerful choruses and piquant couplets, which were popular with French audiences (Rosen 1996, 599–645). In his earlier operas, Berlioz had used Wagner's *"sucreries"* (sweet things) (Berlioz 1971, 323; see 311–333), but not in the serious opera *Les Troyens.*

Before composing *Les Troyens,* young Berlioz made the carnival music of *Benvenuto Cellini* and the Italian folk-tunes of *Beatrice and Benedick*. In this earlier period, when he still lived at home in La Côte-Saint-André, he enjoyed composing light operas. But after leaving home, the opera *The Damnation of Faust* and other later symphonic and operatic works strengthened and intensified his inclination to deal with some of mankind's most profound questions. He showed light operas in the new vein of *opéra lyrique* (Longyear 1969, 87–88). His aim was to create more than dance operettas; he began recreating religious symbols and the political ideals of love and loyalty in musical harmony. It seemed that the French composer Georges Bizet (1838–1875) also followed the same direction in his final opera *Carmen* (1875); like Berlioz, Bizet moved from *opéra comique* to *opéra lyrique* in depicting the romantic story of a Spanish gypsy girl whose life ends in tragic death.

Berlioz's musical and literary work reconsidered the classical dramas of literary history, but the opera *Les Troyens* remained his main opera. The reformed parts of Virgil's original epos the *Aeneid* (Latin: *Aeneis*), written in Latin in dactylic hexameter, were rewritten in poetic form in French. This lyrical opera tone-paints how retranslation, described in Jakobson's terms as a method of vocal translation, aesthetically harmonizes (or even disharmonizes) the target work with the poetic versification of Virgil's source text. Charles Rosen states that "Berlioz often uses a root position when the harmony of the voice leading demands a second and third inversion" (1996, 545). Berlioz invented a new musical technique to create ambiguity of meaning in music but included the imaginative use of notes to transpose the lyrical words, creating a new situation in opera. It seems that the double-bind of music-and-words loosened the lyrical versification. Berlioz met a literal and cultural verse challenge (Raffel 1971, 154–172, 1988).

The anticlassical inclusion of intermittent sounds within the vocal music of Berlioz's versification provided the asymmetrical texture for the simple symmetry of dividing and irregulating the phrase length of words to accompany the previous musical notes. Berlioz's task was to shorten considerably Virgil's epic poetry into the lyrical words of the opera, but it meant that the words of the opera were sung to a tune with a slow tempo and rhythm. Truly, the words of the lyrical interpretation took three times longer than the passage of music. The singing in *bel canto* meant that the asymmetrical tones of the musical notes were more than the symmetrical "wrenched accent" (Abrams 1941/1957, 103). Berlioz had to reduce the singing to accommodate the word length of the musical notes (Kruse 2011). His task was one of vocal gymnastics, of squeezing words into music. The listener does not hear the open vowel of the motif's harmony but rather the irregular and slow harmonization of music and lyrical text as the melody proceeds with disharmonious half-variants before returning to the motif. This tension between musical tones and the length of words is a puzzling combination. Berlioz adjusted the rules of prosody to comply with the tempo of his own libretto, thus re-forming the dramatic flow of the opera.

Berlioz realized that the shock of the singer's vocal performance can lead from harmonious dissonance to basic consonance, raising a passionate interest in the listener (Rosen 1996, 547–556). In the lyrics of the sung texts, Berlioz's technique used and misused absolute synonyms to form the variety of quasi-synonyms, parasynonyms or even antonyms to make sense of his dramatic retranslation. He needed to innerly translate and outerly retranslate from Latin to French, but the aesthetic moment of creating the new combination of sound-and-text melds the total melody of his opera, creating an exciting drama for the audience.

The vocal texture of dissonance and consonance that Berlioz created in his opera was a step further than Virginia Woolf's understated ellipsis of not translating Wagner's *Stabreim* but readapting the rhythm and rhyme in a new style. In the French acculturation of Virgil's poem, Berlioz applied the half-modern figure of the parabole to recode the intercode of music-with-words. He dissolved the figure of the parabole from the unlikeness of meaning between the compounds music-and-text, not through literal synonyms, but through overemphasis of the disharmony to reconcile the two branches of music and lyrics with near- or parasynonyms. The verbal and musical weight and importance of Berlioz's sense of opera overemphasized the music but underemphasized the retranslation.

Berlioz's rhetorical genius constructed *prima la musica e poi le parole*; the musical notes overplayed the music of the words. Bringing music-and-text together, Berlioz reoriented both elements into the combination of musical notes with a "metaphoric" appendix. He moved in the opposite direction, attempting to fit the length and breadth of the words into the musical arias (Goodman 1976/1985, 83, see ill. 82). Whereas Virginia Woolf transported her elliptical version away from the political framework of Wagner's system of lyrical verses, Berlioz's parabole was an extreme version of musicocentrism. The music was Berlioz's primary art, whereas he employed his retranslation of Virgil to dramatize his opera. The moral resemblance of the double lines was an attempt to differentiate the retranslation into primarily hearing the music and secondly hearing the corresponding lyrics of the words of the composition (Shipley 1968/1972, 297, 293).

Olympic Odyssey

Berlioz used Virgil's epic poetry as a source when he composed the operatic music for *Les Troyens* in the period from 1856 to 1859. The music was for him the main element, while the lyrical texts had to follow the melodies. In epic poetry, the Greek "*epos*" initially simply meant "word," then more concretely it was used to refer to a speech or tale, or referred to a song or heroic poem (Shipley 1968/1972, 139). Enlightened by the Homeric epics versified in Greek dactylic hexameter, Berlioz unfurled his musical epos by retranslating the *Iliad* and *Odysseus* into French operatic style. The epic Homeric tradition challenged Virgil to write his *Aeneid*. However, this epos was not written in strict imitation of Homer's verse but re-versified into Latin hexameter. In turn, Berlioz changed the verse by imitating Virgil in the transduction when composing his opera in the French tradition. Berlioz's imitation recognized the achievement and potentialities of Virgil's epic, but Berlioz's imitation was a retranslation (that is, a creative speculation) of the *Iliad* and *Odysseus* into the different art of opera.

As discussed by Hays (2017), Latin literature started with the translation of Greek play scripts into Latin ones to be performed at the Roman festival *Ludi Romani* (Roman Games). The torch of the source country Greece was passed to the imperial Roman Empire. In the late Republic, when Virgil lived, Greek satires and parodies were performed in a different language and needed Latin translators to allow the audience of elite Romans to enjoy the theater of the old Greeks (Hays 2017, 56). In the Roman theater, fragments of the codex with remnants of the translated plays were codified in theater scripts, but the original plays have not survived. Yet it seems clear that the Latin plays borrowed from Greek models retold classical stories of Mediterranean culture to the Roman citizens. Hays' concept of hypertranslation was more than just making word-for-word translations; the literary translators added to the Latin target text "references to Roman institutions, puns that only work in Latin, slapstick humor, and the elaborate aria-monologues known as *cantica*" (that is, the songs of one actor accompanied by music as well as dancing) (Hays 2017, 58). The cultural in-jokes made the retranslated comedy an attractive performance for the Latin spectators. Berlioz continued this ancient tradition in the retranslation of his opera *Les Troyens*.

Virgil's battles for the city of Troy descended from Homer's Greek mythology. The hero Aeneas follows Odysseus' meanderings across the Mediterranean Sea to reach the island of Ithaca. Virgil borrowed this from ancient Greek epics but transferred the translated Latin parts and paraphrases to highlight the "double labyrinth" (Weissbort 1989) in the transduction of parts of the opera. Virgil's original intention was to honor the divine background of Emperor Augustus, probably to ensure his survival in troublesome times in Rome (Hays 2017, 58). Virgil's epic poetry was the classical work, but it was retranslated again and again by later writers to reproduce the translation and retranslation of poetic (even cultural) reproduction from verse in one language into another. Virgil's followers announced the coming or arrival of transitory copies of the *Aeneid* with or without new ideas and thoughts belonging to the mind of the next interpreter (or translator). The work of the literary translators served the source text but readapted the content to remake it in the new target text.

This literary transduction does not mean that the translator steals a verse, play or speech under false pretense from the original author to create a similar (or dissimilar) artwork. Borrowing fragments was standard practice in musical and literary circles of all ages. Even in Berlioz's time, he did not need to legally buy Virgil's literary property, since this belonged to the mythological world, but Berlioz labored to compose the work into his own epos. This double exercise of creating music-and-text was not a problem in his time, since legal permission to freely copy the preferred choices into new works was not required.

As an illustrative example, Dante Alighieri's imaginary wanderings through Hell, Purgatory and Paradise decoded and reinterpreted Virgil's stories to make a modern version from the classical epos (Auerbach 1953/1957, 151–177). The poems in the *Divine Comedy* were therefore not taken *verbatim* by Dante in his literary hypertranslation but were retranslated without committing literary theft from Virgil. Dante presented the *Divine Comedy* as a new and original work in a freer version with a different enjambment of verse meter and in the target Italian versification of *terza rima*. Copyright did not present a problem at the end of the eighteenth century. Later, starting from Berlioz's time, the freedom of the voluntary interface became plagiarism: then, to obtain the mercantile monopoly of an author's published written work, one needed legal permission to re-use the previous material. The ends were not artistic but constituted a simple commercial gain. The requirements of copyright were intentionally designed to redouble the costs. Berlioz (as all other contemporaneous artists) was still relatively free to decide to publish ancient work in a changed form and shape, without requiring any form of legal permission.

Berlioz's libretto for the *Aeneid* retold in retranslation a new story far removed from Virgil's source work. Berlioz revived Virgilian texts in the arias, ensembles and chorus songs of the opera singers. Vergil's story was equally re-narrated in the Italian style of *commedia dell'arte* by the Baroque composer Henry Purcell (1658–1695). He created the first English opera, *Dido and Aeneas* in the year 1689 (*Kobbé's Complete Opera Book* from Harewood 1922/1961, 16–20; Orrey 1972/1987, 52–55). The borrowing of "alien" music had permeated the Elizabethan stage, so Purcell composed *Dido and Aeneas* with fluid melodies sung by a school-girl chorus. The libretto to accompany Purcell's music came from poet Nahum Tate. The première took place at Mr. Josiah Priest's Boarding School for Girls in Chelsea. The story relating to the courtship of Aeneas and Queen Dido was played out in the open air. This one-hour opera charmed the audience, who were enchanted with the light narrative of romance and dances, the seamen's carousels, the masks of the acrobats and the witches' incantations.

The form of Purcell's opera centers on the classical love duet of Aeneas but ends with Dido's grief. The libretto of mutual love compressed "the emotions in a few bars and then reliev[ed] the tension and crystallis[ed] the situation in a set piece for chorus" (Harewood 1922/1961, 16). Emotionally, the ballet with singing has an unhappy end when "Dido hears a distant thunder" (Harewood 1922/1961, 17) and hears the frantic cry of the witches exclaiming their alarming cry "Ho!" (Gorlée 2015a). The witches warn the lovers that love is no paradise. Aeneas decides to leave his beloved Dido to carry his journal to the coast of Italy. Their idyll comes to an unhappy end when Dido's final *passacaglia* song is sung, the moment of truth. The descending melody in soft and slow harmonies announces Dido's lament and her agonizing death.

Berlioz's free "conversation" with Virgil consisted basically in taking the story and readapting and redeveloping the action into the dramatic response of the opera. The key is to observe how Berlioz dramatized what Jakobson described as the poetic aspects of war and love to depict the dramas in his opera. His creative retranslation seemed to follow Peirce's fragmentary sign of "transuasion," which is not drawing a circle of synonyms but finding a transition of parasynonyms between two cultural codes. Berlioz did not simply retranslate the lyrics into one line but redeveloped the circularity from the vocal melodies to produce a poetic novelty onstage.

Berlioz followed Peirce's series "Originality, Obsistence, and Transuasion" (CP: 2.85–2.94). He remodeled a new scheme of categories eventually leading to what Jakobson termed as the level of "poetics," but unwillingly so. Peirce's "Originality" stands for the ordinary mood of the translator as being present in the professional activity that produces the translation. The token was the twoness of the concept of the noun "Obsistence," which borrowed from the Latin verb "*obsisto*," meaning "to stand or place oneself before or in the way of" with the secondary meaning of "to oppose," "to withstand" or "to resist." The Latin root meant that the crucial sign was "to be open" or "to yield" to the energetic action or emotional mood in a personal reaction (CP: 2.42–2.94). The technical word "transuasion" describes the readiness of the quasi-translator to indulge in the individual mode and take a new action to react with a self-translation.

Peirce's "transuasion" comes, like "persuasion," from the Latin verb "*persuado*." Although "persuasion" is used as a real noun, "transuasion" is not the "genuine" translation but a weak or, in Peirce's terms, "degenerate" type of retranslation as the personal conviction of the translator. Transuasion refers to the quasi-mind of the translator giving his/her "partial aspect of the fact that each of the Relates has its Quality" (CP: 2.91). For Peirce,

> *Transuasion* (suggesting *translation, transaction, transfusion, transcendental,* etc.) is mediation, or the modification of firstness and secondness by thirdness, taken apart from the secondness and firstness; or, is being in creating Obsistence. (CP: 2.89, Peirce's emphasis)

Transuasion mediates between the knowledge and the choices of the quasi-translator, leading from the grammatical rules of the language in order to provide the target text. The geographical effects of Peirce's categories represent transuasion as the translator's continuity of following the "circuitous roads" (Gorlée 2015, 32–47), where semiotranslation mediates with the triadic system of the translator's knowledge to reach into the logical reasoning of thirdness. Peirce rejected the possibility of this "hard fact" (MS 478, 29) of circularity, since for the literary translator the metaphor "A door is slightly ajar" can be replied to with "You try to open it," but it seems that the translator sees that "[s]omething prevents. You put your shoulders against it, and experience a sense of effort and a sense of resistance" (MS 478, 29). Indeed, transuasion could never reduce the singularities of the laboratory of separate words or signs to the formal logic of inquiry, because semiotranslation needs to branch out from firstness (mood) to secondness (token), without ever reaching the real level of general thirdness (type) (Gorlée 2015, 12, 38–39). Transuasion is not logic or reason with logical rules but stays in the culture of the "degenerate" art of retranslation, or "self-translation." Take as an example the "ordinary" variety of English translations of Virgil's *Aeneid* composed in rhythmical prosaic verse (Bernard 2017). The dialogue is used in the lyrics of the arias and chorus to give a dramatic sensibility to composer Berlioz's continuous opera *Les Troyens*. He retranslated or self-translated Virgil into music, but the whole lyrical text remained the problem. Transuasion is indeed a choice in mediation.

In a further step, Berlioz evaded the problematic process of translation by retranslating for operatic voices (Peirce's firstness and secondness) to achieve the final voices of the opera (thirdness). Peirce distinguished the internal emotion of firstness and the external energy of secondness, unifying them into the semiosis of translation as thirdness. By 1902, however, what for Peirce evolved into the technical skill of "categories," progressing from unlogical to logical, became for Berlioz merely a retranslation of his earlier prosaic translations to fit the measured lyrics of this opera. Sadly, Berlioz realized that it was beyond his ingenuity to compose the lyrical text for the music of his final opera *Les Troyens*. In the last phase of his life, Peirce abandoned the weaker (that is, "degenerate") semiotic pseudo-types of "belief," "affirmation" and "judgment" (Peirce 1976a, 249–250) to follow the speculative symbolic grammar of semiosis (CP: 3.430). The final category of "judgment" (thirdness) was for Peirce a shifting term, which he reduced to the ambiguous status of "assertion" (CP: 3.432–3.438, Peirce 1976a, 262–263). In Peirce's form of semiosis, which he called the process of "transuasion," he clearly realizes how the two elements of secondness and firstness are the main elements of thirdness but are themselves multiple varieties of semiotranslation. The retranslations and transtranslations of secondness and firstness push thirdness off the horizon.

Peirce's term "transuasion" proposes a variant of "translation." Transuasion is understood as providing choices between inside and outside meanings, allowing double shifts that exchange the proposition for the main argument. The proposition is the source text but stands out to be the same as the target text, yet both represent Peirce's thirdness (like Morris's symbol, see 1932/1946, 282–286, 294–330). While the symbolic third is a mental thought-sign extending the union of sign-and-object to the logical "judgment" of truth, the meaning of the thing signified is not a moral rule meant for every sign-receiver (that is, interpreter and translator). The "assertion" remains an error of "judgment" of failing to observe and analyze the operatic lyrics signified with different ideas. The individual "assertion" is the "speculative grammar" of the knowledge of the receiver, whose quasi-mind may produce confusion or even mistakes in the final opera (CP: 3.432, 3.438). While "judgment" was Peirce's genuine symbol for commanding logical thirdness, "assertion" is the sign-maker's (that is, the translator's) empirical sign endowed with critical and cultural impressions of (outside) secondness and (inside) firstness. Transuasion carries out the definitive experiment of translatology by emerging with "good" and "bad" translations coming from the interpreter's quasi-mind, which can be accepted or rejected as the new target. Beyond knowing the real meaning as an exact symbol, the translator must "degenerate" into the vague feelings of signs to "regenerate" the value of the pseudo-symbol as a real symbol (CP: 3.425–3.455; Gorlée 1990, 2004, 66–67, 129–132, 148).

Transuasion takes Peirce's step of relative truth to mediate what happens in translation (including retranslation and autotranslation), but without providing any proof or evidence, so Berlioz's retranslation bears a question mark. The hypothesis includes the correct concept of necessary reasoning with the final conclusion of logic, but we have to deal with the non-necessary emotional reasoning of the interpreter's quasi-mind. The psychological images inspire and influence the "transaction" of the intellectual translator in "transfusing" emotionality into the target translation. The tools are conscious "judgment" and unconscious "assertion," which judge the continuous process of Peirce's semiosis (CP: 3.432–3.439).

Beyond the dynamic value of suggesting Peirce's non-logical otherness in the varieties of secondness in linguistic units, the translator embodies the two-sided experience of action and reaction, stimulus and response, change and resistance. Transuasion modulates the "suchness" of unanalyzed, instantaneous, immediate and unthought feelings carried by the sign-maker (translator) into linguistic signs. The mental activity of translation indirectly gives the reader (hearer) the translator's personal choices of favorite words in language. The interaction of firstness is the "most primitive, simple, and original" belief (CP: 2.90) that hears the translator's inner voice drawing from the basic ground of the sign's private "*Originality* [which] is being such as that being is, regardless of anything else" (CP: 2.89; Peirce's emphasis). Paradoxically, Peirce's transuasion lacks the conventional truth of his own theory to be able to deal correctly with translation and retranslation. Since there exists no real "methodology" with fixed rules, the whole series of troubling implications and explications in the work of translation and retranslation is instead an opportunity to play the free game of "experiential" procedure. Any choice is possible in such wordplay.

The absence of rules gives Peirce's three categories no standard of cultural rules to conduct Berlioz's "electrical" current from the retranslator to the theatrical transduction. His nuanced conversation with Virgil was more an intellectual lesson in translating and retranslating the differences in length of the lyrics to match the space of the music, rechanging the notes of the music to match the sung lyrics. In creating the opera *Les Troyens* Berlioz firstly refocused the double feeling of the music as a crucial element of the composer's dissonance and consonance. Secondly, by trying to slow the tempo of the actual words sung in order to fit the musical notes underlying the meaningful clue-words that have their own accent and rhythm, he supplied a tension of completeness to arrive at what Jakobson describes as "poetics."

At the beginning of *Les Troyans*, in Act I (Berlioz 1969/2013: I.1, 7–202), Berlioz introduces the chorus of the Trojan people. The chorus sings and dances in the abandoned Greek camp in celebration of their freedom from their oppressors. The wild joy of the people marks the conclusion of the decade-long war against the city of Troy. The Greeks have disappeared, and the Trojan people can feel at peace. The *allegro vivo* music of the chorus, which represents the cheering Trojan multitude, is accompanied by flutes, oboes, double-flutes, clarinets and timpani (or kettle drums) (Berlioz 2002, 107, 145–146, 272). The double dramatic sound of different melodies underlies the mechanical resonance Berlioz creates in the loud cries of the voices (Wilshire 1982, 46–47, 82–83, 130), while the repeated laughter reflects the rhythmic pitch and harmony of collective excitement:

Ha! Ha!
Après dix ans passés dans nos murailles,
Ah! Quel bonheur de respirer
L'air pur des champs, que le cri des batailles
Ne va plus déchirer (6x) (Berlioz 1969/2013, I.1: 9–20)

Ha! Ha!
After ten years spent within our walls
Ah! What delight to breathe
The pure air of the fields, ha!, ha!, which will never more
Be rent by the shouts of battle (6x)
(Berlioz 1973, 1, transl. David Cairns)

Berlioz's lyrical words accompany the metallic exclamations in a metrical construction. David Cairns' translation decomposes the "loose but original" rhythm and tempo (Longyear 1969, 99) into a vocalized, but barely singable, version. The poetic effect is a literal translation, but without observing the poetic variations of the catchwords in musical end rhyme. Troy's massive fortifications (*"murailles"*) are downtranslated by Cairns into the simple noun "walls," while the rhymed end-word *"batailles"* has totally disappeared. The other catchword *"respirer"* has quasi-rhyme with *"déchirer."* Cairns' "normal" translation informs about the libretto's rhythm and tempo without engaging with the proposed poetic tonality and literary meaning characteristic of dramatic music-with-words. It seems that Cairns follows the events, but without endowing Berlioz's verse with much poetry.

In the literary translation, in order to convey Berlioz's unexpected cross-rhythms between the verse lines, there is no obligation to translate either the differences between the initial and final macro-rhythms or the micro-rhythm of individual words or lines. The poetic forms of rhyme and quasi-rhyme in the original Latin led to invariants of choice due to lexical, semantic and syntactic preferences in French. Berlioz followed his own "personal" choices in translating his lyrical text for the target audience. An epic-dramatic versification in the sense of Jakobson's double method of poetically translating the source into English iambic lyrics would perhaps be the following singable translation:

Ha! Ha!
After ten years confined to the fortress
Ah! the luck to forgive and forget
On the encampment, no clamor of battles
but breaths of sea air (6x) (my transl.)

Both tempo and rhythm reach a critical point in the parallelism of the initial and final words of the poetical verse (Jakobson and Waugh 1979, 216, 226–231). Without the strictness of the traditional end rhyme, the poetic translation preserves the cross-rhythms of alliterative poetry, first in the initial interjections with rhymic [a] together with the final quasi-rhythms of the light syllables [fōr], as in *fortress, forgive* and *forget,* and second in the stressed syllables onset with [k] in *encampment* and *clamor.* In the end rhyme, there is the combination of the alliterated stressed syllables onset with [b] in *battle* and *breaths*) followed by the soft vowels [a(ə)] or [e(ə)] in *cries* and semi-vowel *sea air* to embellish the upward sense created in the singable translation from French to English.

Berlioz, the sign-maker of the opera, followed the half-normal and half-poetic symbols of power in his choice of words for the chorus, in order to lend a sense of the old rhetoric, which was still the trend in the eighteenth century. By engaging in the disharmony on a deeper level than that of Virgil's ancient versification, he gave to the sign-receiving audience of the opera *The Trojans* what can be called a "contrastive look" (Steiner 1990, 10). Berlioz chose his own rhythm and tempo in the dramatic verses. His "contrastive" perspective in his transduction enabled him, as the composer and translator, to create an alternative world through the imagery evoked by his choice of alternative words, a world of peace instead of war. In the chorus, he created the linguistic nuances for multiple shades of contrasting qualities in the voices but preferred the energy of the rhythm of his musical setting. Berlioz's best choice was the musical parabole (Sheriff 1984/1991, 40, 123). Berlioz reduced the epic length of Virgil's poem by choosing wordings with a shorter duration than the music, thereby crafting easy verbal lyrics and adding emotional exclamations with musical rhyme and rhythm.

Berlioz must have read Virgil's original works many times, but for Berlioz, Virgil's Book I (1999, 263–315) was second only to his own ideas of creating a more exciting visual performance onstage in Act I of the lyrical text of the opera *Les Troyens*. While composing the opera, Berlioz's sense of music certainly did not find its "absolute" source in primarily remembering the ancient cycle of Virgil's *Aeneid*; his vision as a lyrical poet was to redevelop the half-cycle into an elliptical retranslation of Virgil's *Aeneid*. At the same time, his artistic task was to advance the parabolic trajectory of operatic music, leaving behind Virgil's "ordinary" translation to rewrite his own lyrical text for the opera. In *Les Troyens,* Berlioz composed his own music-drama in a process of electromagnetic transduction of music-with-text. But although Virgil was interweaved in the lyrics as the "illustrative" source of the mysterious interactions of the gods speaking on Olympus, Berlioz also wanted to intertwine the operagoers into his musical genius. The quarrels among the gods after the fall of Troy featured in Virgil's epos were abandoned, and in Acts I–IV Berlioz took the romantic opportunity to musicalize the speech on Aeneas's future life driven by his own divine Fates.

Importantly, the musical elements include Virgil's ancient hexameter. The dactylic hexameter, consisting of a verse of six feet of stressed syllables followed by two light syllables, remained the traditional meter of the scanned rhythm of Virgil's epic poems. The first verse of Virgil's *Aeneid*, "*Arma virumque cano, Troiae qui primus ab oris*" (Virgil 1916/1999, 262), must be recited phonetically in the classical hexameter as *árma vi/rúrumque ca/nó Tro/iái qui/ prímus ab/ óris*—that is, five caesuras with a strong stress at the beginning, softening at the end of the verse. For the singing, Berlioz used the opposite invariant for the lyrical verse: the melodic rhetoric of the iambic hexameter (also called the "alexandrine"), with one light syllable followed by a stressed syllable. This two-unit rhythm allows space for longer syllables, with room for three or four syllables and caesuras, as a standard line for singing operatic arias in French and English. In an iambic hexameter, the singing words are pronounceable and understood by the audience, meaning that

> each vowel represents a *single sound*, and in singing, it must be maintained unaltered during the whole duration of the musical sound, a pure and definite sound. This cannot be sufficiently emphasized, as there is nothing more disturbing than the intrusion of English diphthongs into any other language. (Bernac 1978, 12, Bernac's emphasis)

In French, each vowel is a monosyllabic sound but requires extra space to be sung to accommodate the longer meter and rhythm of combined French words, including the silence of mute syllables [ə] in plural forms, the elision of vowel sounds in adjoining words and the pronunciation of many consonants written separately in one syllable (Jakobson and Waugh 1979, 151–152). Iambic hexameter is flexible for longer lines sung in arias and was the standard dramatic and poetic meter of poetry. When the melody is punctuated by operatic music, the melody can change into the first three or four feet in iambic verses, consisting of a light syllable and a stressed syllable. The last iambic verse has an end rhyme to hold the lyrical stanza together in meaning and underline the electrical effects of the final clue-words of the whole verse. These literary clues construct the framework of Berlioz's vocal poetry.

Berlioz's *Les Troyens* starts with this iambic versification, with stress on the final words and light stress in between:

Ah! Ah!
Après díx / ans passés / dans nos muráilles,

Quel bonhéúr / de respírer
L'air púr / des champs [...] que le crí / des batáilles
Ne va plús / déchirer (Berlioz 1969/2013, I.1: 920)

Virgil's dactylic hexameter is converted into the more elastic hexameter, which has a "rising meter" to dramatize the poetic event of making peace in Troy, as seen in the end rhyme. Berlioz's high point lies in the end of each verse, where the meaning is expressed through the rhymes of the last words. He needed to follow the method of poetizing the end of the line to emphasize the keywords of each verse. This is illustrated in the conquest of the fortress city of Troy with its enormous stone walls. The *"murailles"* tower above the Greek camp, where the Trojan soldiers have fought losing battles (*"batailles"*) against the invading Greek forces. Now the clouds are broken (*"déchirer"*) allowing the people to breathe fresh air (*"respirer"*). Berlioz starts Act I *in medias res* without any flashback to the horrors of the war. He follows Virgil's epic: the Trojans have lost their hero Hector, commander of the Trojan forces, and the Greek warriors Achilles and Patroclus plan to return to Greece.

The ringing *staccato* laugh "Ha! Ha!" [hä] resounds in the mixed chorus of the Trojan people sung by the lighter sopranos and circulated by the deeper tenors (Gorlée 2015a). The exclamations of joy resound as the repetitive word "Ha! Ha!" to represent the Trojan people's pleasure at the conclusion of the war. The people's delight at the dawn of peaceful times is symbolized by the sensuous word "Ha!" transverses into the reversed word "Ah!" followed by "What delight to breathe" (Goodman 1976/1985, 82–83). Berlioz conveys the people's ecstasy in the cries of soldiers, citizens, women and children. They turn the theatrical exclamations into cries of pleasure (Poizat 1992; Jakobson and Waugh 1979, 40–41). The folk dance starts accompanied by the high sopranos and mezzo-sopranos but ends with the forceful bass of the tenors and basses extending the exclamation as "Ha__! ha__! ha__! ha__! ha__! ha__! ha__!" (Berlioz 1969/2013, I.1: 20–21). In this chorus, Berlioz gives rhythmic form to the resonant stage sound of mixed voices, as described in his work *Orchestration Treatise* (Berlioz 2002, 256–264). He gives the high female voices a prominent place on stage. As argued before, in Wagner's opera *The Rheingold*, composed at the same time (1853–1854), the narrow diphthong "Ha!" sung by the Rhinemaidens interplays with Alberich's parabolic cries of *"Heia"* and *"Heiajaheia"* in his pursuit of the maidens.

He has the same pleasure in dealing parabolically with the situation of the Trojan people, who erupt in joy after the Greek soldiers end the war and decide to return home. In Book I of the *Aeneid*, Virgil depicts the epic conversations of the Olympian gods and half-gods as they intervene in the lives of humans. They also quarrel with each other about thwarting the plan to return home held by the virtuous man Aeneas. Virgil's *Aeneid* conveys an enlightened familiarity with the story of the gods, half-gods and mortals in the voice of the poet speaker. The whim of the gods brings adventures and misfortunes from Olympus to the traveler Aeneas. Virgil must invoke and respect the will of the gods for Aeneas to survive the trajectory of his journey home. In Virgil's *Aeneid,* the gods do not act spontaneously on human decisions, but instead the

> Olympians have taken on a dignified and grave look; Virgil proposes to repeat the frivolous tales about them which Ovid so enjoys collecting. Their attitude inspires respect: Jupiter presides over his council with sovereign majesty, and Venus herself is only a mother [of Aeneas] who fears for her son. Just as he deifies moral concepts, Virgil "moralizes" the gods. (Seznec 1953/1972, 86–87)

In Berlioz's opera, the magical miracles are performed by the gods, mainly Venus, the goddess of love, who takes care of her son Aeneas. His decision is to carry his father and son away from Troy to the new world. Apart from the divine voices, the story also brings demonic voices in the human sense of clairvoyance to augur the future Pompeian War. Aeneas's adventures bring about both divine and earthly events to supplement Virgil's original text, producing the highly dramaticized romantic events of Berlioz's *The Trojans.*

In Act I, Troy must deal with the unexpected arrival of the huge wooden horse, stranded in the Greek encampment on Troy's seashore as a "reactor" symbol (Sebeok 1994/1999, 22–23). The visually impressive wooden construction sparks a controversy. King Priam is told that this present is a miracle from the gods. The warrior Aeneas rushes in with bad news: the wooden horse is a clever trick to deceive the Trojan people. He warns that the Greeks are waiting in the next bay to hurry back and destroy the city and enslave the inhabitants. Then, the priest Laocoön hurls a javelin at the horse and two monstrous serpents devour him. Is this magical accident a divine augur or a strange miracle? Act I continues with the high notes of Cassandra's prophecy. She protests forcefully against accepting this dangerous object. Cassandra warns the Trojans that the horse-like engine with its devilish forces will secretly conquer the city of Troy, but her voice is ignored.

The prophetess Cassandra is the primary heroine of *Les Troyens,* emphasizing the *prima donna*-oriented tradition of Berlioz's operas. Cassandra, a figure whom Berlioz borrowed from Shakespeare's *Troilus and Cressida,* is the first of a number of female characters with a key role in this opera. Cassandra is a Trojan princess, the daughter of king Priam and Hecabe, but Apollo gives her the gift of prophecy. In Virgil's Book II, 341, Cassandra is only mentioned once, but Berlioz places her in a leading role in Acts I and II of his opera. For Berlioz, the figure of Cassandra conveys the emotional atmosphere of Troy struggling against the calamity of the city's fall and destruction (Langford 1981). Cassandra is not taken from Homer's epic: this character, with her "unusual sound" signifying her role as a prophetess, (Fogel 1969) is not found in Homer.

Berlioz's first key female singer, Cassandra, is the radical voice warning against the danger of the wooden horse as she foresees the future horrors it will bring. Cassandra's monologues shock and disturb the Trojan citizens. She warns about the riddle of the Trojan horse appearing to the Trojans as a grim seduction *a posteriori* from the Greeks. The Trojan people wheel the horse jubilantly into Troy, but Cassandra's prophesy proves to be right. During the night, a trapdoor opens, and a battalion of Greek soldiers emerges from the wooden horse to destroy Troy, slaughtering and enslaving the citizens.

After the fall of Troy, Cassandra, who has outlived the fall of Troy and the murder of her father, Priam, reminds the Greek oppressors of the darkness hanging over the city of Troy: the Trojans have lost their value and courage forever (Fogel 1969, 15). As a seer, she ironically warns the survivors in the dark shadow of the Trojan hero Hector (Berlioz's homonym), who fell on Troy's battlefield:

> *Les Grecs ont disparu! [...] mais quel dessin fatal*
> *Cache de ce départ étrange promptitude?*
> *Tout vient de justifier ma sombre inquiétude!*
> *J'ai vu l'ombre d'Hector parcourir nos remparts*
> *Comme un veilleur de nuit, j'ai vu ses noirs regards*
> *Interroger au loin le détroit de Sigée [...]*
> *Malheur! Dans la folie et l'ivresse plongée*
> *La foule sort des murs, et Priam la conduit!*
> (Berlioz 1969/2013: I.2.36–38)

> The Greeks have vanished. But what dread plan
> Lies hidden behind this strangely sudden departure?
> All is bearing out my firm forebodings!
> I saw Hector's spirit pacing our ramparts
> Like a watchman of the night: I saw his darkened eyes
> Staring far off towards the straits of Sigeium [...]
> Woe betide them! Drunk with madness
> The people leave the city—Priam at their head!
> (Berlioz 1973, 1, transl. David Cairns)

Cassandra's warning is followed by the melancholy lament in *andante* tempo and slow rhythm:

Malheureux Roi! dans l' éternelle nuit
C'en est donc fait, tu vas descendre!
Tu ne m'écoutes pas, tu ne veux rien comprendre,
Malheureux people, à l'horreur qui me suit!
(Berlioz 1969/2013, I.2.40–41)

Ill-fated King! The die is cast,
You must go down to everlasting night.
Ill-fated race, you heed me not, not wish
To know anything of the terror that haunts me.
(Berlioz 1973, 1, transl. David Cairns)

Cassandra stays on stage during the whole of Act I, trying to persuade her co-citizens not to carry out their foolish plan of bringing the wooden horse into the city. The Greeks will be responsible for the fall of Troy, but once again her prophesies are not believed, and the shadow of Hector is seen as a dream image. In Berlioz's music, the dissonant and consonant chants of the people (Berlioz 1969/2013, I.10.150) about the destiny of the wooden horse transform from discord into the consonant decision to bring the horse into Troy (Berlioz 1969/2013, I.10.184–186).

The Trojan people decide that the wooden horse is a divine offering to save the city of Troy, despite Cassandra's frantic cries. She remains alone on the stage and exclaims:

Arrête! Arrête! Oui, la flamme, la hache!
Fouillez le flanc du monstrueux cheval!
Laocoon! [...] les Grecs! [...] il cache
Un piège infernal [...]
(Berlioz 1969/2013: I.2.40–41)

Stop Stop! Fire an axe!
Search the monstrous horse!
Laocoön! [...] The Greeks! [...] It hides
A deadly trap [...]
(Berlioz 1973, 5, transl. David Cairns)

Cassandra's protest does not flow quite as naturally as her cries. The Trojan people thank the gods for the gift, but the meaning of the gift is not clear.

In Act II, Berlioz's first female figure, Cassandra, has survived the misery of the fall of Troy (Berlioz 1969/2013, II.2.290, 1973, 9, transl. David Cairns). Despite her gift of prophesy, the female figure Cassandra is not believed by the Trojan population, and she is replaced by the male hero Aeneas, who tells the truth of the fatal plan. Despite having been part of the Greek invasion, as a half-god he remains neutral during the war and is not hostile to the Trojans. His divine mother Venus, who is the second key female singer in Berlioz's opera, helps him in his battles against the Trojan heroes. Berlioz's Venus is borrowed from Shakespeare's narrative poem *Venus and Adonis*. Since Berlioz worked on Act IV after the long Act I, the shortness of Act II reduces this chapter to Cassandra's final cry of anguish before she dies. After burning the Greek camp, the hero Aeneas flees to the mountains to desert Troy. Aeneas is concerned about carrying his father, Anchises, and his eight-year son, Ascianius, from Asia Minor across the sea and becoming the patriarch of Rome (Berlioz 1969/2013 II.2.203–294).

Virgil's *Aeneid* concludes with Aeneas, the main narrator, telling the chronological story of his adventures as a wayward foreigner, ending with him being sanctified in the city of Rome. In Berlioz's vocal translation, however, Berlioz inserts the dramatic events surrounding the male protagonist Aeneas into the opera to interest the operagoers—for instance, making use of the symbol of the wooden horse and the voice of the seer Cassandra—while the rest of Virgil's epic is abandoned. As a lyricist of arias and chorus songs, Berlioz had to crisscross the epic poetry of Virgil's *Aeneid* with intersecting lines to find the emotional images he needed for the opera during the process of conduction of the primary text. Then in the process of the transduction, he remade and restructured a new framework with or even without Virgil's lines and verses. This means that the opera *Les Troyens* was obviously not a formal Virgilian retranslation but flourished as Berlioz's own self-translation, both dependent on and independent from Virgil's source text. It seems that Acts I and II were influenced by Virgil, but the key female figure of Cassandra was borrowed from Homer's *Iliad*.

Berlioz took Virgil as his main source, but during the composition of the final opera, he preferred his own lyricized retranslation rather than literally reciting Virgil's poetry. In his paraphrases, Berlioz varied the story with his own romantic inventions of love and hatred. Berlioz's role as retranslator was to apply the "contrastive look" (Steiner 1990, 10), whereby he self-translated from Latin to French to create his own art object in the fairy world of French opera. *Les Troyens* was an "open texture" (Scheffler 1997, 18–21) to be redeveloped from Virgil's poem into Berlioz's dramatic impact of the opera, but Virgil's scale and ambition of epic poetry in Augustan times enlivened Berlioz's version with flashing insights, renewing the art of opera. During the writing, Berlioz intermingled composing the music with a new version of Vergil's rhymed hexameters, re-narrating the source text into the new voyage of Aeneas's lyrical Odyssey.

Act II presents the drama of the violent death of Cassandra under the shadow of Hector. Hector had been killed in the Trojan War but reappears as a shadow to warn Aeneas to leave behind the fallen city of Troy. Now, in Act III (1969/2013, 295–442; 1973, 9–13, transl. David Cairns), Aeneas's sea voyage from the battle scenes of Troy has ended. Berlioz's narrative jumps from the city of Troy to the shipwreck off the city of Carthage. Aeneas appears in the royal palace of Queen Dido. After Cassandra and Venus, Dido is the third female voice borrowed from diverse plays by Shakespeare to be the center of love and disputes in the opera *The Trojans*. In contrast to Virgil, Berlioz adds the heavy storm on the Mediterranean Sea, so that the next day, after the shipwreck, Aeneas lands as a refugee on the African coast.

The city of Carthage is celebrating a folk festival: from the Roman amphitheater, the huge choir of men, women and children are singing the national anthem to laud Queen Dido (Pavis 1980, 58–60). Versified in iambic hexameter, the classical hymns sung on the feast day express the obedience and loyalty of the citizens to their queen. The choir sings the ritual *maestoso non troppo lento* hymn to illustrate the victory and freedom of the city thanks to the royal work of Queen Dido, who raised Carthage to a prosperous city:

Gloire à Didon. Notre reine chérie!
Reine par la beauté, la grâce, le génie,
Reine par la faveur des dieux,
Et reine par l'amour de ses sujets heureux!
(Berlioz 1969/2013, I.3.309–311, no. 18 Chant National)

Glory to Dido, our beloved Queen!
Queen by her beauty, grace, and great spirit,
Queen by the favour of the gods,
Queen by the love of her happy subjects.
(Berlioz 1973, 9, transl. David Cairns)

The high accents of the chorus are at the beginning of the verse, such as "*Gloire*" and three times the word "*Reine*," ending in the rhymes of four alliterated end-verses: "*chérie*," "*genie*," "*dieux*" and "*heureux*." The *allargando* with *un poco ritenuto* singing of the choir is followed by the national anthem. The farm workers process in the streets to thank the Queen. Queen Dido is a widow but tells her sister and confidante Anna that she has unexplained moods of sadness. Anna replies with a smile that she will find someone to fill the emptiness of her mood, saying *"Vous aimerez, ma soeur [...]"* (You will love, my sister); she insists that *"Carthage veut un roi"* (Carthage needs a king) (Berlioz 1969/2013, I.3.371, 373–374; 1973, 11, transl. David Cairns).

At that point, Aeneas has overcome the storm on the seashore and is stranded on the African coast. While the hymn of the Trojan March is being sung, he enters the palace as a stranger disguised as a sailor, hiding his real identity as a hero. When he draws near to Queen Dido's throne *"sous un déguisement de matelot"* (disguised as [a] sailor) (Berlioz 1969/2013, I.3. 393: 1973, 11), he seeks asylum. Aeneas now *"laissé tomber son déguisement de matelot. Il porte un brillant costume de la cuirasse, mais sans casque ni bouclier"* (drops his sailor's disguise. He is wearing a dazzling breastplate, but not his helmet or shield) (Berlioz 1969/2013: I.3.27, 104–105; 1973, 12). The Trojan warrior Aeneas was given by Queen Dido a warm welcome to stay in Carthage. Happy with the royal entrance, Aeneas changed the spirit of his heart from the memories of Troy to a new future.

Berlioz did not follow Virgil's mythological transformation but lent a new inventiveness to the classical play (Pavis 1980, 104–105; Jakobson and Waugh 1979, 204–208). In Virgil's ancient poetry, Aeneas explores the forest of the African coast, but deep in thought he still reminds himself of the horrors of the Trojan War. Suddenly, he meets a huntress, who is really his mother Venus disguised in the double metaphor of Aeneas's mother and his helper in distress (Wilshire 1982, 39). The mythopoetic camouflage signifies a "play on words (*jeu de mots*)" giving a double life to their dialogue (Jakobson and Waugh 1979, 236). Venus comes to console or defy her own son, but masked as a young huntress, with a bow in hand and a quiver on her shoulder; she loves but also fears her son's sadness (Wilshire 1982, 54). Venus pursues Aeneas to awaken in his heart the urge to hunt for the love of Queen Dido. In Virgil's Latin poem,

Cui mater media sese tuli obvia silva,
virginis os habitumque gerens et virginis arma,
Spartanae, vel qualis equos Threissa fatigat
Harpalyce voluqremque fuga praevertitur Eurum.
namque umeris de more habilem suspenderat arcum
ventatrix dederatque comam diffundere ventis,
nuda genu nodoque sinus collecta fluentis.
ac prior 'heus," inquit, "iuvenes, monstrate, mearum
vidistes si quam hic errantem forte sororum,
succintam pharetra et maculosa tegmine lyncis,
aut spumantis apri cursum clamore prementem."

Sic Venus, et Veneris contra sic filius orsus:
"nulla tuarum audita mihi neque visa sororum,
o—quam te memorem, virgo? Namque haud tibi vultus
mortalis, nec vox hominem sonat; o dea certe!
An Phoebi soror? An Nympharum sanguinis una?
Sis felix nostrumque leves, quaecumque, laborem,
Et quo sub caelo tandem, quibus otbis in oris
Iactemus, doceas; ignari hominumque locurumque
Erramos, vento huc vastis et fluctibus acti;
Multi tibi ante aras nostra cadet hostia dextra."

Across his path, in the midst of the forest, with a maiden's face and mien, and a maiden's arms, whether one of Sparta or such a one as Thracian Harpalyce, when she out-tires horses and outstrips the East Wind in flight. For from her shoulders in huntress fashion she had slung the ready bow and had given her hair to the winds to scatter; her knee bare, and her flowing robes gathered in a knot. Before he speaks, "Ho!" she cries, "tell me, youth, if perchance you have seen a sister of mine here straying, girl with quiver and a dappled lynx's hide, or pressing with shouts of a foaming boar?"

Thus Venus, and thus in answer Venus' son began: "None of your sisters have I heard or seen—but by what name should I call you, maiden? For your face is not mortal nor has your voice a human ring; O goddess surely! Sister of Phoebus, or one of the race of Nymphs? Show grace to us, whoever you may be, and lighten this our burden. Inform us, pray, beneath what sky, on what costs of the world, we are cast; knowing nothing of countries or peoples we wander driven hither by wind and huge billows. Many a victim shall fall for you at our hand before your altars." (Virgil 1916/1999, vv. 315–324)

By replacing Virgil's verse with a merely informative translation, the literary translator Allen Mandelbaum reduced Virgil's large epic ornaments to brief modern poetry, giving new verses to the speaking voices to appeal to modern readers. Allen Mandelbaum's lyrical translation of Virgil possesses the new rhetoric of modern certainty, as opposed to Berlioz's old classic text, where the make-believe and fiction create an ambiguous zone of uncertainty (Pavis 1980, 348–349). As an example of Mandelbaum's modern poetics, Aeneas asks his mother for help, but with her secret enchantments, the divine mother, Venus, has a female trick up her sleeve. Translator Mandelbaum gives this lyrical translation:

> But in the middle of the wood, along
> the way, his mother showed herself to him.
> The face and dress she wore were like a maiden's,
> her weapons like a girl's from Sparta or
> those carried by Harpalyce of Thrace
> when she tires out her horses, speeding faster
> even than rapid Hebrus as she races.
> For, as a huntress would across her shoulder,
> Venus had slung her bow in readiness;
> her hair was free, disheveled by the wind;
> her knees were bare; her tunic's flowing folds
> were gathered in a knot. And she seeks first:
> "Young men there! Can you tell me if by chance
> you have seen one of my sisters pass—she wore
> a quiver and a spotted lynx's hide—
> while she was wandering here or, with her shouts,
> chasing a foaming boar along its course?"
> So Venus. Answering, her son began:
> "I have not seen or heard your sister, maiden—
> or by what name am I to call you, for
> your voice is not like any human voice.
> O goddess, you must be Apollo's sister
> or else are to be numbered with the nymphs!
> Whoever you may be, do help us, ease
> Our trials; do tell us underneath what skies,
> upon which coasts of earth we have been cast;
> we wander, ignorant of men and places,
> and driven by the wind and the vast waves.
> Before your altars many victims will
> Fall at your hands, as offering to you."
> (Vergil 1981, I.444–473, transl. Allen Mandelbaum)

Aeneas tells his mother he has abandoned his Trojan life of battles, but during the sea voyage he completely failed to do the right thing and lost the battle against the bad weather:

> "Now I am left with scarcely seven galleys,
> ships scattered by the waves and the east wind;
> and I myself, a needy stranger, roam
> across the wilderness of Libya; I
> am driven out of Europe, out of Asia."

> But Venus had enough of his complaints,
> And so interrupted his lament:
> "Whoever you may be, I hardly think
> The heaven-dwellers hold a grudge against you:
> The breath of life is yours, and you are near
> A Tyrian city. Only make your way
> Until you reach the palace of the queen."
> (Virgil 1981, I.543–555, transl. Allen Mandelbaum)

For his mother, Aeneas is still a hero. Venus's poetic imagery is more than a magical enchantment transvested into a miracle (Warner 2020, 27–28). Her divine persona goes beyond the protection of her son, who deeply suffered from the horrors of Troy; instead, she imagines intimate feelings of love, since she, in her special function as the goddess of love arts, hopes for a possible love affair between her son Aeneas and Dido. Queen Dido is the third female singer in Berlioz's opera. Indeed, she falls deeply in love with Aeneas and is a major protagonist of the opera *Les Troyens*.

Allen Mandelbaum's literary translation employs the concept of Jakobson's "poetics" in the use of lyrics in a contemporary sense so that the meaningful words can display an informal feeling of rhetoric rather than the formality of the old source in Virgil. Mandelbaum was freer than Berlioz, since he had no reference to music to accompany the words. He moved further away from Berlioz's sung lyrics, which were still bound to the rhetoric of eighteenth-century France. Mandelbaum's translation is a hypertranslation of words. Berlioz wanted to suit the music to the very short lines of operatic verse, but this adapted style meant that his vocabulary was not aimed at composing poetic music, but at poeticizing music. Berlioz produced unconventional figures of half-poetic sound to accompany his melodies, but his lyrical words remained formal and not creative.

Hunt and Storm

In line with Virgil's epic, Act I of Berlioz's opera is full of *staccato* interjections of joy and *tristesse*, separate or linked together in the dynamic chorus of the Trojan people and the prophetic words of Cassandra. Act II encompasses static performances of personal arias and national hymns. Act III tells the story of Aeneas telling Dido of his pathway of trials. Dido is captivated by the mysterious adventures of Aeneas' survival and falls in love with him. In Acts IV and V, Berlioz's tone differs from Virgil's undramatic plot of narratives, and Berlioz includes his own dynamic scenes (Cairns 1988, 86–87). Act IV (Berlioz 1969/2013 IV.2.443–590) starts with a dramatic storm and rain, focusing the attention on composing and decomposing the meaning of music-without-words. Berlioz arranged the visual scene onstage with musical thrills in *crescendo* with *arpeggio, tremolo* and *staccato* (Berlioz 1844/2002, 8–16). In the tones, half-tones and semitones of the stormy weather, Berlioz demonstrates Aeneas' spiritual rising from being the poor victim of a shipwreck to experiencing his second birth, when he falls in love with Queen Dido.

The emotional level of Act IV is ritualized through pantomimic ballets that encode meanings and movements of love to express the frenzy of love between Aeneas and Dido. Berlioz expresses the amorous passage of Act IV in the tonal harmonies that fill his own nineteenth-century heart (Newman 1972, 229–233) to achieve his tonal harmony. Whereas Brecht reflects away from the text to musicalize the sound shape and color the emotional movement of nature and love as the center point of his opera, Berlioz's tender form of translation is defined as music-without-words. Berlioz reduplicates the speech sounds as evocative, even illustrative, sound gestures of the music-with-words to craft the love-act of Act IV. Berlioz's self-translation exchanges the dialogue of words-to-words to resound with the sensitive variations of what Jakobson describes as "poeticalized" music, played not only in words but mainly in the feeling of the symphonic orchestra (Jakobson 1960/1964, 367).

The set of Act IV transitions to the African forest. The scene is provided with rocks, a stream, several waterfalls and the grotto where the nymphs, harpies, satyrs and fauns swim in the pool and join in grotesque dances. With the forest-demons shouting and gesticulating in wild pantomime, Berlioz follows Wagner's opera *The Rheingold*, which he composed in the same period. Both of them show the poetical pandemonium of the singing and dancing Rhinemaidens, as played on the theatrical stage. During the gestures of this mythological play, the Dido's party including Aeneas takes over the stage. The mythological scene is transformed into the royal hunt, where Thyrian huntsmen pass with dogs on leashes to change the scene. In the horn theme of the hunt, the trombones, flutes and oboes (from Berlioz 1969/2013, IV.2.453) along with the choir change from the "natural" dance in the *larghetto non troppo lento* tempo of the ballet to singing in a *crescendo* tone to reflect in music the discordant rhythms (*arpeggios* express the upcoming storm). The royal hunt is forcefully interrupted by the menacing signs of the distant rumblings of the torment and the upcoming of the storm. Dido, who is dressed as Diana the huntress, follows her guest Aeneas, clothed in military dress, to look for refuge from the bad weather. The grotto is their hiding place, where hidden fantasy rests from the tumult of the storm and dissolves into romantic love—a feature that was Berlioz's specialty.

The next scene is set in Dido's garden by the sea, where Dido is met by waves of cheers. The choir sings the national hymn of Carthage and ballets are performed by Egyptian dancing girls and Nubian slave girls. Queen Dido interrupts the vocal and visual festival of music and singing by asking Aeneas to retell the story of the fall of Troy. Now, different from Virgil's rendition of the narrative, Aeneas seems to avoid telling this story, but instead he encourages Dido to enjoy the romance of love. Aeneas sings:

Mais banissons ces tristes souvenirs.
Nuit splendide et charmante!
Venez, chère Didon, respirer les soupirs
De cette brise caressante
(Berlioz 1969/2013, IV.2.564–567)

But no more of these sad memories.
Night of splendour and enchantment!
Come, dear Dido, breathe the sighing whisper
of the caressing breeze (Berlioz 1973, 16, transl. David Cairns)

The romantic tale of Aeneas and Dido unfolds with the love duet sung to arouse their feelings in the moonlit royal garden. They embrace each other, and their undulating waltz (French: *valse*) is accompanied by them singing solo and in duet the "*Clair de lune*" (1969/2013: IV.2.575–589):

Nuit d'ivresse et d'extase infinie!
Blonde Phoebé, grandes astres de sa cour,
Versez sur nous votre lueur bénie;
Fleurs des cieux, souriez à l'immortel amour!
(Berlioz 1969/2013, IV.2.575–577) (Berlioz 1973, 16)

Night of boundless extasy and rapture!
Golden Phoebe, and you, great stars of her court
Pour on us your enchanted light;
Flowers of heaven, smile on our immortal love.
(Berlioz 1973, 16; transl. David Cairns)

Through the mythological metaphors and metonymies (Shipley 1968/1972, 268–269, 271), the duet is both a formal poem of mythological figures and the informal embrace of Aeneas and Dido within Berlioz's real embrace of music-with-words.

Par une telle nuit, fou d'amour de joie,
Troïlus vint attendre aux pieds des murs de Troie
La belle Cressida. [...]
Par une telle nuit la pudique Diane
Laissa tomber enfin son voile diaphane
Aux yeux d'Endymion. [...]
Par une telle nuit le fils de Cythérée
Accueillit froidement la tendresse enivrée
De la reine Didon! [...]
Et dans la même nuit hélas! L'injuste reine,
Accusant son amant, obtint de lui sans peine
Le plus tendre pardon. (Berlioz 1969/2013, IV.2.577–588)

On such a night, mad with love and joy,
Troilus awaited, under the walls of Troy,
The lovely Cressida. [...]
On such a night the modest Diana
At last let fall her gauzy veil
Before Endymion's eyes. [...]
On such a night Cytherea's son [Aeneas]
Responded coldly to the passionate love
Of Queen Dido! [...]
On that same night, alas, when the Queen
Unjustly accused her lover, he gladly gave her
The tenderest forgiveness. (Berlioz 1973, 16; transl. David Cairns)

Berlioz readapted this mythological duet from Virgil's Book IV but drew equally from Shakespeare's *The Merchant of Venice* (Cairns 1988, 83). Shakespeare's play also figured as a source for Virgil's *Aeneid* (with Ovid's *Metamorphoses*). The Shakespearean couple Lorenzo and Jessica (the Jew's daughter) proclaim the passage "On such a night" to each other several times in their lyrical duet in the moonlit garden at Belmonte (Act V Scene 1) (Shakespeare 1598/1987, 627). To maintain the allusion, Shakespeare's couplet must be included in the translation of the scene from Berlioz's opera into English. The double "play with sound" (Jakobson and Waugh 1979, 218–219) means that for Berlioz's Act IV, David Cairns's purely functional translation certainly requires a higher standard of lyricism to give this love duet more than the basic formality of mythological metaphors and metonymies. The theatrical effect of the love duet requires us to reflect on the sexual intimacy between the lovers to create the dramatic scene onstage.

Although Berlioz followed Virgil as his model for his description of the love affair (1916/1999, IV: vv. 2238–2278), he suddenly has the statue of the god Mercury, messenger of the gods, come to life onstage. Mercury strikes Aeneas's shield with his golden staff three times as he intones *"Italie! Italie! Italie"* (Italy! Italy! Italy!) (Berlioz 1969/2013, IV.2.589; 1973: 10). The intense exclamations of love are gone. The *andante molto sostenuto e maestoso* music ends the lovers' ecstasy, warning them that Mercury is the bearer of bad tidings from the gods reminding Aeneas of his mission to go to Italy.

In the final scenes of Act V (Berlioz 1969/2013, V.2.591–751; 1973, 16–23), Aeneas departs from Carthage. He responds to the dark shadows of the gods and the uncomfortable portent of "Italy! Italy! Italy." In the harbor of Carthage, the ships are ready to leave this place of refuge to embark on the final voyage to Italy. Aeneas, who is still in love with Queen Dido, finds himself in despair over the decision of whether or not to leave, while Dido is hopelessly troubled by his departure, which ends their love affair. The signs of Act V continue as signs of grief and mourning. Aeneas comes to the stage alone and deeply emotional and slowly sings some fragments of his troubled thoughts, not ready to take the final decision:

Inutiles regrets! […] je dois quitter Carthage!
Dido le sait […] son effroi, sa stupeur,
En l'apprenant, ont brisé mon courage […].
Mais je le dois […] il le faut! […].

Futile regrets! […] I must leave Carthage.
Dido knows […] Her terror, her amazement,
When she learned it have shattered my nerve […]
But I must, it has to be.
[…]
Ah! Quand viendra l'instant des suprêmes adieux.
Heure d'angoisse et de larmes baignée,
Comment subir l'aspect affreux
De cette douleur indignée? […]

But ah! When the moment comes
for the last farewell,
Moment of anguish and tears unstinted,
How to bear the dreadful grief?
(Berlioz 1969/2013: V.2.621–628; 1973: 18, transl. David Cairns)

Aeneas again sees the ghosts of the Trojan king Priam, Cassandra and Hector repeating to him Mercury's warning cries to leave Dido and Carthage, but he is bewildered by the puzzle. In the next scene, Aeneas, as the commander of the fleet, gives the decisive orders to prepare the fleet for sailing. Accompanied by Berlioz's wild music, Queen Dido's heart overflows with grief, and she announces in slow tempo that her life is over. She sings with emphatic rhythm this farewell:

Ah! Ah! [...] Je vais mourir [...].
Dans la douleur immense submergée
Et mourir non vengée! [...]
Mourons pourtant! Oui, puisse-t-il frémir
A la lueur lointaine de la flamme de mon bûcher!

Ah! Ah! [...] I am going to die [...]
Drowned in my great grief—
And die unavenged! [...]
Yet I must die. Could he but tremble
When he sees from afar the glow of my funeral pyre!
(Berlioz 1969/2013, V.2.705–706; 1973, 21, transl. David Cairns)

The next scene happens on the day of Dido's death, when she looks out over the sea for the departed Aeneas but sees him no more. For the funeral rite, a pyre has been set up, while Dido *"parcourt la scène en s'arrachant les cheveux, se frappant la poitrine et poussant des cris inarticulés"* (runs about the stage, tearing her hair, beating her breast and uttering inarticulate cries) (Berlioz 1969/2013: V.2.703; 1973: 21). After her cries of terror, she gathers herself and says goodbye to her sister Anna and her minister Narbal. In a half-dream, Dido announces the dark moment of her own death, singing that

C'en est fait [...] achevons le pieux sacrifice [...].
Je sens rentrer le calme [...] dans mon cœur

All is over [...] let us finish the holy sacrifice [...]
I feel peace returning [...] to my heart
(Berlioz 1969/2013, V.2.728; 1973: 22, transl. David Cairns).

Dido's last words in the primary source, Virgil's *Aeneid*, are the following:

"*dulces exuvia, dum fata deusque sinebat,*
accipe hanc animam meque his exsolvite curis.

Vixi et, quem dederat cursum Fortuna, peregi
et nunc magna mei sub terras ibit imago.
urbem praeclaram statui, mea moenia vidi,
ultra virum poenas inimico a fratre recepi,
felix, heu! nimium felix, si litora tantum
numquam Dardaniae tetigissent nostra carinae!"
dixit et os impressa toro, "moriemur inultae,
sed moriamur," ait. :sic, sic iuvat ire sub umbras. […]"

Dido's funeral rite switches around the mood and action of the dramatic scenes from passionate love to ritual acts ruled by the rigidity of their "formalized and relentless fixity" of structure and text (Scheffler 1997, 152). Certainty in life gives degrees of uncertainty, but at the end of the opera *Les Troyens*, the dramatization culminates in the climactic moment of Dido's suicide. The final scenes are no happy surprise for the audience but instead depict the declamation of disaster and intense mourning. The funeral rite is accompanied by the paraphernalia of Aeneas's toga, shield and arms to indicate a direct reason for Dido's despair. With Dido's suicide transpiring directly onstage, her drama is emoted through the vocal allure of her dramatic song. In her heroic aria, she stabs herself and falls wounded on the bed of the pyre to die.

Dido's death is accompanied musically by Anna and Narbal and the choir of the Carthaginian people, who provide the emotional sound backdrop to capture the immediate uncertainty of the tragic situation (Scheffler 1997, 131). The violent cries of this background ring out as

Ah! Au secours! (5x)
La reine s'est frappée!
Ah! Help, help! (5x)
The Queen stabbed herself!
(Berlioz 1969/2013, V.2.737–738; 1973: 23, transl. David Cairns)

The French interjections "*Au secours*" [ósekúr] are complex, being written with two vowels but pronounced as monophthongs (Malmberg 1954/1963, 38–39). In French, the first accent is on the open vowel "*au*" [o] and the second is on the half-closed vowel "*ou*." Cairns's English translation "Hélp! Hélp!" [hélp], with extra emphasis on the front open vowel and both rhyming with each other and the end rhyme "herself," adds drama to the situation onstage. As a poetic translator, I would translate "*La reine s'est frappée!*" as "The Queen killed herself" (my transl.) to overemphasize the rhythmical stress of consonant [k] in "secours" [sekur], "queen" [kwén] and "killed" [kil-éd].

Dido's last words are completely different from Virgil's nostalgic words (as mentioned). Dido's final cry reveals one last vision: "*Rome [...] Rome [...] immortelle!*" (Rome [...] Rome [...] eternal!) (Berlioz 1969/2013, V.2.743, 1973: 23, transl. David Cairns). The final words of Dido's prophesy announce the fall of Carthage with the victory of Rome, even anticipating the later struggle of the Punic Wars. At the same time, Berlioz reveals a political manifesto publicizing the eternal life of the Roman Empire. All this art, and even kitsch, is accompanied by the African people singing the triumphal *Trojan March* as the final chorus. At the end of the opera, Berlioz presents the moral of the opera as a cautionary tale by spelling out the lesson to be drawn: "evil" is rescued and "good" is punished. Certainly no happy ending.

Morality in the artistic form of "good" or "bad" is not so clearly drawn in the events and images of Berlioz's opera and is almost never pointed out. The heroes and heroines are the victims of the Olympic team of gods who decide their destiny, but they can also pull some evil tricks to explore the mystery of human hearts that can lead to the very edge of the world. Morality seems to be what humans enjoy or love, which may be virtuous or sensuous or a mingling of the two. The storytelling produces dramatic resonances and emphases of meetings and goodbyes to get what the operatic aficionados desire from adventures in fairy tales. Berlioz's reality of love ends in tragedy, when Aeneas abandons his Dido to travel on to Italy, leaving the audience with the inevitable farewell to Queen Dido.

To establish a final criterion for Berlioz's opera *The Trojans*, this opera is the overstatement of a romantic crisis, which was composed by Berlioz in a state of ecstasy (Jourdain 1997, 300–333). During the nearly five years he spent on composing the new *opéra lyrique*, he had to struggle with demons of words in the interaction of music-and-words. Berlioz's wild emotionality was actively in play in this double process, functioning as a repetitive intensification of the two lines of thought, the musical and the linguistic. Composing the music was not problematic, but inventing new lyrics was the challenge. Berlioz was not a poet, nor a novelist. His violent impulse focused on the harmony of tonal verses, but the lyrical rhythm of untonal words created a sense of disharmony (Jourdain 1997, 100–105).

Berlioz attempted to reassemble the two parts (the Trojan War and the royal love) into a recognizable plotline but found no consistent tone to pull together hatred and love in one opera. The tensions created by the tonal and untonal dichotomy intensify the "poetic" displacement of musical notes in the mind of the listeners. The "spirit and sensitivity and beauty" (Kerman 1956/1989, 16) of the opera was not the untonal lyrical words, but the music in itself (Meyer 1956/1970, 229–232). It was clear that the music itself was Berlioz's priority, but in his preparation of the *opéra lyrique*, the "poetic" words of the story and songs were understated and could hardly be said to have reached Jakobson's poetical level of new words.

The opera *Les Troyens* is a double labyrinth of music-with-words, but Berlioz was more a musicocentrist than a logocentrist. His language was transposed from Virgil's long poem the *Aeneid* to form a *pasticcio* of new ideas or concepts that were usable in his verses. But the uninterrupted medley of songs required from the composer Berlioz the artistic vision of one style to construct the novelistic scene onstage, bringing the melodious accuracy together with the "poetic" rhyme and rhythm of language. Although Berlioz worked for his living as a music critic and music arranger, his working abilities did not extend to redacting "poetic" verse for the opera *Les Troyens*, as would be desired by the concept of Jakobson's "poetics." We can conclude that Berlioz was a "bad" poet, who was put to the test by writing this libretto in music-with-lyrics (Labie 1990, 134–135). It seems that Berlioz may have been an excellent translator from Latin to French, but his retranslation into the poetry of libretto resulted in a disappointing self-translation.

Berlioz's hypertranslation of the libretto functioned as his parabole focused on the music (musicocentrism). The double-lined parabolic curve of Virgil's epic poetry could not harm the music, but Berlioz focused on the music as the main element of his lyrical work, distancing the words from the music (logocentrism). Berlioz as a poet and novelist always buried himself in the extravagant overtranslation of music, but he undertranslated in the sense of Jakobson's "poetic" forms and shapes. His lyrical verse was self-translated, yet the invariants of operative speech were not really "poetic" variants but instead "ordinary" invariants. In Jakobson's book *The Sound Shape of Language* (1979), he wrote in the section "Language and Poetry" that the "direct interplay of the speech sound with meaning" is the problem that poets impose on their creation. In the combination of music with poetry, the real poet needed

> to overcome the palling flatness and univocity of verbal messages, to curb the futile and impoverished attempts aimed at "disambiguation," and to affirm the creativity of language liberated from all infusion of banality. (Jakobson and Waugh 1979, 230–231)

Jakobson concluded that the spell of the sheer sound of words

> which bursts out in the expressive, sorcerous, and mythopoeic tasks of language, and to the utmost extent in poetry, supplements and counterbalances the specific linguistic device of 'double articulation' and supersedes this disunity by endowing the distinctive features themselves with the power of *immediate s*ignification. (Jakobson and Waugh 1979, 231)

It seems that in Berlioz's time it was probably too early to see the perfect parabole in the "*mediate* way of signification [which] totally disappears in the poetic experiments of the early twentieth century, which are parallel to the abstract trend in painting and akin to the magic ingredient in oral tradition" (Jakobson and Waugh 1979, 231, Jakobson's emphasis).

Berlioz as a poet and novelist was a parabolic player who was filled with the joy of innovative structure, melody, rhythm and instrumentation of music, but as an interpreter of the poet Virgil, he retold his life's adventures in his own transduction. Accompanied by the harmony and disharmony of modern music, Berlioz "played" with the new traditional rhetoric of literary speech to create a set of close-ups in a strange montage. Berlioz's elliptical version was hardly an operatic vision of translation or retranslation. He recast the beloved lines of Virgil and Shakespeare in *bel canto* song but followed the language of the old-fashioned style of French rhetoric.

Berlioz was like the electrical "thermostat" of his world. He attempted to maintain the double perspective of music-with-words to maintain his euphoria and energy as he composed the opera *The Trojans*. On the one hand, Berlioz's electric temperament was the main driver for him to compose the operatic music, but unfortunately the lyrics did not achieve the same power of meaning as the music. On the other hand, the words and sentences had to embellish the music to give a "magnetic temperature" to their flow (Sheriff 1984/2002, 147–151, 245). Berlioz lived in an age too early to be acquainted with the less dramatic atmosphere conjured up by the choice of merging the fine arts in the reformulation of the lyrical words. Berlioz seemed to foreshadow the movement of modern Cubism. Cubism does not seek to represent the whole phenomenon of the object but divides it into the fragmented movement of "cubes," which is reflected in Berlioz's opera. After depicting Dido's separation from her lover Aeneas, Berlioz did not go on to describe the founding of Rome as the holy capital of the Roman Empire, as Virgil did. Instead he focused on the scenes of Queen Dido's ceremonial self-inflicted death, giving the opera an unhappy ending, which was not fashionable in Berlioz's time. This opera creates a "playful" image of music-and-words but is notoriously unfaithful to Berlioz's literary model Virgil. Berlioz divided the invariants into dismembered fragments of holiness. Dido's ceremonial death was pictorialized in her own suicide as the unhappy end of the opera. These different "wave forms" (Bunn 2002) played a visible role in the circle of Virginia Woolf's waves. However, Berlioz wanted to embrace his scientific (mainly musical) talent in the aesthetic vision of his opera. Cubism provides a playful cultural reimaging, with Berlioz providing the illusion of different perspectives through the complexities and ambiguities of "cubes" as visual clues in his operatic hypertranslation.

Chapter 4

THE THREEPENNY OPERA: JAKOBSON'S POETICS RETRANSLATED IN THE SPIRIT OF BRECHT'S WORK-PLAYS

New Tongues for Brecht's Language

The dramatic genre of opera in its modern form has abandoned the old, static poetry of formal text-with-music in response to the attraction of dynamic and unconventional rhymes, dramatic sounds and satirical melodies, thus introducing new art forms (Kerman 1956/1989, 203–213). Alternative opera developed from the operatic tradition in its exploration of new subjects and themes, accepting contemporary vocabulary and speech to intensify the lyrical effect in conjunction with modern rhyme and tempo. This allowed a remix of scenic effects to create new dramas (Kerman 1956/1989, 214–228). Indeed, the new form of contemporary drama with songs and music, along with new sets, different lighting and a readaptation of the costumes, revived the stages of opera and operetta by emphasizing the emotional gestures of the actors (Pavis 1980, 133–134, 191–195, 262–263, 354–356). Brecht's new song-play genre featured an unconventional, modern style of declamation (*Sprechstimme*). This "speech song" consisted of a half-singing, half-speaking recital of lyrical texts which were similar to the twentieth century's harmonic, but dissonant, arias. *Sprechstimme* echoed the eclectic and dissonant schizophrenia of the international politics that formed the backdrop of reality in the twentieth century. Brecht personified the new voices in his sketches using variations to and elaborations on German theater, a process which Jakobson termed as cryptanalytical hypertranslation.

Onstage, the dramaturgic effects of modern opera were altered through the mimetic involvement of playwrights in order to move away from the old, familiar tradition of the audience being amused by the amorous events depicted in Italian opera which resolved into a happy ending. Instead, Brecht manipulated his modern dramas in educative theater by offsetting the pleasure of the audience with a contrastive feeling of displeasure. Brecht coined the term *Verfremdungseffekt* (alienation effect) for his method. He used (and abused) the emotionality of the German music drama (*Singspiel*) genre while preaching the sacred and secular themes of the melodramatic action by recoding the language in the popular speech spoken by the "street" classes. Jakobson splendidly discussed the contrastive structure of Brecht's lyrics in his article, "*Der grammatische Bau des Gedichts von B. Brecht 'Wie sind sie'*" (Jakobson 1963/1981). The use of music aside, Jakobson discusses parallelism and the recurrence of words and sentences, which must include alliteration, inversion and contrasts of sounds, and how they are held in balance by Brecht's dialectical commitment to his didactic lessons.

Brecht's theory was about more than intermixing poetic verses to create a new version: he broke down old dogmas to generate a dramatic action. With a sense of humor, he revolutionized the art of theater performance by incorporating Marx's social antiphilosophy and transforming it into a new form of theatrical cabaret. In his songs and narratives, he captured the misery of the masses, which was not due to their own wickedness, but might be used to preach new rules for the survival of humanity. Brecht proclaimed that there were capitalist economic laws in operation that ruled society and seemed to exclude the working class. Capitalism was, according to Brecht, "merely one stage of historical development, one soon to be destroyed by its internal contradictions" (McInnes 1967/1972, vol. 5: 172). Brecht's work was basically a commandment or moral imperative to society to change its way of thinking.

Brecht assimilated Marx's laws into his spiritual evolution to introduce a new world and revive the human spirit in a process characterized by the electrical entropy of conduction. Brecht shifted away from moral conduction to transduction, far removed from just writing poems in order to perform musical pieces. In terms of style, he seemed to covertly return to his Protestant upbringing in Augsburg (Bavaria), but now the dramaturg changed his social model. During his student years in Munich, the young artist rebelled strongly against his Christian education, forming a bohemian group of underground artists to shock bourgeois society. His early poems and songs reflect the political basis of his later theater pieces.

In the 1920s, Brecht was attracted to Marxism as the grounding for his theatrical works. As argued before in the case of Virginia Woolf's "nontranslation" and Hector Berlioz's retranslation of Virgil, Brecht's form of theater offered his transductive version of translation, which he transferred into the dialectic triad of social development. In the crude language of his song-theater, he expressed his protest against the rise of Nazism in Germany, revealing his telescopic vision of Marxist dialectics; for him, all classes were equal in non-capitalist morality. Brecht argued that the principal "thesis" behind his use of street language in his work-play was its power to convey compassion for the working classes, which leads to the "antithesis" of helping the working classes and solving the problems of class conflict (Kesting 1959/1967, 97). The "antithesis" leads to transduction for depicting the "synthesis" between the social classes (McInnes 1967/1972, vol. 5: 175) in the sociocritical rebellion, with the aim of mentally influencing the audience to embrace an equal and just society. Brecht's electrical wires were his "antithesis" to characterize the language of *Die Dreigroschenoper* (1928/1955), cited here in the English title *The Threepenny Opera*. Brecht included street language in his play to embrace an equal and just society. Brecht's electrical wires for composing *Die Dreigroschenoper* allowed the audience to arrive at the total synthesis of literary-and-musical hypertranslation as an aftereffect of what Jakobson termed "poetics."

Brecht's early play *The Threepenny Opera,* which premiered in 1928 in the Theater am Schiffbauerdamm in the German capital of Berlin, offered the bourgeoisie a realistic kind of German sung theater as in the *Singspiel*. The stories were not performed as in old opera but in a contemporary version of the German tradition of fairy tales, upgraded to Brecht's modern dramatic style with lyrical songs, gestures and even ballet. The content that Brecht circulated in the songs presented a sharp social satire of the bourgeois audience to prompt them to learn the lessons of Marxism, now transferred into theatrical actions. The actors were *chanteurs* (*chanteuses*) who used their untrained voices to perform the songs, reading the lyrical text not in their proper tone but readapting their voices to Brecht's alternative tongue. Brecht coached the singers to punctuate the sounds and raise the pitch of their voices in order to reflect the symbolic emotional experience of the language. He manipulated and managed language to give the expectant audience the myth of spiritual transduction to recode his message into another dialect (Wilshire 1982, 14; Zazzali 2018, 36).

Bertolt Brecht (1908–1956) was a dramatist, poet and theatrical director. After the First World War, he took on the role of restructuring the old form of opera into modern forms of singing theater. As a playwright, he struggled with the ancient background of theater and, during the dramatic democracy of the German Weimar Republic, he created a new operatic canon. His theater strongly countered the old tradition of operatic performances, which had pleased the audience with their dramatic illusion of quasi-reality and a happy ending. His political cry in the theatrical performances was intended to alienate and confuse the theatergoers with a new vision of reality depicting the struggles of postwar society. Brecht's double messages of thesis and antithesis gave the audience a dialectic lesson of simultaneously realist and formalist [performance]: realist, because it makes it possible to experience a segment of reality which has become unrecognizable as the response to it has become automatic; formalist, because it exploits the artifice of art to revive and stimulate perceptions which have grown dull and stereotyped—in other words, by disrupting conventions and schematized practices to some extent, it recreates the power of fresh, original perception. (Dahlhaus 1985, 79)

The radical conceptualization of the struggles of the bourgeois class presented the wrong image of the working classes. Brecht's formalist vision rearranged the image of the German lower class, giving them the alien process of transduction, moving from bad to good. With the help of his theater group, he moved the artistic quality of the collective work of drama away from the old opera and operetta. In the modern song-play, he readapted the working reality of folk balladry to suit his political "play with music" in contemporary revue and musical. The theater audience listening to the realistic folk song enjoyed the popular ambience of the dancing saloons telling the folk stories. In this highbrow move upward for the German working classes, his model revived the short and personal "work songs" (Koch 1994, 106–110, 299–305) from the old British ballads to embody the street music of ordinary people in Germany. Brecht's work-play had to find a way to express the crude lives of the German proletariat transferred into a new theatrical world.

In the gulf between the two social worlds, Brecht the scriptwriter functioned as a contemporary conductor, leading this movement away from traditional theater into an alternative translation of the old source play *The Beggar's Opera* by John Gay (1685–1732). Gay's British ballad opera was produced in London in the year 1728. Brecht re-used the underworld figures of London from this musical play. When Brecht was 22 years old, he set himself the task of being a modern playwright and of transforming the time-held cultural attitudes of the audience by giving them the new process of transduction. Brecht moved from indoor music to outdoor, street music. He gave the content a renewed, alienating interaction in the form of the dialogue of popular or crude songs. He combined fine arts with graphic pictures and other examplars of non-art. The result was the clownesque craft of cabaret (Gorlée 2015, 9–11). Brecht's melodramatic form of artistic transduction provided the historical, theoretical, formal, political and so on, senses of human empathy on all fronts enabling the audience to identify living persons with the actual poverty, crime and prostitution suffered by the German working class in their society.

In his satirical lessons on the stage, Brecht forced the audience to transfer rational Marxist argument into the dramatic ambience of the proletariat's vulgar language. He caused the audience to feel genuine shock at the destitution of the German laboring class. Brecht's music-play made the spectators ready to understand the ironic, observant and alert tone of his songs, enabling them to see the vision of a world with social equality. His view was that the audience needed associative thinking to emotionally and intellectually understand that the characters' motives and desires were those of reasonable men and women fighting against the hostility of the social structure of capitalism (Pavis 1980, 44, 50, 125–126, 203, 209–211; Müller 1980, 162–173).

In his experimental form of theatrical song-play (that is, the "light" form of the modern theater revue), Brecht reacted strongly against the "grand" opera of Italy and Wagner's operas about German gods and heroes. Brecht's theater embodied the cultural renaissance of opera in the reversible transduction of his invention of song-play, which converted social words-with-music into a new realism of art and non-art revealing a different truth. After the horrors of the First World War, this method of transduction made all drama into a truthful message of social justice. Brecht satirized the dark influence of Marxist doctrines by using the transductive form of ballet and dance, which he himself remade into a new genre of theater in his *Lehrstücke* (teaching-pieces). He explained and discussed the dialectics of realism and formalism in the fashionable art of *The Threepenny Opera* (1928/1955), continuing this in later plays as well (Brecht 1957/1962). Brecht's prolonged exercise in the aftermath of the tragic war was an exercise in overcoming the crisis of democracy by giving political lessons on the human value of consciousness, courage, ethics and political aesthetics in the 1920s. With his social transfer function, he expected to offer an image of socially acceptable dialogue for transforming the traditional disunity of German politics back into the cultural response of artistic transduction. The Weimar Republic, founded in 1924, intended to contribute democratically to countering the postwar depression in Germany.

The German working class was split into a majority supporting the Social Democrats and a radical minority supporting the German Communist Party. Extremists threatened to overthrow the government after the economic collapse of paper money, which had disrupted the political atmosphere in the Weimar Republic due to devastating shortages and poverty. Street attacks by Nazi groups hostile to other parties increased the hysteria of the populace. The Communist and Fascist Parties surged in popularity in Germany, and the German *Kaiser* left Germany in exile. The moderate Social Democrats declined into the underworld in the face of the Nazi Party. When *The Threepenny Opera* was being composed during 1927–1928, it was becoming clear that the parliamentary democracy established by the Weimar Republic in an effort to enforce democracy in the wake of the First World War could no longer cope with the turbulence and poverty suffered by the working classes.

The first radical movement in Europe was communism in Russia following Lenin's revolutionary victory (1917). Communism spread to other European countries, including Germany, as the democratic revolution of the proletariat against the power of the capitalist class. The radical activities of the communists in Germany were darkly overshadowed by the growing threat of National Socialism. In the 1920s, Brecht was drawn to the study and teaching of Karl Marx's theories. Brecht was basically a poet but, as discussed in his *Schriften zum Theater* (1957/1962, 13–212), he rejected the usual tradition of narrative art (as used by Berlioz) and turned toward developing the proverbial expression of his "epic" theater (Müller 1980, 19–20). This culminated in Brecht's "epic" nature positioning the educational idea of the music-and-words interaction in one paradigm to explain and remedy the situation of economic inequality existing between the social classes. This narrative poetry was not about the struggle of Homeric heroes but was a popular, even vulgar, kind of "epic" poetry (Shipley 1968/1972, 139–140).

Brecht followed Marx's social opinion in his artistic method, proposing that, in theater, the meaning of true reality is never the most obvious one, but is built into the illusionary but artificial sense of unreality in the role of the poetry. The nature of social truth elaborated in the criminal fiction of *The Threepenny Opera* builds on the hope of society understanding and healing the social evils of capitalistic structures (Müller 1980, 23). For all literary genres, including new cinema, the Cubist gestures of such representatives as Charles Chaplin and Sergei Mikhailovitch Eisenstein build up a social model for a class remedy (Jakobson and Halle 1956/1971, 92). The "epic" problems raise the pressure on the human characters to a fighting pitch, fluctuating between feeling and reason, but this is then resolved by the good sense of Brecht's political message integrated in the theatrical action onstage. Brecht's didactic method required integrating the code of these political rules into the linguistic subcodes in the audience's minds to build the "epic" transduction. To make *The Threepenny Opera*, Brecht spliced the separate tableaux of theatrical scenes into separate "shots" to build a "montage" that assembled the text-with-music (Müller 1980, 88–89).

Finally, Brecht's theater replaced the dialect of feeling and reason depicted in theatrical scenes with literary codes (and subcodes) to reflect how epic theater could be reworked into low language or crime language (Crystal 1987, 53). Brecht's plays were "adorned" with popular speech to arouse pity for the ordinary workers and fear of the absolute power exercised by the police, the courthouse and the government. In Brecht's epic alienation, the colloquial codes directly construct the workers' code of "survival of the fittest." His epigraph to *The Threepenny Opera* was "*Erst kommt das Fressen, dann kommt die Moral*" (First comes food, then comes morality). In the epic metaphor of his music plays, Brecht therefore presented the street sense of the "culinary opera" (Schuhmann 1964, 156). The audience is expected to recognize the economic and social conditions of the working classes, draw swift conclusions and thus aim toward building a just society (Schumann 1964, 156). Brecht's sharp line "*Doch die Verhältnisse, sie sind nicht so*" (But the circumstances are not like that) reflects his mobilization to employ the power of lyrical words in order to change the minds of the audience and create in them an "epic" *catharsis* (Brecht 1957/1962, 243; see Pavis 1980, 57; Wilshire 1982, 28).

In Brecht's *Schriften zum Theater* (1957/1962, 215–278), the triadic pattern of thesis, antithesis and synthesis was presented in the singing and declamation of the lyrics as a transductive model to explain the "epic" workings of modern dramatic theater. Brecht's ultramodern form of poetic theater sharpened the didactic material into Marxist ideology. To learn the new ways of playing and singing, the actors needed to understand the progress of thesis and antithesis to arrive at the synthesis of rethinking the dramatic play through their gestures and speaking. This was the way in which Brecht's group revealed the mystery of Brecht's theater. The culturally explosive theater group needed a stable organizer to maintain the continuity of Brecht's theatrical approach. Due to the sociopolitical activities of the group, Brecht as its leader appeared to be a communist agent. He was presented antithetically as the scriptwriter and dramaturgist, but his extravagant attitude defied the poverty, crime and prostitution of his theatrical program. In his musical plays, Brecht liberated the songs and gestures from formal poetry to give the audience the liberty of conscience to be free.

Brecht led the group like a Marxist chairman, teaching them how to play the crime scenes in keeping with his approach. Brecht's outward persona was eccentric: his head was clean-shaven or with little hair. He had piercing eyes and wore metal-rimmed glasses, giving him the air of a teacher or agent. His usual attire was an old leather jacket worn over a white shirt. He smoked cigars, giving him a playful, theatrical pose (Kesting 1959/1967, 112). In his Leftist "disguisement," he was a "born contrarian" to the values of his society (Hofmann 2018–2019). Brecht donned the attire of a political policeman or even people's commissar to function as the intellectual, literary and Marxist leader of the theater group (Kesting 1959/1967, 112).

The revolutionary impact of Brecht's stage works was almost a paradox. His realistic plays brought his ideological propaganda to the attention of the public. Using witty wordplay and new gestures, he symbolically realized the codes of the proletariat classes. Simultaneously, the moral function of his plays stood in contrast to Brecht himself, since he was the sensuous lover of many of the female singers, actresses and other women he knew in the theater environment. The many love affairs in his life were somehow part of his eccentric personality playing in his own drama. His spirit seemed to embody austere, clearheaded energy in his programmatic thesis of teaching "epic" life for the theater; but the erotic transduction of his love sonnets also served as his fetish to "epically" integrate the antithetical idea of free love into the declamation and singing of his theater group (Schuhmann 1964, 177–189).

Brecht was a literary man who, as a poet, wrote the lyrical text of songs for the theater. For the musical compositions of his "epic" songs, he needed the collaboration of an inspired composer. He found the lyrical composer in the specialist Kurt Weill (1900–1950). Weill was a disciple of composer Engelbert Humperdinck (1854–1921), who abandoned the mode of Wagnerian operas to write dramas in the form of *Singspiele*, a vocal technique of sung and spoken dialogues used in German folk songs. Humperdinck used *Sprechgesang*, combining singing and speaking, as a new technique for modern operas. For example, Humperdinck's fairy-tale opera *Hansel and Gretel* (1893) combined 16 songs to accompany a puppet show, loosely based on the fairy tale collected by the Brothers Grimm.

Kurt Weill, a composer of modern operettas, radio dramas and film music, now wanted to score a success with the comic-opera tradition of Brecht's *The Threepenny Opera*. Weill was the son of a Jewish cantor and wore horn-rimmed spectacles which lent him an intellectually dark and serious demeanor; yet he was a well-educated, humorous composer and converted the old operas into playful operettas. He seemed to follow the popular numbers of Jacques Offenbach but went even further, using modern jazz music for stage and, as a new alternative, film music. Playful theater for "practical purposes" (*Gebrauchsmusik*) was Weill's "commodity" version for creating a new theatrical performance using popular and jazzy melodies, which were ideologically uncompromising but basically romantic tunes. Weill used evergreen and forgotten melodies rearranged in a folk-rock rhapsody. Like Brecht, Weill challenged the audience and critics with his dissonant and consonant melodies, endowing musical symbols with a deeply felt social and political message. Weill's music had little impact on contemporaneous music as such, but for the German theatrical world, he successfully created brilliant music to spur the revolution of mass culture and advance the art form of revue to a new stage, later called the musical.

Brecht was lucky to find Weill as his librettist for *The Threepenny Opera*, and Weill was happy to work with Brecht to formulate the clear purpose of the modern music drama. As Weill wrote in 1932 in his articles "*Das Formproblem der modernen Opera*" and "*Wirklich Opernkrise?*" (1990, 102–105), their immediate mission was to jointly invent a new form of music drama as the work-play. Weill re-used old cotillon, waltz and polka melodies in addition to ragtime, blues and jazz music. He was the perfect composer for transforming the

Brechtian gangster sound into exciting music. Kurt Weill was brought into the group by Brecht's wife, the radical singer Lotte Lenya (1838–1981), who worked with Brecht as a singer and speaker. Although Lenya was a radical, vibrant and exciting young woman from a working-class background in Vienna, she had a singular ambition, which was to become a revolutionary actor on stage. In Brecht's experimental theater, Lenya's high, thrilling voice flourished in performing Brecht and Weill's revolutionary songs.

Lotte Lenya and Kurt Weill fell in love and got married (see the letters of Lenya and Weill edited in *Speak Low (When You Speak Love)*, edited by Simonette and Kowalke 1996). Weill's musical genius brought Lotte sentimental security, while she brought him into contact with Brecht to compose the revolutionary music for Brecht's song-play. Together they launched the popular and uncompromising success of Brecht and Weill's *The Threepenny Opera*, with Lenya becoming the star, enchanting the German public with her rendition of Brecht's cynical and satirical lyrics. Weill's style radiated modernism and garnered an outstanding response from the public (Farneth 1998, 41–88).

Elizabeth Hauptmann was Brecht's literary co-worker. Prior to this she worked as a college teacher and literary translator, but she chose to become a close collaborator or secretary of Brecht's dramatic group. As the male theater director, Brecht saw himself as the active leader and superior to his collaborators, but the income was meager. From *The Threepenny Opera,* 62 percent of the earnings went to Brecht, 25 percent to Kurt Weill for the whole composition, and just 12.5 percent to Elizabeth Hauptmann for her translation (Hinton 1990, 9, 20). Hauptmann was barely noticed as a special individual in Brecht's performances, but she was Brecht's long-term partner, silent collaborator and vigilant shadow reinterpreting, recreating and readapting all his works from the 1920s (Hanssen 1995, 7–18; Kebir 1997, 5–17).

In Brecht's theater group, Elizabeth Hauptmann was the only one able to speak and translate foreign languages. The truth was that it was she who first read about the London success of the revival of John Gay's play *The Beggar's Opera* (1728, republished in 1937). She roughly translated the mixture of witty dialogues and popular ballads into German herself, proposing the burlesque cabaret as a source for Brecht's works-in-progress. Brecht was enchanted. With the literary help provided by Elizabeth Hauptmann's translation, Brecht transformed Gay's old opera in the electrical sense of transduction: he retranslated it into lyrical slang. Brecht rewrote Hauptmann's German translation in criminal argot (the speech of thieves, rogues or beggars, German: *Gaunersprache*) (Pohl 1969: 40–43).

John Gay's (1685–1732) *The Beggar's Opera* was based on country ballads and belonged to a witty genre of entertainment for the theatrical world of London. In the eighteenth century, Gay moved away from the fashionable

Italian and French trends of making opera presided over in England by the composer Georg Händel. Gay refreshed the interest of the audience by using British folk tunes. He was a poet as well as a dramatic performer. Gay started out as the apprentice of a silk-merchant in London, at ease with urban life. Like Samuel Pepys (1633–1703) (Gorlée 2020a, 88–93), Gay was eager to advance himself socially and began to frequent literary circles and the taverns of the city of London to gain a better understanding of "ordinary" people's speech and worker's language in London. After writing collections of poems, Gay wrote a "tragicomical farce" about aristocratic gangsters; the farce was a success in English theaters and revived his interest in semi-literate and illiterate speech, as well as high and low speech.

Gay was appointed secretary to the Duchess of Monmouth and later to Lord Clarendon and the Duchess of Queensbury. These secretarial positions in aristocratic life not only provided him with an income but also propelled him into higher circles. In his free time, he befriended Jonathan Swift, dean of St. Patrick Cathedral and the author of the satire *Gulliver's Travels*, who used many colloquialisms but little real slang. Gay also befriended the poet and satirist Alexander Pope, who, as a man of letters, was the English translator of *The Iliad* and *Odyssey*, but who also wrote social pamphlets denouncing the low idiom of the London underworld (Partridge 1933/1972, 65–68, 71). Gay spent time with his new circle of literary friends to find inspiration.

Gay's characteristically comic level of popular speech was combined with a bold experiment to put into writing the speech of street life (Partridge 1933/1972, 64–79). He used the folk genre of British ballads as "pastoral" melodies to accompany the folk verse couplets. In his greatest work, *The Beggar's Opera* (1728), the crisp sense of humor in the songs and the narrative stories were prodigiously successful in the theater. The main protagonists, Captain Macheath and Polly Peachum, became household names in England at the time. In later life, Gay began to indulge in gambling and drinking in public houses, producing no more works. When he died in 1732 in London, John Gay was given a grand funeral.

After Gay's death, the folk tunes were readapted with new melodies, composed by musical editor Johann Pepusch (1667–1752). Dr. Pepusch was a German *émigré* living in England, working as a music copyist and choir director and even working on the "serious" historical and biblical subjects of royal composer George Händel. He also remade the music to Gay's "light" parody of homely songs, adding new texts to the libretto narrative. The new musical version was later revived by vocal composer Benjamin Britten (1913–1976), who produced a contemporary musical version of *The Beggar's Opera* for performance by the English Opera Group in 1948. Britten used the full Gay/Pepusch text of the earlier edition, but in the new continuum he dispensed with extra introductions and postludes to give more emphasis to the "sweetness of the tunes and the bitterness of the words" (*Kobbé's Complete Opera Book*; see Harewood 1922/1961, 23).

John Gay's portrayal of London in *The Beggar's Opera* (*Kobbé's Complete Opera Book*; see Harewood 1922/1961, 21–30) starts in the Prologue, in which the organist walking the streets of London transports the scene into the vernacular. Gay wrote in the spirit of the "unnatural" opera (1728/1937, 2), abandoning the popular fashion of Italianized opera and instead performing a folk play. The language used was not standard language, but the criminal speech used by beggars and criminals in the London milieu of thieves. In the folk jargon, the aim of the criminals was "to deceive, to defraud, to hide their dishonest and illegal activities from potential victims" (Hellar-Roazen 2013, 13; for the history of criminal slang, see Heller-Roazen's *Dark Tongues: The Art of Rogues and Riddlers* 2013, 19–43).

Act I (Gay 1728/1937, 3–35; see 1728/1948, 15–30, with 18 songs) initially describes the background of the characters. In both Gay and Brecht, Mr. Peachum seems to combine the professions of police informer and fence, and he receives and frees prisoners from jail. Gay narrates the story of Captain (shortened to "Captn") Macheath as the well-dressed leader of a gang of highwaymen. In Brecht's version, Macheath (later dubbed Mackie the Knife or Mac the Knife by Brecht) had the ambition of being a businessman or even a bank director. Peachum and Macheath come into personal conflict with each other, which is compounded by the intervention of the police (Lockit and the constables), who arrest Macheath and lock him up in Newgate prison.

Beyond money-making, Macheath embodies the romantic highwayman, enjoying the company of beautiful women, particularly Polly Peachum, daughter of Mr. Peachum. Macheath wants to conduct his criminal activities free from police intervention. Mr. Peachum and his wife upbraid their daughter Polly for flirting with a highwayman, but the couple grasps any opportunity to plot together. They plan for Macheath to be arrested and hanged, so that Polly will inherit his ill-gotten gains. Indeed, Macheath and Polly Peachum get married, and their love duet is sung in Act 1.

MACH. Pretty Polly, say
When I was away
Did your Fancy never stray
To some newer Lover?
POLLY. Without Disguise,
Heaving Sighs,
Doting Eyes,
My constant Heart discover.

Fondly let me loll!
MACH. O pretty, pretty Poll
(Air XIV: Gay 1728/1937, 30; see 1728/1948, 28)

In Act II (Gay 1728/1937, 36–73; see 1728/1948, 28–49), Macheath also has an amorous affair with Lucy, the daughter of Lockit, the jailer of Newgate prison. Macheath visits a tavern where Lucy works as a prostitute hired to entertain the criminal gang. The gangsters are known by their criminal nicknames: Money Matthew, Hookfinger-Jakob, Robert the Saw, Wally the Weeper, Lemmy Twitcher, Crook-finger'd Jack, Wat Dreary, Robin of Bagshot, Nimming Ned, Harry Paddington and Ben Budge (Danesi 2014, 92–93). The burglars and thieves get together to drink, sing and plot new criminal deeds. Captain Macheath orders the pleasurable company of some women to entertain them. The gang welcomes Mrs. Coaxer, Dolly Trull, Mrs. Vixen, Betty Doxy, Jenny Diver, Mrs. Slammekin, Suky Tawdry and Molly Brazen to entertain the gentlemen. In Brecht's later version, the sinister Lockit has been replaced by a corrupt sheriff, Jackie Brown, who eventually captures Macheath and incarcerates him.

Lucy enters to see her lover Macheath behind bars. She calls him a "perfidious wretch!" and his wife Polly calls him a "barbarious husband," while Lucy adds, "Hadst thou been hang'd five months ago, I had been happy" (Gay 1728/1937, 65; see 1728/1948, 45). Macheath's two lovers sing the following song:

POLLY. I'm bubbled.
LUCY. [...] I'm bubbled.
POLLY. Oh how I am troubled!
LUCY. Bamboozled and bit!
POLLY. [...] My Distresses are doubled.
LUCY. When you come to the Tree,
Should the Hangman refuse,
These Fingers with Pleasure,
Could fasten the Noose.
POLLY. I'm bubbled, etc.
(Air XVIII: Gay 1728/1937, 67; see 1728/1948, 46)

Polly and Lucy are cheated and tricked, indeed "bubbled," which meant in the English workers' speech of the eighteenth century "cheated, perhaps from being like an air bubble, filled with words, which are only wind, instead of real property" (see entry in Robert Cromie's *1811 Dictionary of the Vulgar Tongue* 1811/1971). Polly accuses Lucy of being a flirting wench, committing to men's folly, and reminds her of the sacred bonds of marriage:

POLLY. No Power on Earth can e'er divide
The Knot that Sacred Love hath ty'd.
When Parents draw against our Mind,
The True-Love's Knot they faster bind.
Oh, oh ray, oh Amborah—oh, oh, etc.
(Air XXI: Gay 1728/1937, 71; see 1728/1948: 48)

Gay seemed to flirt positively and negatively with the sexual content of *The Beggar's Opera*. Free love for men means that female prostitution and marriage serve as commercial products of the sexual dependence of women on men. Brecht wanted Lucy to turn her destiny upside down. She would be able to gain some property when her lover Mac the Knife is put under arrest, because she could take over as the head of the criminal business. Lucy hopes, as an upstart with money, to become a decent lady.

In the last act, Act III (Gay 1728/1937, 74–113; see 1728/1948, 50–68), Gay's *The Beggar's Opera* reaches its climax onstage. Lockit confronts Lucy wanting to share the bribe he thinks she has taken from Macheath to let him go free. Lucy admits that she did it out of her love for Macheath, but if Macheath does not pay up, he will be imprisoned and hanged. In a gaming-house, Macheath does indeed pay Lockit to keep the police off his back.

In Gay's songs of *The Beggar's Opera*, Macheath is in the "Gaming-House" elegantly dressed in "a fine tarnished coat." He seeks to make a good living, despite the corruption of the police:

MACH. The Modes of the Court so common are grown,
That a true Friend can hardly be met;
Friendship for Interest is but a Loan,
Which they let out for what they can get.
'Tis true, you find
Some Friends so kind,
Who will give you good Counsel themselves to defend.
In sorrowful Ditty,
They promise, they pity,
But shift you for Money, from Friend to Friend.
(Air IV: Gay 1728/1937, 80–81; see 1977/1948, 53)

Gay's drama continues with a satirical depiction of the hypocrisy and extortion of the English police and courthouses, which transform the criminal networks of London's underworld into a real mafia hub (Herbert 1948). In *The Beggar's Opera*, parliamentary opposition includes the capitalist tricks played by the Walpole administration. With royal support, the Whig prime minister Sir Robert Walpole (1676–1745) held Parliament together with bribery and corruption. Walpole was convicted of corruption and spent time behind bars in the Tower of London. Gay referenced Walpole's life of drinking and off-color stories in his satirical cabaret of *The Beggar's Opera*, which was directed at bourgeois listeners. Gay probably had Walpole in mind when he created the theatrical figures of Peachum and/or Macheath.

Macheath's wife Polly wants to reconcile with Lucy. Both women realize that Macheath desired both of them, but the love of any woman is a dangerous venture for any independent male. Lockit and his constables disturb the reconciliation of Lucy and Polly. They enter the drinking scene to prepare Macheath to be hanged, guilty or not, at the Old Bailey. Macheath, in distress, sings his farewell in trio with Lucy and Polly (with chorus):

LUCY. Would I might be hang'd!
POLLY. [...] And I would so too!
LUCY. To be hang'd with you,
POLLY. [...] My Dear, with you.
MACH. O leave me to Thought! I fear! I doubt!
I tremble! I droop!—See, my Courage is out. [Turns up the empty bottle]
POLLY. [...] No token of Love?
MACH. [...] See, my courage is out. [Turns up the empty Pot]
LUCY. No token of love?
POLLY. [...] Adieu.
LUCY. [...] Farewell.
MACH. But hark! I hear the Toll of the Bell.
CHORUS. Tol de rol lol, etc.
(Air XVI: Gay 1728/1937, 108–109; see 1728/1948: 66)

Four more "wives" appear to claim Macheath as the father of their children. The old beggar from the Prologue returns to announce that Macheath is going to be hanged. Rather than having the play end with the execution, Gay introduces a more positive note in the form of an alternative ending. In this version, Macheath is freed and he dances with his wife Polly to celebrate the bonds of marriage (Act III Scene XVII: Gay 1728/1937, 111–113; see 1728/1948, 68–68).

The simple ballad entered British literature in the sixteenth century in the verse form used by Gay. Coming from French lyric verse, balladry enlivened the folk narrative in the eighteenth century. The ballad is a short form of verse often set to music that appeals to the mystery and suspense of the people's feelings. The rhyme pattern is generally *a b c b*, but it also comes in variations, as in *a b a b* and *a a b b*. The rhythm is low in the first verse but rises in the second verse and remains at a high level in the third verse, before moving down in the final fourth verse. The meter is four iambic lines (that is, light and stressed syllables) alternating in four or three-foot lengths. Each verse has five stressed syllables, which can be employed as meaningful clues to stress the epic, lyric or dramatic forms of ballad. The ballad can be transposed with minor adjustments and repetitions, so that the text can shift to eight lines instead of four. The long ballad is sung in *parlando-rubato* folk music, that is, the half-singing, half-reciting style of *Sprechgesang*. This style of half singing and half reciting includes elongation and shortening of the tones, restructuring the double meaning of the verses (Nettl 1965/1973, 66–70; Shipley 19681972, 34–35; Koch 1994, 15–18).

Gay polished the popular folk ballad into a metrical verse form that expressed a mock-heroic attack on the civilized language by the street life of London, with the aim of popularizing low and vulgar speech. In his noble effort, Gay criticized the indecency of public houses and the habit of gangsters giving bribes to stay out of prison. Gay's picturesque style of literary writing was characterized by his unconventional exposition in Cockney rhyming slang as spoken in the East End of London (Lunde 2009, 132–133, 135). Gay did not write "ordinary" songs for the London music halls but specialized in the vivid prose of folk speech for thieves and pickpockets, satirically remaking it into rhyming "poetry" with parallel syntax and rhythm, metaphor and alliteration. In *The Beggar's Opera*, Gay sometimes used expressions from vulgar slang—but he used very few expressions from thieves' cant, unlike Brecht later does in the 1920s.

Brecht Juggling with Gay's *The Beggar's Opera*

Two centuries after John Gay composed *The Beggar's Opera*, Brecht adapted the British ballads of the source play for *The Threepenny Opera* (1928). Brecht wanted to gain public acclaim not only in his own country but throughout the civilized world, but his adaptation of Gay's play caused him legal problems. On August 28, 1928, the *chanteuse* Lotte Lenya described Brecht's process for *The Threepenny Opera* as follows:

> As his admirers have it: to adapt, reinterpret, re-create, magnificently add modern social significance; or in his detractors' eyes: to pirate, plagiarize, shamelessly appropriate—to borrow at will from the vanished great like Marlowe and Shakespeare and Villon, and even from his actual or near contemporaries like Kipling and Gorky and Klabund. Critical storms have crashed around Brecht's close-cropped head for more than thirty years—some say the inevitable result of a singular

talent, while others snort that they have been shrewdly provoked by a charlatan. "Why deny that Brecht steals?" said a Berlin friend last summer. "But—he steals with genius." Brecht generally has disdained self-defense and held to an enigmatic, smilingly scornful silence. (Lenya 1956/1960, v–vi)

Brecht's transductive translation was controversially a retranslation from Gay's workplay, but Brecht's literary theft reconstructed and overplayed Gay's social story. He modernized *The Beggar's Opera* performed in 1728 into a modern self-translation (also called autotranslation) by reverting Gay's criminal songs and fables with an alienation effect to make them intellectually acute (Müller 1980, 141–146, 153–162). Brecht guided the literary composition of theater into the "epic" poetry of intercultural hypertranslation. There was for Brecht no question of plagiarism, since he did not willfully steal Gay's original. The assistant Elisabeth Hauptmann had translated Gay's *The Beggars Opera* herself to give a rough retranslation to prepare the way for Brecht's to recreate the self-translated version of *The Threepenny Opera*.

In the article "Editorial notes," Brecht's translators Ralph Mannheim and John Willett stated that Brecht only used some parts of Gay's original text, basically some parts of Act 1 scenes 1 and 3, Act II scenes 4, 5 and 6, Act III scene 8, and the Finale representing Mac the Knife's execution (Brecht 1979/2000, 106–107; Hinton 1990, 21–22). Apart from that borrowing, the rest is Brecht's work, for which he replaced Gay's songs and narratives with his own epic poetry (Shipley 1968/1972, 139–140) and added new scene titles. With consideration to the characters, Brecht exchanged Gay's Mr. Peachum for J. (that is, Jonathan Jeremiah) Peachum, and Mrs. Peachum for Celia Peachum; then he replaced Lockit with police commissioner Brown, alias Tiger Brown, the High Sheriff of London. Brown is friendly with Macheath, also called Mac the Knife, until the latter is captured in a whorehouse and held prisoner in the Old Bailey until he presents his account-book. Lucy, who is Brown's daughter, sings a popular song about a girl called Jenny. Further characters are Reverend Kimball and the young beggar Charles Filch, as well as Brecht's ballad singer, the criminal gang of thieves, beggars, whores, constables and other minor actors.

Brecht shifted Gay's eighteenth-century piece into a Victorian setting for *The Threepenny Opera*. He changed the whole stage design, but Gay's satirical spirit is still there in the poetic (that is, the textual and musical) reproduction of *The Threepenny Opera*. Brecht lifted and altered Gay's burlesque cabaret with entirely new words, bringing socially aggressive songs to the stage. Composer Weill completely abandoned the tunes of Gay's ballads to compose light jazzy melodies to fit the musical *Zeitgeist* of the twentieth century. Weill strongly reacted to the old Wagnerian operatic tradition by advancing the melodies into light, but serious, revue music. The evolution from Gay to Brecht and Weill is firstly demonstrated by the introduction of the Prologue, which means the play does not open in Peachum's house, as in Gay's opera, but at a fair in Soho with a barrel organ player singing "The Ballad of Mac the Knife."

To start the Brechtian festival, the Prologue rings out with the impious tunes of an Italian vagabond musician playing his barrel organ on the streets of London to earn a living. The musician sings a *Moritat*, that is, a murder ballad, from *Mord* meaning "murder" and *Tat* as "deed"). Brecht's wordplay employed "criminal [speech] and other spectacular events of little poetic value (often on a low and vulgar level), especially addressed to the lower classes" (Koch 1994, 17; see Pearsall 1973, 189–195, and 64). The rest of Brecht's spoken text is a poetic renewal with entirely revised lyrics to accompany his own poetry. Brecht did not compose a sung version of Gay's earlier speech but refurbished it as a new text to echo the tragic world of the Victorian era. All this was penetrated by Weill's harsh melodies to make a unity of music-and-text.

The Threepenny Opera had a political message for the audience. The success of Brecht's music-play is reflected in the fact that they intended to make a film of *The Threepenny Opera*. However, as Nazi oppression grew in Germany, with Hitler coming to power, the popularity of Bertolt Brecht and Kurt Weill ended. When Hitler became German Chancellor in 1933, performance of *The Threepenny Opera* was officially forbidden. The day after the *Reichstag* fire in February 1935, democracy in Germany was over. Jewish composer Kurt Weill and his wife Lotte Lenya were forced out of Hitler's Germany. They fled to Paris and emigrated to New York. There, Weill eventually built a new career composing musicals. Weill and Lenya were befriended by lyricist Ira Gershwin (brother of George Gershwin, who died in 1937) and the young director Leonard Bernstein. Lotte Lenya became a well-known singer performing in musicals. Weill's premature death at the age of 50 brought more problems for Lenya, who, in the controversy of the Cold War period, struggled to get a just settlement from the communist regime in East Berlin for the copyright of Weill's music.

As for Brecht, he too was placed on the Third Reich's banned list. To escape from the German brownshirts, he looked for safety in Finland, which was, however, occupied by the Russians and not safe. He then emigrated to Hollywood to write film scripts and stayed there for six years but had little success with the film producers. In 1945, Brecht wanted to return to East Germany. Luckily, his wife, Helene Weiger, was later appointed as theater director (*Intendantin*) of the newly founded Berliner Ensemble in East Berlin, at that time the communist capital of East Germany. In her official function as director, Weiger, in collaboration with her husband Brecht, staged productions of his repertoire in this theater.

In 1942 in Los Angeles, Brecht met with the young English composer and music critic Eric Bentley (1916–2020), who had studied at the University of California. As an absolute fan of Brecht, Bentley wrote (in collaboration with Desmond Vesey) the first English translation of *The Threepenny Opera* in 1949 (Vesey, Desmond and Eric Bentley 1949/1960). Several other translations would follow, but the value and quality of the translations are rarely discussed in research on Brecht's theater. The translation by Marc Blizstein in 1952 was produced after Weill's death during the McCarthy era. *The Threepenny Opera* was under suspicion of being influenced by communism and did not become popular in the ensuing crisis of the US government. Marc Blitzstein befriended Weill's widow Lotte Lenya, and she sang "Pirate Jenny" herself in the first performance after her husband's death (Farneth 1998, 130–134; for the song libretto, see Brecht 1928/1955). Michael Feingold made a new translation of *The Threepenny Opera* in 1954. Feingold was a drama critic, playwright and dramaturg, who produced a poetic performance of *The Threepenny Opera* (Weill and Brecht 1928/1999). In the same year (1954), Ralph Manheim made a literary translation of Brecht's text of *The Threepenny Opera* (edited by John Willett), resulting in a grittier version with ample commentaries and editorial notes (Brecht 1928/1979).

The qualities and nuances of these translations shall be discussed on the basis of the following examples, first according to Brecht's lyrical texts, accompanied by Weill's popular music. In the Prologue of *The Threepenny Opera*, gangster Macheath, nicknamed Mac the Knife (*Mackie Messer*), makes a spectacular entrance onstage. The opening song, "The Ballad of Mac the Knife," is accompanied by the disagreeable nasal mechanical whine of the beggar's barrel organ and serves as the leitmotif of Brecht's music-play. The first stanza is:

Und der Haifisch, der hat Zähne
Und die trägt er im Gesicht
Und Macheath, der hat ein Messer
Doch das Messer sieht man nicht.
(Brecht 1928/1955, 7)

And the shark he has his teeth and
There they are for all to see.
And Macheath he has his knife but
No one knows where it may be.
(English transl. Desmond Vesey 1949, see Vesey, Desmond and Eric Bentley 1949/1960, 3)

Oh, the shark has pretty teeth, dear
And he shows them pearly white.
Just a jack-knife has Macheath, dear
And he keeps it out of sight.
(English transl. Mark Blitzstein 1952, 5; see libretto Weill/Brecht 1928/155, 5)

Oh, the shark's teeth, you can see them
Always ready to attack.
But you don't see Macheath's knife blade
Till you feel it in your back.
(English transl. Michael Feingold 1954; see record Weill/Brecht 1999, ed. Stephen Hinton).

See the shark with teeth like razors.
All can read his open face.
And Macheath has got a knife, but
Not in such an obvious place.
(English transl. Ralph Manheim 1979, see Brecht 1928/2000, 3)

Since Brecht was indoctrinated with Marxist principles, the sharply formulated theisms of "epic" theater were intended to save the world from social inequality. Skeptically and even paradoxically, Brecht's style of writing was compatible with fragments from biblical texts (Hinton 1990, 187–188; Pohl 1969, 55–61). Brecht reverted to the old style of his parents' education, drawing from the religious education he received in the Protestant Church (Schuhmann 1964, 9), but in addition he found instructive teachings in his own folk poetry, which provided enough literary material for dynamic poetry (Jakobson 1963/1981, 661–662). The formal literary styles of the Bible provided Brecht with the constructive elements of biblical metaphors, parallel expressions, alliterations and inversions. However, as will be discussed later, Brecht expanded this style of language to include slangy speech encrypted with special lyrical and criminal words (Danesi 2014, 89–91; Crystal 1987, 53).

In the lyrics of the first ballad in Act I, Brecht employed special idiolects couched in a closed structure with the old quasi-rhyme of *a b c b* but materialized this in each verse of the *Moritat* as the "electrical wires" (Schuhmann 1964, 35) of his special process of transduction, shifting from the old picturesque style into the modern lyrics. Simultaneously, the content of Brecht's musical songs played with the use of oral poetry to provide epic sermons to the audience. When asked by a German magazine what "the strongest influence" on his work was, Brecht replied, "You'll laugh: the Bible" (Jakobson

1963/1981, 662). According to Hinton, Brecht was a tongue-in-cheek poet, using "sacred means" to reach "profane ends" (Hinton 1990, 187).

Brecht's *Moritat* is the introductory piece to *The Threepenny Opera* and presents Macheath as Mack the Knife. The *Moritat* was originally marked to be played in a blues tempo, but Brecht altered it into a fanfare. He adjusted the mood of the melody by including the *fortissimo* sounds of basses and percussion to evoke the pseudo-military signs of a funeral procession. The first translation of *The Threepenny Opera* made by Desmond Vesey in 1949 (with Eric Bentley) is an accurate and literal version of Brecht's work, but this version failed to evoke the lyrical quality of Brecht's original. Mack Blitzstein's translation (1952) creates the sense of a love poem, twice adding the rhyme of the odd word "dear" as a form of address. This vocative is addressed to the unknown receiver of the ballad, but Blitzstein's poeticized dialogue seems out of place in the context of Macheath's dramatic entrance, which presents him as a shark in order to raise a sensational response in the audience of *The Threepenny Opera* (Nida 1964, 232–233).

However, the third and fourth translations, produced by Brecht (1979/2000) respectively, contrast the thesis of Macheath's speech with Brecht's antithesis of singing the lyrics when he transformed the invisible weapons of Gay's ballad into signs that allow the audience to understand the epic libretto as a funeral march reminiscing on the crimes committed by a mafia-like organization. Feingold and Manheim carefully explore the separate value of the words, drilling the meaning of the sentence into a lyrical stanza. They form a poetic diction, not in poetry but in prose to be sung with music (Feingold), rather than being a lyrical wordplay in the sense of Jakobson's rhyme and rhythm, to align the songs in poetic harmony (as in Manheim's translation).

Importantly, the sarcastic figure of Captain Macheath is, in Brecht's piece, called the "shark," a semantic and syntactic metaphor derived from his moniker "Mack the Knife" (Danesi 2014, 94–97). The word "shark" is not used as such in scriptural texts, but the predaceous fish with its dangerous rows of sharp teeth is referred to in the parable of Jonah and the whale (Jon. 1:17–2:10). In the Bible reading, Jonah is swallowed by a whale or shark at sea and prays to the Lord to be liberated from his dark confinement and suffering. In a reversal of the Bible text and in keeping with Brecht's "epic" doctrine of alienation, Macheath instructs his gang in the art of engaging in criminal activities (Pohl 1969, 57–58). In contrast to the teachings of biblical morality, Mack the Knife teaches his "good" works in line with a non-Christian immorality. Macheath employs sharp, crude language when ordering the gangsters to kill their human victims (Herbert 1948). Brecht, the disbeliever, turns the biblical world upside down, reversing the story of Jesus' miracle with the fishermen in order to create the wisdom of his prophetic work.

Brecht irreverently alludes to the biblical story of Jesus pragmatically "fishing" Simon, James and John out of the Sea of Galilea to be his first disciples. He taught them to be fishermen for the salvation of others. In the biblical text, Jesus brings the fishermen the divine message of God when they catch the "great multitude of fishes" (Luke 5:6) for now they will go out as fishers of people. Jesus' good work was, so to speak, public news to be divulged in the "tabloid newspaper." Brecht revived this miraculous day that had taken place in the first century of our era. Brecht the disbeliever called the "gang" of fishermen the believers that had to live on a moral knife edge as disciples throughout their lives doing good (that is, spiritual and divine) works. Brecht seems to have rewritten the story of believers for disbelievers (Hinton 1990, 187–188).

The vivid metaphor of the "shark" that is used to refer to Macheath alludes to the "knife" he uses to brutally kill his enemies. A "shark" is defined in the *1811 Dictionary of the Vulgar Tongue* as a "sharper," which in turn is defined as a "cheat, one that lives by his wits." The entry for "shark" goes on to define it as someone who lives from "preying upon any one he can lay hold of," and states that the word is also used the designate "the first order of pickpockets" (Francis 1811/1971). Eric Partridge, who was an expert in underworld speech, generally defines "shark" as a "sharper" sense in "a swindler or a sharper" (1933/1972, 400). Macheath represents the double meaning of the knife as an ironic metaphor by showing that the shark is both a visible and an invisible weapon of pickpockets. Brecht builds in special metaphors with double meanings by using what Jakobson calls a mixture of linguistic signs transformed into "poetical" watchwords. Jakobson wrote (in Danesi's words) the following technical definition:

> All these figurative processes (metaphor, metonymy, irony), however, show association as the underlying cognitive mechanism, so all three have the structure *X is Y*, either by mapping one domain onto another (conceptual metaphor), using one domain to stand for another (metonymy), or using one domain contrastively to another (irony). (Danesi 2014, 95)

In the history of translation, the analysis of metaphors has been tackled in the works of many Bible translators. The original source texts in the Scriptures seem to "shift from a metaphor to another metaphor, a metaphor into a simile, or a metaphor to non-metaphor" (Nida 1964, 219–221). In this complex task of metaphor to non-metaphor and back, the translator cannot lose sight of the original sacred text to create other forms of new metaphors. The panculture of mythology in the target language can be different from that of the source language, but the translator stays cautious about culture. This is illustrated, for example, in the article "Kings are lions, but Herod is a fox" by Bible translator Hermanson (1999), where he discusses the likeness of and difference between translations of animal metaphors into different code-languages. The metaphor "shark" can stand for a human person in order to guide the moral reason of emotion toward the logical reason for death. But when humans are viewed as unlogical animals, this metaphor works well combined with the metonymical nickname of Mac the Knife (Shipley 1968/1972, 268–269, 271).

In 1928, Brecht used this metaphor in the *Moritat* ballad in the Prologue to present Mac the Knife as the main protagonist of the play. Jakobson's article about Brecht (Jakobson 1963/1981, 662) refers to the parallelism, alliteration and contrastive structuration that guided Brecht's sound symbolism in a similar mode to the poetry of the Bible (Hinton 1990, 187–188; see Jakobson and Waugh 1979), stressing the keywords of the ballad verse. In the first verse, he uses the metaphor "shárk" (*Haifisch*) and "tééth" (*ä*), in the second line "cárries" (*trägt*) and "fáce" (*Gesicht*), in the third line Brecht goes back into "Machéath" (*Macheath*) and his tool, the "knífe" (*Messer*). In the last verse, the "knífe" is there, but out of sight ("*[sieht man] nícht*"). The internal syllables of the rhyme in the fourth verse (*Gesicht–nicht*) are alliterated: the German vocal [ä] in *Zähne* (teeth) and *trägt* (carries) along with the repeated consonant [m] in the proper name Macheath and the word *Messer* (knife) carry these key words beyond themselves to create the mythopoeia of a secret world of thieves. Transduction comes from both contiguity (being nearby) and similarity (being almost the same) (Jakobson and Waugh 1979, 204–208, 230–231, 236), suggesting Peirce's quasi-semiosis in metaphors of firstness and secondness, but the feeling and force have no logical thought (thirdness) of real semiosis.

In the structure of the story, the Brechtian songs start by repeating the syntactic structure of the conjunction "*und*" (and) in synonymous phrases being formally sung in the separate verses (Nida and Taber 1969, 134–135). The thesis of "*und*" is followed by "*doch*" (but) or other conjunctions used as stylistic antithesis (Nida and Taber 1969, 135–137). This formal and informal structure was borrowed from biblical poetry, such as the songs, hymns, lamentations, proverbs, wisdom and prophetic speeches of the Bible (Pohl 1969, 60). Even the narrative of Jesus Christ in the parable of Luke 5:6 and other gospels (Matt. 4:16 and Mark 1:18) was informally poeticized into the work of the unscrupulous murderer Mack the Knife, who starts the poem with the initial "and." In the gospel of Luke, examples of such use are as follows:

> *And* it came to pass, that, as the people pressed upon him to hear the word of God […].

And saw two ships standing by the lake: but the fishermen were gone out of them, *and* were washing their nets.

And he entered into one of the ships [...]. *And* he sat down, *and* taught the people out of the ship.

Now, when he had left speaking, he said unto Simon, Launch out into the lake [...].

And Simon answered said unto him, Master, we have toiled all the night, *and* have taken nothing [...].

And when they had this done, they enclosed a great multitude of fishes: *and* their net broke.

And they beckoned unto their partners [...]. *And* they came, and filled both the ships [...].

When Simon Peter saw it, he fell down at Jesus' knees [...]. (Luke 5:1–8, emphasis added)

Brecht's dialectics reflect traditional biblical style in its contrast of thesis and antithesis. Brecht followed the formal style of the gospel, but he employs epic parallelism by starting each verse with the unconventional additive conjunction "and" (Jakobson 1963/1981, 664–666). In later verses, Brecht uses the negative conjunction "now" or "when" to tell the story of the biblical wonder (Nida 1964, 232–233). By introducing the preliminary thesis with *"und"* followed by the adversary conjunction *"doch,"* Brecht attempts to communicate the opposition in the positive and negative story presented by the dynamic or even ironic part of the dirty deeds: the "shark" catches and kills human victims. In *The Threepenny Opera*, Brecht desired to relate both the "good" and "evil" parts of the biblical story: he tells of how the lost sheep can fall into the hands of tax-collectors, whores, drinkers, adulterers and other sinners (Schimmel 1992).

Brecht employed this dynamic procedure to communicate some of the portions of Gay's text as part of the twentieth-century list of songs in *The Threepenny Opera*, but most of the songs he wrote himself, employing his own dynamic technique (Nida and Taber 1969, 224–225). For example, in the source text by Gay, the marriage of Macheath and Polly provokes a conflict with Polly's parents, Peachum and his wife. Brecht's text closely adheres to the ensuing discussion in Gay's work. After a storm of speculations to contradict the arguments of the parents, Polly is happy to get married, as it gives her a state of some security. The source text by Gay provides a metaphor for Polly's life when she sings:

> POLLY. I like a Ship in Storms, was lost;
> Yet afraid to put in to Land;
> For seiz'd in the Port the Vessel's lost,
> Whose Treasure is contraband.
> The Waves are laid,
> My Duty's paid.
> O Joy beyond Expression!
> Thus, safe ashore,
> I ask no more
> My all is my Possession!

Polly feels as if she is a woman alone, like a ship in the storms, but the marriage promises to give her the certainty of fair weather. With Macheath's status and income, she feels "safe ashore," meaning looked after. Later, the marriage turns into a disastrous series of conflicts with Lucy, who has taken her place as Macheath's mistress. Then, Lucy re-uses the reversed allusion of bad weather on the sea:

> LUCY: I am like a Skiff on the Ocean tost,
> Now high, now low, with each Billow born,
> With her Rudder broke, and her Anchor lost,
> Deserted and all forlorn.
> While thus I lye rolling and tossing all Night,
> That Polly lyes sporting on Seas of Delight!
> Revenge, Revenge, Revenge,
> Shall appease my restless Sprite.
> (Air VII: Gay 1728/1937, 89–90; see 1728/1948, 58)

Brecht adopts Gay's symbol of the ships in a storm in his poeticized lyrics for "Pirate Jenny" (*Seeräuber-Jenny*), which (with Weill's melodies) became the German hit of *The Threepenny Opera* (Brecht 1928/1955, 27–29). To describe the fate of Jenny, Brecht uses the scene from Gay's opera in which Captain Macheath visits the tavern to hire some whores for his sexual pleasure and that of the gangsters (1928/1937: II.1–5, 41–49; see 1928/1948, 33–37). This visit to the whorehouse illustrates the perils that existed for unmarried women trying to survive on the streets of London. At the end of Brecht's theatrical juxtapositioning of thesis and antithesis, the repellent Peachum and the constables rush into the tavern to arrest Macheath and put him in prison.

Brecht's *chanson* "Pirate Jenny" was transformed to echo the inner thoughts of a woman serving as a prostitute. Brecht returned to the history of the English pirate ships in the seventeenth century, when the pirates into the ports of the Atlantic Ocean and were entertained by whores. Brecht's scene is curiously reminiscent of Gay's time, in which seaborne commerce enriched Europe's colonial economy. The British buccaneers on the Atlantic Ocean lived the adventurous life of drinking and fighting vagabonds, striving to protect overseas trade from the Dutch, Spanish, and other rivals. But life under the black flag of piracy announcing the unscrupulous adventurers at sea was transformed by the dramaturg Brecht into a London whorehouse. Macheath and his gangsters come here to drink, sing and gamble, while indulging in amorous escapades with their hired mistresses (including Macheath's paramour Polly Peachum).

The lyrics of "Pirate Jenny," sung by Polly in the tavern (performed by Lotte Lenya in her hard, penetrating voice), are couched in the merciless voice of tavern worker Jenny, when she, fed up with the men's flirtation and fornication, breaks into full revenge. In the first stanza, Jenny reveals her working situation to the *allegretto* dynamics of the music, while in the second stanza, Weill's composition responds in tempo to Brecht's dark vision, with the dynamics becoming a "slow march," echoing a funeral march. Then, in the refrain, Jenny sweeps aside her fears, mustering up her courage to tell the truth of her troubles. Brecht's first and last stanzas of the lyrical text are:

JENNY. *Meine Herren, heute sehen Sie mich Gläser abwaschen*
Und ich mache das Bett für jeden.
Und Sie geben mir einen Penny und ich bedanke mich schnell
Und Sie sehen meine Lumpen und dies lumpige Hotel
Und Sie wissen nicht, mit wem Sie reden.
Aber eines Abends wird ein Geschrei sein am Hafen
Und man fragt: Was ist das für ein Geschrei?
Und man wirde mich lächeln sehen bei meinen Gläsern
Und man fragt: Was lächelt die dabei?
   Und ein Schiff mit acht Segeln
   Und mit fünfzig Kanonen
   Wird liegen am Kai.
[...]
Und es werden kommen hundert gen Mittag an Land
Und werden in den Schatten treten
Und fangen einen jeglichen asus jeglicher Tür
Und fangen ihn in Ketten und bringen vor mir
Und fragen: Welchen sollen wir töten?
Und am diesem Mittag wird es still sein am Hafen
Wenn man fragt, wer wohl sterben muss.
Und dann werden Sie mich sagen hören: Alle!

Und wenn dann der Kopf fällt, sag ich: Hoppla!
   Und das Schiff mit acht Segeln
   Und mit fünfzig Kanonen
   Wird entschwinden mit mir. (Brecht 1928/1955, 27–29)

The four English translations of Jenny's work song are the following versions:

Gentlemen, today you see me washing up the glasses
And making up the beds and cleaning.
When you give me p'raps a penny, I will curtsey rather well
When you see my tatty clothing and this tatty old hotel
P'raps you little guess with whom you are dealing.
One fine afternoon there will be shouting from the harbor.
Folk will ask: what is the reason for that shout?
   They will see me smiling while I rinse the glasses
   And will say: what has she to smile about?
   And a ship with eight sails and
   With fifty great cannon
   Sails in to the quay.
[…]
   And a hundred men will come ashore before it's noon
And will go where it's dark and chill.
And every man they find, they will drag along the street
And they'll clap him in chains and lay him at my feet
And they'll ask: now which of these are we to kill?
And when the clock strikes noon it will be still down by the harbor
When folk ask: now just who has got to die?
You will hear me say at that point: All of them!
And when their heads fall, I'll say: Whoopee!
   And the ship with eight sails and
   With fifty great cannon
   Will sail off with me.
(English transl. Desmond Vesey 1949; see Vesey 1949/1960, 324–25)

You gentlemen can watch, while I'm scrubbin' the floors, while I'm scrubblin' the floors while you're gawkin', and maybe once you tip me and it makes you feel swell, on a ratty day waterfront in a ratty hotel, and you never guess to who you're talkin', and you never guess to who you're talkin'. Suddenly one night, there's a scream in the night, and you yell, "What could that a-been." And you see me kinda while I'm scrubbin'. And you say "What the hell's she got to grin?"

>And a ship, a black freighter,
>with a skull on its mast
>will be coming in.

[…]

By noontime the dock is all swarmin' with men, comin' off that ghostly freighter. They're moving in the shadows where no one can see, And they're chainin' in up people and bringing them to me, askin' me, "Kill them now or later?" Noon by the clock and so still on the dock, you can hear a foghorn miles away, In that quiet of death, I'll say [*spoken freely*] "*Right now!*" "*That will learn you!*"

>Then a ship, the black freighter,
>disappears out to sea,
>And on it is me.

(English transl. Mark Blitzstein 1952, 5; see libretto Weill/Brecht 1928/155, 14–19)

Well, today you men see me rinse out the glasses
And I make up the beds you're messin'
And you throw me a lousy penny and I say "thanks" fast as And you see my crammy outfit and this crammy old hotel /he!
And you never know you are addressin'
No, you never know who you are addressin'
But one night you'll hear them all yellin' down by the harbor
And you'll ask, "Do they have to yell that way?"
And you'll see me smile and rinse another glass out
And you'll ask "What's made her smile today?"
>And a fifty-gun galleon
>With its eight sails a-waving
>Slips into the bay.

[…]

They'll be landing by the hundred as soon as it's light
And hide where none of you can see 'em
They'll run in ev'ry door and grab the first man they see,
They'll throw them in chains and they'll drag them to me
And ask me, "Should we kill 'em or free 'em?"
As the clock strikes noon there's not a sound in the harbor
When they ask which ones have to die

And then loud and clear you'll hear me saying "All of them"
And when your heads roll, I'll say: Whoops there!
>   And that fifty-gun galleon
>   Keeps the eight sails a-waving
>   Till it's vanished with me.

(English transl. Michael Feingold 1954; see record Weill/Brecht 1999, ed. Stephen Hinton, 24–25).

Now you gents all see I've the glasses to wash.
When a bed's to be made I make it.
You may tip me with a penny, and I'll thank you very well
And you see me dressed in tatters, and this tatty old hotel
And you never ask how long I'll take it.
But one of these evenings there will be screams from the harbour
And they' ask: what can all that screaming be?
And they see me smiling as I do the glasses
And they'll say: how she can smile beats me.
>   And a ship wit eighty sails and
>   All its fifty guns loaded
>   Has tied up at the quay.

(…)

And a hundred men will land in the bright sunny midday sun
Each stepping where the shadows fall.
They will look inside each doorway and grab anyone they see
And put them in irons and then bring him to me
And they'll ask: which of these should we kill?
In that noonday heat they'll be a hush round the harbour
As they ask which has got to die.
And you'll hear me as I softly answer: the lot!
And as the first head rolls I'll say: hoppla!
>   And that ship with eight sails and
>   All its fifty guns loaded
>   Will vanish with me.

(English transl. Ralph Manheim 1979; see Brecht 1928/2000, 20–21)

Jenny's work is quite alien to her real character, so "Pirate Jenny" reduces or even eliminates the feeling of alienation toward her working life, identifying with her emotional self. Brecht's alienation process is not about the blues Jenny has through her troubles at work, but he overemphasizes the contextual story to integrate her alienation into the murder of her employers. This crime of murder will heal her and turn her into a sensitive persona. Pirate

Jenny stands in contrast to the care-worn Jenny of real life (Pohl 1969, 57–59), who describes the virtues of a wife of noble character in terms of the biblical Proverbs:

> She will do him good and not evil all the days of her life.
> She seeketh wool, and flax, and worketh willingly with her hands.
> She is like the merchant ships; she bringeth food from afar. [...]
> (Prov. 31, 12–14)

Brecht follows Gay's ballad pattern and even provides the verse with the initial repetition "She" (*Sie*) to describe the many qualities of the biblical woman (Prov. 31: 10–31). However, Brecht's *Lehrweisheit* (moral instruction) contrasts the virtues of the Bible with the ultramodern twist of forcing the gentlemen to pay with their lives for her services.

The rhyme structure consists of nine lines followed by a final triplet of three short lines to mark the momentum of the final refrain. Biblical archaisms are reflected in the use of "*und*" (and) at the beginning of each line followed by "*aber*" (but), "*wenn*" (when) or other syntactical conjunctions, lending a certain reverence or dignity to the violent scene of death that Jenny recounts, but importantly for Jenny's song, the repetition at the beginning of the lines is excellent conduction for singing the string of verses. Brecht's final rhyme is basically two times *a b c d b*. In the triplet, there is no end rhyme, but the internal rhyme of interconnected stressed words has the same sound and rhythm as the song itself. In Brecht's refrain, the stressed consonant [ʃ] with the frictional stress of [k] as in *Schiff* (ship), *Segeln* (sails), *Kanonen* (cannon) and *Kai* (quay) evokes Jenny's fierce love of freedom, and drive to be liberated from male tyranny. Jenny realizes her desire in her vision of the deadly ship with eight sails.

Concentrating on the possible literary translation of Brecht's "Pirate Jenny" (Vesey/Bentley 1949/1960, 324–325), this first English translation made by Desmond Vesey (with Eric Bentley) is a literal, even scholarly version, but does not function well as a theatrical performance. The translation follows Brecht, with an iambic verse of short syllables imitating ordinary English speech. In the 6-foot verse, the end rhyme (*cleaning/dealing, shout/about, chill/kill*) patterns meaningful clues in Jenny's narration, but the euphony of Vesey's sounds in English is a lesser product than Brecht's original poetry, which works up to the momentum of the refrain. Although the initial repetition in the first stanza is overplayed with other conjunctions (*when, perhaps,* etc.) with a lessor role than Brecht's "*and*," the loss is remedied in the last stanza by repeating the initial word "*and*." Despite the ploy of speaking (not singing) the iambic exclamation "Whoopee!" (standing for Brecht's *Hoppla!*)

(Gorlée 2015), Vesey's translation lacks the ecstasy of Brecht's text, which hurries forward with speed and velocity from the first stanza to the refrain of the ship with eight sails to provide Jenny's final solution. Vesey's first translation is indeed more prose than poetry, but the prose is spiritlessly framed (according to composer Weill) and made hardly singable, as it distorts the melodies (Farneth 1998, 138–139).

Marc Blitzstein's American translation of "Pirate Jenny" (see libretto Weill/Brecht 1928/155, 14–19) readapts the libretto of *The Threepenny Opera* as it was performed in the concert version (that is, without acting, costumes, or scenery) in 1952 at Brandeis University. Blitzstein was a composer who worked together with Weill, and after Weill's premature death, he performed this concert version (Hinton 1990, 36–40; Farneth 1998, 130–140). Blitzstein was not only Brecht's translator but acted onstage as the *Sprecher,* the narrator between songs. In the concert version, Lotte Lenya sang the songs, while the orchestra was directed by longtime friend Leonard Bernstein. This stage play led the composer and dramaturg Blitzstein to compose a song album from Weill's ragtime melodies, placing the American English words in the libretto. It seemed that composer Blitzstein affected not to respond to Brecht's poem, but appeared to concentrate entirely on the musical version, which needed to be sung as one line to catch the clue-words. In this wordplay, Blitzstein shifted back and forth between the two pronunciations of American English and Cockney English. He used contractions of the verbal suffix -ing (*scrubbin', gawkin', talkin', swarmin', comin', chainin', askin'*) to produce an understandable version of street language (Farb 1974/1975, 57–59).

For Brecht's epic poetry, Blitzstein included elliptical code-words in colloquialisms to maintain the crudity of the street speech. He left the end rhyme in the short metrical pattern (*gawkin'/talkin', a-been/grin, freighter/or later*), but at the end of the stanza, Blitzstein's refrain varied the diction to reinforce the emotional power and meaning of Jenny's dream. He translated the dream as a "black freighter, with a skull on its mast." Perhaps a "freighter" is not the right poetic word, referring as it does to an ordinary cargo ship; it seems that in Jenny's dream, the nautical symbolism must be a ship to save her life from eternal servitude.

Important elements are Jenny's loud interjection "*Hoppla!*," which was not sung but "recited freely." The interjection has no standard semantics but must be translated into English in a free cultural version to denote Jenny's impelled mortal movement pushing through her heart. Translator Blitzstein translated "*Hoppla!*" as "Right now!," freely complemented with his own interjection "That will learn you!" This double refrain was a courageous and bold move to reproduce Jenny's alienation from her working life, but Blitzstein's prosaic addition emerged as adding his own words, by copying himself with a technical trick. Blitzstein wanted to influence the audience with Brecht's epic conclusion, but the alienation sounds clearer in German than in English. A solution to the additional interjection would be to use "Hi hi hoppla" in the German style of epic poetry.

For the vocal translation, the translation of drama critic Michael Feingold (1954), who (like Brecht himself) worked as a playwright and dramaturg, gave to *The Threepenny Opera* the dramatic action of Jenny's alien song with refrain. Feingold's focus was to evoke the drama by using meaningful clue-words to improve the thrill of Jenny's song. Feingold filled the verses with rhyme and rhythm as an internal method to accelerate the tempo of the alliteration and parallelism, creating the speed and thrill of Jenny's future. The dramatic events recounted by Jenny were both the interrogative and emotive signs of her wish harm to the "gentlemen" she had served hand and foot. The refrain of Jenny's song secretly prepares for her leaving this state of subjugation to become a free woman. One can conclude that Feingold's translation recast Brecht's epic narrative as Jenny's rallying cry, changing Brecht's German "*Hoppla!*" into a new, spoken interjection in English.

Within Feingold's version, the plural form of "gentlemen" has been downgraded to "you men" or simply "he." Jenny describes the troubles of her working situation using the biblical-style parallelism of "and" in series, repeated until the last "but" replying with a "no." The end rhyme is more complex than Brecht's alternative rhyme in employing internal rhyming words to emphasize the meaning. The basic *messin'/addressin', see 'em/free 'em*, and *way/today* is redoubled in "addressin'" to emphasize the "messin'" of his bed. Jenny leaves the brothel and moves back to the harbor. There, she is twice "yellin'" and twice "smilin'" in response to the final iambic interjection "Whoops there!" The interrogative and emotive cries introduce the marvelous refrain of the last stanza: "And that fifty-gun galleon / Keeps the eight sails a-waving / Till it's vanished with me" (English transl. Michael Feingold 1954, see record Weill/Brecht 1999, 25). The refrain dwells on the mystical gesture of images of the future, in which the epic death scene in typical Brechtian alienation is expressed in the image of the tensely waving flags of the warship, with the soft [w] and [v] consonant sounds of *a-waving, vanished with me* (Jakobson and Waugh 1979, 139–146).

Feingold's verbal art is full of emotional power. He brings comfort with the symbol of the waving flags and poeticizes the transformation of Jenny's life as represented by the warship disappearing after the massacre. The most recent translation was made by Ralph Manheim (1979) (Brecht 1928/2000, 20–21). This translation reflects the lyrical poetry of Brecht's songs. For example, Manheim's speech does not "imitate" Brecht's "low" street speech, nor does it maintain the parallelism of "and." Manheim took the liberty of exchanging the repetition of "and" at the beginning of each line of the first stanza with the more narrative conjunctions "now," "when" and "but." Yet, the metrical foot of the separate verses was enlarged from short (three) to long (four), with two to three stressed words to add extra meaning as catchwords. Brecht applied the final rhyme pattern to every line in both real and quasi-rhyme.

The effect was to formalize Jenny's song into a socially aggressive pamphlet consisting of brief words in a contemporary style. The brief words of the four translations require extra space, for example, four iambic verses in the first stanza "Now you gents all see I've the glasses to fill" from three verses in *"Meine Herren, heute sehen Sie mich Gläser abwaschen"'* in the last stanza, and "And a hundred men will land in the bright midday sun" from *"Und es werden kommen hundert gen Mittag an Land."* Manheim changed the subject matter in the first stanza "And you never ask how long I'll take it" from Brecht's *"Sie wissen nicht mit wem Sie reden"* or "In that noonday heat there'll be a hush round the harbour" from Brecht's *"Und am diesem Mittag wird es still sein am Hafen."*

Manheim's sense of translation is not literal but dynamical, moving the translation far away from the first three translations into a more verbose version, containing more words than Brecht needed to express thoughts and narratives. Singing requires extra space in the melodies, which was considered in Weill's precise composition of Brecht's German original but overtranslated in Manheim's version. The effect of this modern translation is that the thoughts of Brecht's characters are portrayed with more dramatic "bubbles," contributing to the typical themes and techniques in an essentially ironic vision. Since this translation is phrased in a more meaningful idiom than the narrative stories of Brecht's "closest possible equivalent" (Nida and Taber 1969, 159–160), Manheim's translation is certainly no "formal equivalence model" but progresses into the "dynamic equivalence model" of a new vocabulary and grammar (Nida and Taber 1969, 165–171).

One example is the translation of Brecht's German interjection *"Hoppla!"* into "Whoopee!" (Vesey), "Right now! That will learn you!" (Blitzstein), "Whoops there!" (Feingold) and even left untranslated as "Hoppla!" (Manheim). In the exclamations, cries and shouts, there is no fixed meaning, and the possible translations depend on the cultural nuances of the emotional and affective experience of the translator in question and the pancultural environment of their translation. The vagueness of meaning represents a high-pitched metaphorical alarm cry due to the immediate fear caused by the potential danger (Gorlée 2015). My translation would not be concrete as in the normal interjection "Hurrah!" but more general, as in "Hooray!" Indeed, "Hip! Hip! Hurrah!" has a modern twist, since it invites other bystanders to join in with their own rhyme and rhythm to metaphorize Jenny's cry as representative of all women in danger.

The response as a positive interjection differs from the parasynonyms in the lyrical metalanguage of Jenny's song (Nida and Taber 1969, 44–45; Cherry 1957/1966, 82–85, 220, 307). In their metalanguages, the translators offer their own critical-and-lyrical versions to ritualize the song-with-music in terms of Jakobson's intersecting types of communicative speeches for transduction (see Chapter 1: *Forked Tongues: Theory from Translation to Transduction*). The translations rework the content in reference to Brecht's modernity of style in singing, chanting, recitation and gesturing—or even shouting and dancing (Cherry 1957/1966, 12, 109 fn., 121–122). But the translators employed their figurative and metaphorical metalanguages to achieve their effect and create a dramatic impact with a new kind of language in the translation. The personal and nonliteral versions were a retranslation of Brecht's forms of epic "outside the system," creating in autotranslation new "phonemes" as minimal elements to depict the double technique used by Brecht both as an explorer of the known language code and a cryptanalyst of unknown language codes (Jakobson and Halle 1956/1971, 28–40; see Chapter 1: *Forked Tongues*).

Returning to Jakobson's semiotic history, his article on Brecht's poetry (1963/1981) was written when Jakobson was away from Prague and the censorship of the Soviet Union. His objective at this time was to transcend Saussure's simple division into sound and image, but his new pictorial and poetic experiments in linguistic sign codes refer not only to "ordinary" speech but also to the "lyrical" expressions of non-standard languages. Jakobson referred to the language of the proletariat with its own form of poetry (Partridge 1933/1972, 148–281). Jakobson's discovery was shaped during his exile in the United States, when Jakobson became acquainted with Charles Sanders Peirce's edition of the *Collected Papers* (from 1960). Saussure's soundimage theory became for Jakobson a speculative theory of the outer parts of phonetic language and excluded the emotional novelty of poetical language both outside and inside. Jakobson seemed to accept that language has two aspects, "outer" and "inner," such that

> [t]he addressee perceives that the given utterance is a *combination* of constituent parts (sentences, words, phonemes, etc.) *selected* from the repository of all possible constituent parts (the code). The constituents of a context are in a state of *contiguity*, while in a substitution set signs are linked by various degrees of *similarity* which fluctuate between the equivalence of synonyms and the common core of antonyms. (Jakobson 1971, 243–244; 1987, 99, 171)

Jakobson seemed to compare Saussure's formal and syntagmatic theory of outer sounds to the associative theory of Peirce's communicative method, which added to the outer sign the inner stress, duration and pitch of the vocal system. While Jakobson was in the United States, he read Peirce's works. Saussure's laws of language disappeared from Jakobson's vision of literature to be replaced by Peirce's "pseudo-laws" that govern the feeling of "sentences, words, phonemes, etc." This discovery of emotionality allowed Jakobson, in his article "On linguistic aspects of translation" (1959/1966), to discuss the possibility of how the meaning of any linguistic sign could transform into an alternative meaning creating not a single meaning (Saussure) but Peirce's three further possibilities of sign meaning. Jakobson code-switched simple translation into the literary activity of conduction by changing his concept of parts of speech into the development of transduction, accepting the involvement of all art and gestures into language codes.

Jakobson's seminal book *Fundamentals of Language* examined the variety of features from the outer sounds of Saussurean phonology to reveal the inner meaning of Peirce's phonemics. The inner features of the "phoneme" move from phonetics into phonemics (Jakobson and Halle 1956/1971, 18, see 18–30; see Cherry 1957/1966, 85–101). The term "phoneme" comes from Saussure, who wrote that the minimal sign of a phoneme is "the sum of the auditory impressions and articulatory movements, the unit heard and the unit spoken, each conditioning the other: thus it is a complex unit with a foot in each chain" (1959/1966, 40). Then, Saussure analyzed

> a sufficient number of spoken chains [sound sequences] from different languages, the phonologist [linguist] is able to recognise and classify the elements with which each language operates. Then, if he ignores acoustically unimportant variations, he will find that the number of species is not indefinite. Special works list these species and describe them in detail. Here I [Saussure] wish merely to show the simple, invariable principles upon which any such classification is based. (Saussure 1959/1966, 40)

Jakobson shifted from the single-language phonetics of Saussure to the multiple languages of Peirce's methodology. Jakobson renounced Saussure's concept of the sound unity of the French language by describing Peirce's categories with differences and variations to the multilingual phoneme. In his primary article "On linguistic aspects of translation" (Jakobson 1959/1966), Jakobson evoked the energetics of the double or triple concept of the linguistic sign, images and symbols. Interjections are good examples of phonemes, because they denote the attitude or emotion of the translator and speaker. For example, "the word 'what?' (a mere interrogative) is distinct from the sudden shouted exclamation 'WHAT!' (denoting amazement), both phonetically and semantically" (Cherry 1957/1966, 86). Not talking *in* Saussurean stylized sound-language but musing *about* the emotional language in Peirce's logical and non-logical forms of making and remaking elements of language makes Jakobson's hypertranslation possible in the epic shape of lyrical language (Shipley 1968/1972, 139–140).

From Speech to Criminal Slang

Brecht's procedure was to generate a new dialect in *The Threepenny Opera* from parts of Gay's *The Beggar's Opera*. Brecht's hypertranslation echoed the poetical language of the proletariat's "low" speech to distinguish as "many as 15 different reasons for the use of slang" (Crystal 1987, 53). Slang is used creatively

> for the fun of it
> as an exercise in wit or ingenuity
> to be different
> to be picturesque
> to be arresting
> to escape from clichés
> to enrich the language
> to add concreteness to speech
> to reduce seriousness
> to be colloquial
> for ease of social interaction
> to induce intimacy
> to show that one belongs
> to exclude others
> to be secret. (Crystal 1987, 53)

This simple division differs from Eric Partridge's expert treatise *Slang Today and Yesterday* (1933/1972, 6–7), where slangy code is amply discussed both historically and socially. In this case here, the multiple code-switching went further than remaking Gay's "outer" folk ballads into Brecht's "inside" poetry, overplayed with criminal metalanguage to give the language of slang a double or triple sense of meaning in rhyming slang, paraphrases and street talk. As argued, Brecht re-used Elizabeth Hauptmann's rough translation of Gay's opera to offer lyrical poetry with a modern twist, but he also had to prepare the lyrical base for composer Weill's musical rhyme and rhythms. Brecht was engaged in the more complex hypertask of exploring (in Jakobson's sense, see Jakobson and Halle 1956/1971, 28–30) modern epic poetry today. Gay's "ordinary" lowlife constructions from eighteenth-century Cockney speech could be retranslated as autotranslation into the crude German dialect of "*Plattdeutsch*" in the twentieth century. For Derrida, Brecht seemed to write "against" the German speech, more precisely against the institutionalized language of Berlin, which was not, strictly speaking, his mother tongue (Derrida 1985, 111).

Jakobson's functional phonology had replaced outer phonemics with the inner function of (re)translating the emotional variant of the code of the message. With the publication of Jakobson's *Fundamentals of Language* (Jakobson and Halle 1956/1971, 18–30), the term "code" (and "subcode" as a mixture of codes) became a distinctive feature of Jakobson's poetic vocabulary. Brecht's painstaking efforts to encode and decode produced contextual variants and invariants. He refreshed his conduction making it into transduction to enliven the linguistic message of *The Threepenny Opera* with new codes. Brecht reworded and exchanged the subcodes of word, sentence and phoneme to create a different co-dialect or idiolect, building up the same function of informative directness as in "ordinary" human speech to create the drama as an art form on the stage (1959/1966, 233, re-edited in 1959/1971a, 261).

Jakobson acknowledged that the technical procedure of recoding and rewriting did not create a general cryptology or a secret writing (as described in Gorlée 2020a) but rather a cryptanalysis of transduction (Jakobson and Halle 1956/1971, 28–30, see 18–30). Cryptanalysis exists for rewriting a semiotic subcode and code to create the third element in the cryptolect of speech, in Brecht's case, the German language of crooks, criminals, beggars and tramps (Partridge 1933/1972, Wolf 1985/1993). In short, Jakobson reformulated the style of literary translation by converting the code of the translation into the transduction of the subcode. Transduction transformed one code of energy into another subcode in Brecht's epic piece. In his article about Brecht (1963/1981), Jakobson concluded that:

> Stylistic variations, particularly in phonology, gradually have begun to disturb students of language who until recently had been possessed by the isolationist idea of a monolithic verbal code. The variety of functional, convertible subcodes requires a careful and consistent structural analysis. Such an analysis makes possible a synchronic study of the phonemic and grammatical changes in progress, which initially present a necessary coexistence of the older and newer form in two related subcodes, and thus there emerges a bridge between descriptive and historical linguistics. On the other hand, the inquiry into the system of subcodes encompasses the various forms of interdialectal and even interlingual code-switching and thus establishes an intimate bond between

the description of an individual of local dialect and the vast horizon of linguistic geography. (Jakobson 1963a, 161, reprinted in 1971a, 283)

Beyond the code-switching between Gay's English and Brecht's German languages, the juxtaposition between Gay and Brecht established the process by which Brecht learned the third art of cryptoanalysis. The cryptanalyst needs to break the codes of dialects into new subcodes for the first process of transduction. The code variability between the code-writings gives evidence of what Jakobson described as transcription from source to target texts (1961/1971a, 578–579). In his learning process, Gay used for his source text the vivid prose of the street language of London that was current in the eighteenth century, while Brecht used a different cryptotext: the proletariat's "vagabond" speech of thieves spoken in Germany in the 1920s (Pohl 1969, 40–43). Jakobson observed that code-switching between the idiolect of "ordinary" speech and dialectal speech applying the direct similarity of Saussure's method, but the poetic languages of literature can switch between real and artistic word-codes, and Peirce's dynamic method can develop the infinity of forms and meanings (Jakobson 1953/1971a, 560–566). This code-switching included Brecht's use of epic alienation of literary gangster jargon. Brecht employed the farcical humor of tough guy fiction to precurse the style of the detective novel or the gangster movie that became popular throughout the twentieth century.

Gay's opera even had a political argumentation, but his frivolous tone lent a sexual plot of love and betrayal to the drama. The special nicknames and the story of *The Beggar's Opera* referenced the political tricks of Parliament and court playing out in Gay's time, but the language expressions were borrowed from early forms of street slang. Gay used colloquial forms in rhyme and other forms of Cockney. This slang adopted new words to correspond to poetry, creating new elliptic forms. For example, Mr. Peachum tells his daughter Polly that her flirting with gentlemen to get the "Business" going and obtain their money is a "moral" game, but marriage is for her totally "immoral":

PEACH. You know, Polly, I am not against your toying and trifling with a Customer in the way of Business, or to get out a Secret, or so. But to find out that you have play'd the fool and are married, you Jade you, I'll cut your Throat, Hussy. You know my Mind.

Then, Mrs. Peachum "in a very great Passion" sings the refrain of her song "Our Polly is a sad Slut! Nor heeds what we taught her" and ends the song in some swearwords to curse her daughter's attitude to love:

MRS. PEACH. You Baggage! You Hussy! you inconsiderate Jade! Had you been hang'd, it would not have vex'd me, for that might have been your Misfortune; but to do such a mad thing by Choice! The Wench is married, Husband. (Gay 1728/1937, 17–18)

In the terminology of highwaymen, informers and pickpockets, Gay added the word "baggage," meaning "a worthless woman: from 1700" and "hussy," meaning "a forward woman: from ca. 1750. Respectable earlier" (Partridge 1933/1972, 352, 170). Gay called women in his vocabulary whores or, in modern parlance, prostitutes or even sex workers. The word "hussy" is mentioned in Grose's slang dictionary as "an abbreviation of housewife, but now always used as a term of reproach" (1985/1971, without pages). Peachum and Mrs. Peachum call Polly a "Jade," meaning a "lazy woman," and "Baggage," downgrading her as worthless. In the song, Mrs. Peachum uses the ordinary word "Slut," meaning a hired woman, the same as the modern term for prostitute.

Frances Grose's old *1811 Dictionary of the Vulgar Tongue* (printed in 1985, reprinted in 1971) hardly indicates any sexual connotations, but these sexual expressions were widely used in Gay's opera—not so much in the ballad songs but more in the Cockney narratives intertwining the songs in prose. Eric Partridge's standard treatises *Slang To-Day and Yesterday* and *Dictionary of the Underworld* demonstrate how the vocabulary of poor man's prose and poetry worked in Gay's eighteenth century (1933/1972, 64–79; 1950/1995). In the nineteenth century, under the influence of the character and trends of slang, "ordinary" expressions were embellished with terms from "miscellaneous" areas such as baby-talk, card-games, sports and fashion (Partridge 1933/1972, 80–108; see 270–272), but sexual expressions and attitudes were not openly discussed. Sexual habits and erotic phenomena were displayed in the diaries of Gay's contemporary Samuel Pepys, but his diaries were devoted to his private hobby of amorous intimacy, discussing it outside social convention and encrypted in secret code (McCormick 1980, 27–32; Gorlée 2020a, 88–93). Yet, Gay's sexual slang glorifies the speech of "outsiders," while street slang was a novelty in the literature of the eighteenth century.

The rough Cockney dialect is far from standard English (Lunde 2009, 132–133): London speech as spoken in Gay's time was a form of back-slang. The elliptical dropping of the half-mute vowel [e] in "play'd," "hang'd" and "vex'd" was accepted, together with the same variant omitting [ai] in "Capt'n" (Jakobson and Waugh 1979, 151–153). Cockney was inspired over the ages and was rich in idiomatic forms of double language expressed in disvariants of actual words (subcodes). This is reflected in the rhyming slang of Gay's "toying and trifling," echoing "toing and froing" (Phythian 1955/1979, 195) as the interaction of two alliterated verbs to give the associated words a vulgar meaning. This is also demonstrated in the gliding enunciation of the consonant [s] in "sad Slut" and the consonant [t]) in "toying and trifling." Following the literary success of Gay's *The Beggar's Opera*, during the nineteenth century, Cockney slang became recognized as a brilliantly satirical mode of speech consisting of words (subcodes) dealing with the tension between the language of the high bourgeoisie and the "aspirational" speech of low society. The variants and invariants of social class were even used in Charles Dickens's literature. His journalistic series of novels refreshed the English novel with folk colloquialisms, which certainly caused excitement in the bourgeois readership of his literature. To decode the apparently (un)connected words in his novels, the reading public had to engage in the free play of a word game, learning to connect separate words together to understand the ambiguity of meaning which described social certainty in uncertainty.

With the exception of two of Gay's songs, which Brecht re-used, Brecht's songs were new works made by himself. He used the *"Platt"* dialect of the German street abundantly in *The Threepenny Opera* but did not often use it in his high-speed songs, because it seemed that the combination of the lyrical text with the musical rhyme and rhythm presented enough problems for the poet Brecht to solve. In Act 1, there are exceptions, such as *"Das Hochzeitslied für arme Leute"* (Brecht 1928/1973, 25–26). The criminal gangsters sing a cheerful chorus song together to celebrate Captain Macheath's marriage to Polly Peachum. The loud voices of the gangsters echo the formal interjections of joy. Brecht's ritual verse *"Hoch sollen sie leben, hoch, hoch, hoch!"* was echoed in the final rhyme word *"Hoch!"* to give a certain irony about sharing a wedding feast at which stolen goods are consumed.

This scene has been translated and even untranslated by the four literary translators in different ways. Brecht's ritual sentence was left untranslated by Vesey, who added in brackets "(A toast!)" (1949/1960, 17) to make up for the omission. Translator Blitzstein omitted the brief song from the libretto. Translator Feingold's fine sentence "Three cheers for the happy couple, rah, rah, rah! With final "Rah!" (Weill/Brecht 1999, 24) demonstrates the conventional translation of the symbol of marriage, reflecting not the personal feeling of the masculine singers, but the reiteration of the ritual pattern of "shouting and prancing" (Scheffler 1997, 131) to celebrate the mythical cries of getting married. Translator Manheim did not translate the sentence into English, but simply added "Hooray" (Brecht 1928/2000, 14). It seemed that the structural laws of the proverb diminished the vocal sounds to interior rhymes, which were non-translatable, even taboo signs (Jakobson and Waugh 1979, 204–211).

Another lyrical procedure lies in Brecht's attempt to learn the German "vulgar tongue" in the context of Act 1. The "Cannon Song" (also called "The Song of the Heavy Cannon" or "Army Song" [*Kanonensong*]) (Brecht

1928/1973, 31–32) is a military song played in foxtrot tempo. The speedy delivery of the whole text coupled with the military march rhythm is complicated for the chorus of soldiers trying to sing Brecht's words. The main purpose of the military subcode used here is to record the clear message that the soldiers have been reduced to carnal flesh, which is emphasized three times in the final sentence (almost a refrain). Brecht's "*Beefsteak Tartar*" is adorned with iambic verse accompanied by heavy rhythms. However, the "Cannon Song" was Brecht's "epic" pamphlet speaking out for Marx's ideology, and the content hardly belongs to the story as a novelistic element but instead alludes to post–World War I calamities.

The first English translation, made by Vesey, offered the conventional, but most literal version "They'll maybe chop them up to make some beefsteak tartare" (1949/1960, 28–29). Translator Blitzstein used a carnal version in his libretto, "we chop them to bits because we like our hamburgers raw" (Weill and Brecht 1949/1960, 25). The third translator, Feingold, situated the military jargon in the vulgar subcode "I betcha we get steak tartare for breakfast next day" (Weill/Brecht 1999, 26–27), but unfortunately the code word "steak tartare" is placed not at the high end of the verse, but situated in between, making the culinary element less conspicuous. Translator Manheim's English version "They quick as winking chop him into beefsteak tartare" (Brecht 1928/2000, 23–24) offers is very rhythmical version, but the subject "They" is grammatically unclear, probably referring to the soldiers John, Jim and Georgie or just indicating the strategy of the army itself.

Brecht's jargon of lyrical subcodes and codes is ordinarily situated in the narrative stories intertwined between the songs. They form the communicative dialogues using ordinary, emotional and sometimes "vulgar" words to embellish them with poetic kitsch from the twentieth century. In the dialogues, we listen to the language rituals of Macheath's highwaymen and the stories of the ladies of the whorehouse when they dialogue with each other in "vulgar" speech. Of particular interest are the terms used to address Macheath. He is nicknamed Mac the Knife and is variously addressed as "*Herr Macheath*" (Mister Macheath), "*Captn*" (Captain), "*Mac*" (abbreviation for Macheath), "*Lieber*" (dear), "*Geliebter*" (sweetheart), "*gemeiner Schuft*" (wretched scoundrel), "*hinterhältiger Lump*" (underhanded lowlife), "*Ungeheuer*" (monster) and other subcodes to characterize the protagonist differently during the onstage conversations. Depending on the dramatic context of the scenes, these epithets are associated with the specific social relationship Mac the Knife has with crime, love and marriage in Polly and Lucy's emotive salutes, the gang's courtesy's names, the policeman Brown addressing Mac the Knife first in friendship and later in hostility and other dramatic figures speaking out freely.

THE THREEPENNY OPERA

Brecht's theatrical language is a mixture of ordinary and special speech. Ordinary speech was the low-standard speech used for speaking normally by the working class, which was mostly illiterate. These terms were marked as "vulgar" elements in the High German dictionaries. The special speech was the idiolect of thieves' cant used by criminals after World War I and not mentioned in High German dictionaries (but see Wolf 1985/1993). This double milieu created independent standards of language construction, giving the actors the dramatic authority to refer to the special social milieu of rogues, swindlers and tricksters. Dramaturg Brecht needed to write scenes replete with an epic kind of in-jokes for the audience of *The Threepenny Opera*.

Brecht's expressions of the mixed "vulgar" languages had Captain Macheath saying to the drunken Money Matthew: "*Halt die Schnauze, Deine Zoten kannst du bei deiner Kitty absetzen, das ist die richtige Schlampe dafür*" (Brecht 1928/1973, 21). "*Schnauze*" is "snout" but in vulgar speech meaning "mouth," together with the alliteration "*Schlampe*" as "slut." German "*Zoten*" means "obscenities" or "dirty stories." Parts of codes (subcodes) figure in the standard dictionary, but the part in thieves' cant (Wolf 1985/1993, 293, 351). Vesey translated this coded sentence into the longer sentence: "Hold your trap. Keep your dirty jokes for your Kitty: she's the right slut for them" (1949/1960, 18), while Manheim's translation gave a splendid version, "Shut your trap. Keep that filth for Kitty, she's the kind of slut that appreciates it" (Brecht 1928/2000, 16). Unfortunately, both alliterations are missing in the English translations.

In terms of thieves' cant, the most commonly known terms that Brecht used are "*hops gehen*" and "*dünne machen*" (Brecht 1928/1973, 88). These expressions juxtapose bodily meanings such as dying and making oneself scarce to avoid arrest by the police (Wolf 1985/1993, 84,139). In Act 1: "*Das wäre ulkig, wenn an einem Tag alle Hochzeitsgäste hopsgingen*" (Brecht 1928/1971, 25) was translated by Vesey into "It'd be funny if all the wedding guests were copped today!" (1949/1960, 23) and by Manheim as "A fine joke on a day like this if all the wedding guests were pulled out" (Brecht 1928/2000, 18). In Act 2, Macheath escapes from the police, and Robert comments: "*Um Gottes willen, will man Sie hopsnehmen?*" (Brecht 1928/1973, 48) translated by Vesey into "What? Are they going to nab you?" (1949/1960, 45) and by Manheim as "Good God, are they out to nab you?" (Brecht 1928/2000, 37). In the tango ballad with Jenny, Macheath remembers his time in the whorehouse with Jenny, who states that: "*War ich ja dann auch einmal hops von dir*" (Brecht 1928/1971, 56), translated with the double meaning in "One day I felt beneath my heart a young Macheath" (Brecht 1949/1960, 53) and in Mannheim's translation "Once I was pregnant, so the doctor said" (Brecht 1928/2000, 44), but—alas!—against the will of the father Mack the Knife. In Act 3, Macheath is "*hops*" (as good as dead) when incarcerated in a prison cell, waiting to be hanged. The excited gangsters propose "making [themselves] scarce" (English translation by Vesey and Bentley in Brecht 1949/1960, 86) (*sich dünnzumachen*, Brecht 1928/1971, 88), or leaving the criminal milieu (English translation by Mannheim and Willett in Brecht 1928/2000, 71).

The words of address used to each other vary from the women calling Macheath a "*gemeiner Schuft*" (wretched scoundrel) to the thieves calling the police "*Polente*" (Wolf 1985/1993, 251–252). Brecht's language is mainly low-standard speech, with the addition of proverbial expressions in thieves' cant to highlight the strangeness of criminal jargon for the audience (indeed, Brecht's "alienation").

Brecht was keenly aware of retaining and reviving the disappearing language of thieves to capture the dramatic scenes on the dangerous streets of the city of London, including the dramatic locations of the empty stable, the brothel and the cell where Macheath is imprisoned, waiting to be hanged. Brecht refreshed the political mood of Gay's cabaret by means of the actor's gestures and the decorative costumes. For example, Brecht, as a visual artist, illuminated the scene by exploiting the aesthetic possibilities of electric light in the form of projections from behind a translucent screen or multicolored fluorescent lamps programmed to change from red to green. The artificial light becomes the principal material on stage when the title of the next song is projected on a sign-board above the head of the performer as an announcement to the audience seated in the dark room (Kostelanetz 1993, 134–135). Brecht sought contrarian ways to shock and amuse the audience to highlight the gravity of the problematic situation depicted in this opera.

Brecht drew an official line between "artist" and "artisan" (Tallman 2021, 4). As a poet, he juggled with Gay's source text, but not to reinterpret, recreate and readapt Gay's work. The superficial translation from English to German was done by Elizabeth Hausmann. She presented Brecht with a new source text, like a Jakobsonian "transcription" from English to German (Jakobson and Waugh 1979, 27–28). Brecht's spirit transformed the transcription into an electrified "conduction" to juggle with some songs and scenes from Gay's poetry and prose, but mainly to rethink and reoppose these conductive features in his special "epic" theater.

Brecht's production applied all the audience's energies to the "transductive" task of overturning capitalism, but it did not defeat the rise of Hitler. Brecht set himself the complex task of being the expansive improviser, re-composing his cultural, lyrical, novelistic and ideological target text (in interplay with the music composed by Kurt Weill) to be performed on stage. The task was to produce a new "transduction" that met the appetite of a different *Zeitgeist*. On top transducing a lyricized and rhymed version, Brecht taught

Marxist alienation to the bourgeoisie, and he also integrated a different criminal slang into the play to make the content of *The Threepenny Opera* into both an alien and familiar artifact of fine arts and applied arts in costume and gestures.

Brecht as the poet who penned *The Threepenny Opera* taught himself the slang of the criminal underworld. In this readaptation of the language, Brecht's electrical spirit increased the disorder of the original folk theater (thesis) to deal with the dissimilitude of the electrodynamically charged slang of thieves (antithesis). The goal was to propagate alienation in "epic" language. He increased the electrodynamic tension between Gay's form of speech and the antithesis of criminal codes to transform the criminal "poetics" into a new language code using unambiguous rules. In making an organic whole out of separate parts, he was not a real novelist (*raconteur*) engaged in recounting the programmatic scenes of a drama; instead, he was a hyperbolic poet, who gave form to his ideological emotions in order to call the bourgeois audience to arms. In the writing of the ballad cabaret, he transformed the language into a high-speed elliptical crime scene. He persuaded the audience to understand the uses of vulgar slang through the fractures of his words and the juxtapositions of proverbial words and expressions. He resituated the words, phrases and sentences in unexpected ways to create criminal scenes using an extreme form of modern lyricism. One can conclude that Brecht was a hyperbole of Jakobson's phonology and phonemics in transforming himself from an explorer into a cryptanalyst (Jakobson and Halle 1956/1971).

Epic Epilogue

As discussed in this book, *From Mimetic Translation to Artistic Transduction: A Semiotic Perspective on Virginia Woolf, Hector Berlioz, and Bertolt Brecht*, the transformation undergone through the process of transduction is the transformation of one form of energy into another (Sebeok 1984a, 30). The basic principle is intersemiotic transmutability, meaning that a linguistic code may be translated into all other semiotic structures (Sebeok 1974/1977/1985, 295). The structural forms of opera, novel and music-play had to "differ essentially in what they *must* convey and not in what they *may* convey" to each other and other code-languages (Jakobson 1959/1966, 236), so that the movement from mimetic translation into transduction intertwines parasitic or restricted derivatives with other behavior to create new formations of art (Sebeok 1974/1977/1985, 297–298).

This book demonstrates that the rhythmic sound of Virginia Woolf's prose poem *The Waves* is far removed from any imitation of Wagner's stylized method of *Stabreim*, such that no uniform field flows between the two language codes. The parallelism was activated indirectly by the moving wave field, which led to the polarity between Wagner's operatic scenes and the fragments of Woolf's novel. Hector Berlioz's challenge was inherent in his self-imposed task: his genius lay in composing extravagant music, but composing this opera entailed his working as a librettist or even a novelist in order to knit the two parts of his opera together into one story. Again the operatic effect fell short of the grand lyrics of the source Virgil. The music had to suit lyric poetry to be sung not recited. Berlioz wrote an imperfect opera: grand in the music, but defective in the lyrical poetry. In this chapter, Bertolt Brecht was crowned as a hypertranslational poet. He overcame the emotional difference to Gay's source play in the English language with more than an artistic conclusion. His language codes focused on a logical conclusion.

These chapters pursued the story of the entropic law of acceleration caused by the artist's conduction leading to artisanal transduction. After the elliptical art of Virginia Woolf and the lines of parabolic music of Hector Berlioz, Bertolt Brecht's complex and multiple retranslation and self-translation were the perfect hyperbole of transduction. Brecht cross-related old into new theater by bringing his electric energy into the political novelty of the "epic" cabaret, structuring the drama of theater into a learning process for the modern audience. Brecht, in his transductive personality, opened the audience to a high-speed change of arts by retranslating the cryptanalytic code and decoding into a dramatic parody, making in his own selftranslations "dexterious manipulations" of the coded message for high and low levels of society (Jakobson and Halle 1956/1971, 28). The scenic effect of Gay's cabaret stayed in place in Brecht's *The Threepenny Opera*, but Brecht's innovation was to cross-switch the translated English target text with different unknown coded messages. The transductive re-formation of re-formation and the introduction of parasites into the source texts were previously undertaken by Virginia Woolf: her target variation gives a parallel perspective of Wagner's source text. Brecht's task distorted the vertical parallels of retranslation or autotranslation to come out into vertical hypertranslation with different rules, as argued here.

Woolf's expression of radiant energy in phonetic words was not merely a translation of Wagner's poetical *Kitschlyrik* into an English prose novel. Her exercise in translation was both an anonymous and an elliptical work. Woolf covertly transferred the Wagnerian technique of leitmotifs to the ground level to create the wave-like sound waves she employed in the novel *The Waves*. To achieve the musical power of the words, Woolf neutralized Wagner's lyrics in her target text. The *différance* between the source text and her target text colored her polyphonic speech, making the rhythms of musical chromatism.

Woolf pseudo-imitated Wagner's poetry in the moving waves, shifting away from ordinary translation into the transduction of rhythmic sound.

The vocalized music "arrives in our nervous system and causes our brains to generate a flood of anticipations by which we make sense of melody and harmony and form" (Jourdain 1997, 329). Composer Hector Berlioz had to deal with his own music when writing the Trojan opera, but he made little use of his own translation of Virgil's for the French lyrics. The setting conjured up when the operatic arias of *The Trojans* are sung is completely different from that evoked when reading and reciting the source code of Virgil's *Aeneid*. Berlioz's non-verbal transduction of the theory of music influenced his verbal conduction when translating Virgil into his native French, but the two lines of thought of music-and-language introduced a fracture into his operatic translationese. As parabolic composer, Berlioz firstly concentrated on writing extravagant melodies for *The Trojans*, but the second element of making poetically poignant lyrics lagged behind.

Woolf's source of information on international events was limited. At the time she was writing *The Waves* (published in 1923), communication by telegraph was possible, but the telephone was a novelty. Woolf's vision of what happened in the *Sturm und Drang* of warlike Germany was based on the press pictures of Nazi patrols on the streets of German cities. Woolf's image of the world was limited, but she wanted to change her previous image of idyllic visits to Germany to see Wagner's Ring cycle in Bayreuth and cultivate her militant character, as if changing through literature the model of the political and social role of the old society. Wagner became an antimodel, which was not translated but remodeled into an elliptical revolution.

Berlioz's opera *The Trojans* was a lifelong challenge against himself and the world. He lived in the nineteenth century, in an earlier age of candlelight, in which the theater introduced a magic lantern to play out the signals of storm, wind and thunder. The theater was bathed in gaslight. Berlioz was a revolutionary musician desiring to write a magical fairy tale. His operatic genre attacked provincial life, French self-centeredness and the grand illusion of French operas. His model was not the internal rhymes of Wagner's verses, but the military successes of Napoleon creating a new revolution.

Wagner's *unendliche Melodie* circled in geometrical and ambiguous figures following the tides of the operatic waves. His operas explore the double coding of words-and-poetry, but his frequent wave was his stylized versification, which gave his lyrics an unromantic depth. Woolf re-imagined her wavy design in an unromantic rupture with Wagner's waves. She deconstructed the vocal drift of Wagnerian words and ideas and reread the continuity of the waves to create the experimental novelty of her elliptical vocal style of writing. Berlioz was a child of the French Revolution who followed the waves of Napoleon and the Commune. The warlike temperament of Napoleon gave him the bold waves of his musical melodies, but juggling with the lyrical text of the opera *The Trojans* was his radical element. He reinterpreted Virgil's poetry, but his lyrics were mediocre. In his musical melodies, Berlioz was a parabolic artist with extravagant compositions, but in his lyrical texts he lagged behind in elliptical waves of language. Berlioz had the double lines of music-and-text to work with, but he tried to follow the waves of transduction of Napoleon's revolution to change the cultural awareness of France in the world.

Indeed, Woolf and Berlioz seemed to rework (redress, refit, reconstruct) at different times and in different places the mythological stories of Wagner's anti-art, thus making the revolution of pro-art. Brecht's pro-artistic vision suffered under the crisis of political exile. The totalitarianism of Nazi Germany threatened both personal initiative and artistic individualism, creating an authoritarian culture that coerced Germany into Fascism. The criminal work-play *The Threepenny Opera* had an open structure that played freely with the meaning of the epic images of Brecht's political transposition, but Brecht's electrical hyperbole overplayed—that is, it did not underplay—his retranslation and self-translation, distancing it from Gay's cabaret and creating the hyperdynamics of cryptanalytical transduction.

BIBLIOGRAPHY

Abbate, Carolyn. 1991. *Unsung Voices: Opera and Musical Narrative in the Nineteenth Century*. Princeton, NJ: Princeton University Press.
Abrams, M.H. 1941/1957. *A Glossary of Literary Terms*, 4th edition. New York: Holt, Rinehart, and Winston.
Anderson, Myrdene, John Deely, Martin Krampen, Joseph Ransdell, Thomas A. Sebeok, and Thure von Uexkull. 1984. "A Semiotic Perspective on the Sciences: Steps Toward a New Paradigm." *Semiotica* 52, no. 1/2: 7–47.
Antović, Mihailo. 2016. "From Expectation to Concepts: Towards Multilevel Grounding in Musical Semantics." *Cognitive Semantics* 9, no. 2: 105–138. DOI: 10.1515/cogsem-2016-0005.
Apter, Ronnie and Mark Herman. 2000. "Opera Translation: Turning Opera Back into Drama." *Translation Review* 59: 29–35.
———. 2016. *Translating for Singing: The Theory, Art and Craft of Translating Lyrics*. London: Bloomsbury Academic.
Arnheim, Rudolf. 1954. *Art and Visual Perception: A Psychology of the Creative Eye*. London: Faber and Faber.
———. 1971. *Entropy and Art: An Essay on Disorder and Order*. Berkeley and Los Angeles, CA and London: University of California Press.
Attili, Jacques. 1977/1985. *Noise: The Political Economy of Music*. Minneapolis, MN: University of Minnesota Press.
Aucoin, Matthew. 2019. "Making Shakespeare Sing." *The New York Review of Books* 66, no. 20: 8–14.
Auerbach, Erich. 1953/1957. *Mimesis: The Representation of Reality in Western Literature*. New York: Anchor Books in association with Princeton University Press.
Barnstone, Willis. 1993. *The Poetics of Translation: History, Theory, Practice*. New Haven, CT and London: Yale University Press.
Beaugrande, Robert de. 1991. *Linguistic Theory: The Discourse of Fundamental Works*. London and New York: Longman.
Berlioz, Hector. 1844/2002. *Berlioz's Orchestration Treatise: A Translation and Commentary* (Cambridge Musical Texts and Monographs), edited and translated, with commentary, by Hugh MacDonald. Cambridge: Cambridge University Press.
———. 1853/1971. "L'état actuel de l'art du chant." In *A Travers Chants*, edited by Léon Guichard, 113–127. Paris: Gründ (in association with the Centre National de la Recherche Scientifique).
——— 1969/2013. *Les Troyens (The Trojans)*, 2 vols. Munich: Musikproduktion Höflich (Study Score 2023) (1863 vocal scores, 1969 full score of libretto).

——— 1973. Libretto *Les Troyens* Metropolitan Opera Translated by David Cairns. New York and London: G. Schirmer.
Bernac, Pierre. 1978. *The Interpretation of French Song*. New York and London: W.W. Norton & Company.
Bernard, April. 2017. "Virgil Revisited." *The New York Review of Books* 64, no. 18: 40–43.
Bernhart, Walter and Axel Englund, eds. 2021. *Arts of Incompletion: Fragments to Words and Music*. Leiden: Brill.
Black's Medical Dictionary. 1987. Edited by C.W.H. Havard, 35th edition. London: A & C Black.
Bloom, Harold. 2002. *Genius: A Mosaic of One Hundred Exemplary Creative Minds*. New York: Warner Books.
Bloomfield, Leonard. 1933/1967. *Language*. London: George Allen & Unwin.
Borges, Jorge Luis. 2000. *Labyrinths: Selected Stories and Other Writings*, edited by Donald A. Yates and James E. Irby. London and New York: Penguin Group.
Bostridge, Ian. 2018. "Crying Out Loud." *The New York Review of Books* 65, no. 13: 16–18.
Brecht, Bertolt. 1928/1955. *Die Dreigroschenoper*. Berlin and Frankfurt am Main: Suhrkamp.
———. 1949/1960. *Bertolt Brecht: The Threepenny Opera*. Translated by Desmond Vesey and Eric Bentley, Foreword Lotte Lenya. New York: Grove Weidenfeld.
———. 1957/1962. *Schriften zum Theater: Über eine nicht-aristotelische Dramatik*. Berlin and Frankfurt am Main: Suhrkamp Verlag.
———. 1979/2000. *The Threepenny Opera*, translated and edited by Ralph Manheim and John Willett. London: Methuen.
Brendel, Alfred. 2016. "The Growing Charm of Dada." *The New York Review of Books* 63, no. 16: 22–25.
Bunn, James H. 1981. *The Dimensionality of Signs, Tools, and Models*. Bloomington, IN: Indiana University Press.
———. 2002. *Wave Forms: A Natural Syntax for Rhythmic Language*. Stanford, CA: Stanford University Press.
Carlson, Lauri. 1983/1985. *Dialogue Games: An Approach to Discourse Analysis*. Dordrecht: Reidel Publishing Company.
Cairns, David. 1989/1999. *Berlioz, Vol. 1 The Making of the Artist 1803–1832*. Berkeley and Los Angeles, CA: University of California Press.
———. 1988. "Berlioz and Virgil." In *Les Troyens*, edited by Ian Kemp, 76–88. Cambridge: Cambridge University Press.
——— 1999. *Berlioz, Vol. II Servitude and Greatness 1832–1869*. Harmondsworth, Middlesex: Penguin Books.
Campbell, Joseph. 1949/1971. *The Hero with a Thousand Faces*. Princeton, NJ: Princeton University Press.
Cassirer, Ernst. 1957/1966. *The Philosophy of Symbolic Forms, Vol 3: The Phenomenology of Knowledge*. New Haven, CT and London: Yale University Press.
Casti, John L. 1994. *Complexification: Explaining a Paradoxical World Through the Science of Surprise*. New York: HarperCollins.
Chambers, Robert. 2010. *Parody: The Art that Plays with Art*. New York: Peter Lang.
Chambers, Ross. 1984. *Story and Situation: Narrative Seduction and the Power of Fiction*. Minneapolis, MN: University of Minneapolis Press.
Cherry, Colin. 1957/1966. *On Human Communication: A Review, a Survey, and a Criticism*. Massachusetts, MA and London: MIT Press.Merops found 2 states in this address. One is probably an error.Merops found 2 states in this address. One is probably an error.

Clüver, Claus. 1989. "On Intersemiotic Translation." *Poetics Today* 10, no. 1: 55–90.
———. 2009. "Interarts Studies: An Introduction." *Media inter Media: Essays in Honor of Claus Clüver*, edited by Stephanie A. Glaser, 497–526. Leiden: Brill.
Coleman, Julie. 2012. *The Life of Slang*. Oxford: Oxford University Press.
Crossland, Rachel. 2012. *Modernist Physics: Waves, Particles, and Relativities in the Writings of Virginia Woolf and D.H. Lawrence*. Oxford: Oxford University Press.
Crystal, David. 1987. *The Cambridge Encyclopedia of Language*. Cambridge and New York: Cambridge University Press.
Culler, Jonathan. 1982. "Literature and Linguistics." In *Interrelations of Literature*, edited by Jean-Pierre Barricelli and Joseph Gibaldi, 1–24. New York: The Modern Language Association of America.
Dahlhaus, Carl. 1985. *Realism in Nineteenth-Century Music*. Cambridge and New York: Cambridge University Press.
Danesi, Marcel. 2014. *Signs of Crime: Introducing Forensic Semiotics*. Berlin and Boston, MA: De Gruyter Mouton.
Darcy, Warren. 1993. *Wagner's Das Rheingold*. Oxford: Clarendon Press.
Deleuze, Gilles and Félix Guattari. 1987. *A Thousand Plateaus: Capitalism and Schizophrenia*. Minneapolis, MN: University of Minnesota Press.
Derrida, Jacques. 1985. *The Ear of the Other: Otobiography, Transference, Translation*. Translated by Christie McDonald, Avital Ronell, and others. Lincoln, NE: University of Nebraska Press.
Dewey, John. 1934. *Art as Experience*. New York: Minton, Balch & Company.
———. 1946. "Peirce's Theory of Linguistic Signs, Thought, and Meaning." *The Journal of Philosophy* 43, no. 4: 85–95.
DiGaetani, John Louis. 1978. *Richard Wagner and the Modern British Novel*, 109–129. London and Cranbury, NJ: Associated University Presses.
Donington, Robert. 1963/1976. *Wagner's 'Ring' and Its Symbols: The Music and the Myth*. London: Faber and Faber.
Dretske, Fred I. 1981/1982. *Knowledge and the Flow of Information*. Cambridge, MA: MIT Press.
Eco, Umberto. 1985. "Producing Signs." In *On Signs*, edited by Marshall Blonsky, 1976–183. Oxford: Basil Blackwell.
———. 2000. *Experiences in Translation*. Translated by Alistair McEwen. Toronto: University of Toronto Press.
———. 2003. *Mouse or Rat: Translation as Negotiation*. London: Weidenfeld & Nicholson.
Ehrenzweig, Anton. 1967/1968. *The Hidden Order: A Study in the Psychology of Artistic Imagination*, 2nd edition. London: Weidenfeld & Nicolson.
Elliott, Ralph W.V. 1959/1980. *Runes: An Introduction*. Manchester: Manchester University Press.
Emre, Merve. 2020. "The Imperfect Telescope." *The New York Review of Books* 67, no. 1: 32–34.
Esposito, Joseph L. 1980. *Evolutionary Metaphysics: The Development of Peirce's Theory of Categories*. Athens, OH: Ohio University Press.
Evans, Ivor H. 1870/1989. *Brewer's Dictionary of Phrase and Fable*. London, New York, Sydney, and Toronto: Guild Publishing.
Farb, Peter. 1974/1975. *Word Play: What Happens When People Talk*. New York: Bantam.
Farneth, David. 1998. *Lotte Lenya: Eine Autobiographie in Bildern*. Cologne: Könemann.
Fiordo, Richard A. 1977. *Charles Morris and the Criticism of Discourse*. Bloomington, IN: Indiana University and Lisse: The Peter de Ridder Press.

Flannery, Tim. 2020. "In the Soup." *The New York Review of Books* 67, no. 19: 37–38.
Fogel, Susan Lee. 1969. "An Unusual Sound." *Opera News*, September 20: 14–16.
Freud, Sigmund. 1930/1979. *Civilization and Its Discontents*. Translated by Joan Riviere and James Strachey. London: The Hogarth Press and The Institute of Psycho-Analysis.
Garner, Philippe. 1974. *The World of Edwardiana*. London: Hamlyn.
Gay, John. 1728/1937. *The Beggar's Opera*. Introduction by A.P. Herbert. New York: The Heritage Press.
———. 1728/1948. *The Beggar's Opera*, edited by Benjamin Britten. London: The English Opera Group.
Glaser, Stephanie A., ed. 2009. *Media Inter Media: Essays in Honor of Claus Clüver*. Leiden: Brill.
Goodman, Nelson. 1976/1985. *Languages of Art: An Approach to a Theory of Symbols*. Indianapolis, IN: Hackett Publishing Company.
Gorlée, Dinda L. 1990. "Degeneracy: A Reading of Peirce's Writing." *Semiotica* 81, no. 1/2: 71–92.
———. 1994. *Semiotics and the Problem of Translation: With Special Reference to the Semiotics of Charles S. Peirce*. Leiden: Brill.
———. 1997. "Intercode Translation: Words and Music in Opera." *Target* 9, no. 2: 235–270.
———. 2004. *On Translating Signs: Exploring Text and Semio-Translation*. Leiden: Brill.
———. 2005. "Prelude and Acknowledgments." *Song and Significance: Virtues and Vices of Vocal Translation*, edited by Dinda L. Gorlée, 7–15. Leiden: Brill.
———. 2005a. "Singing on the Breath of God: Preface to Life and Growth of Translated Hymnody." In *Song and Significance: Virtues and Vices of Vocal Translation*, edited by Dinda L. Gorlée, 17–101. Leiden: Brill.
———. 2008a. "Jakobson and Peirce: Translational Intersemiosis and Symbiosis in Opera." *Sign Systems Studies* 36, no. 2: 341–374.
——— 2008b. "Wittgenstein as Mastersinger." *Semiotica* 172, no. 1/4: 97–150.
———. 2012. *Wittgenstein in Translation: Exploring Semiotic Signatures*. Berlin and Boston, MA: De Gruyter Mouton.
———. 2015. *From Translation to Transduction: The Glassy Essence of Intersemiosis*. Tartu: University of Tartu Press.
———. 2015a. "From Words and Sentences to Interjections: The Anatomy of Exclamations in Peirce and Wittgenstein." *Semiotica* 205: 37–86.
———. 2016. "On Habit: Peirce's Story and History." In *Consensus on Peirce's Concept of Habit: Before and Beyond Consciousness*, edited by Donna E. West and Myrdene Anderson, 13–33. New York: Springer.
———. 2016a. "Intersemioticity and Intertextuality: Picaresque and Romance in Opera." *Sign Systems Studies* 44, no. 4: 587–622.
———. 2020. "Paraphrase or Parasite? The Semiotic Stories of Translation." *Chinese Semiotic Studies* 16, no. 1: 1–46.
——— 2020a. *Wittgenstein's Secret Diaries: Semiotic Writing in Cryptography*. London: Bloomsbury Academic.
———. 2021. "Linguïculture: Thomas A. Sebeok as a Revolutionary Ethnographer." *Chinese Semiotic Studies* 17, no. 4: 525–550.
Greimas, A.J. and J. Cortès. 1982. *Semiotics and Language: An Analytical Dictionary*. Bloomington, IN: Indiana University Press.

Groot, Adriaan D. 1969. *Methodology: Foundations of Inference and Research in the Behavioral Sciences*. The Hague and Paris: Mouton.
Grose, Frances. 1811/1971. *1811 Dictionary of the Vulgar Tongue. A Dictionary of Buckish Slang, University Wit, and Pickpocket Eloquence*, reprint edited by Robert Cromie, with a Foreword by Robert Cromie. Northfield, IL: Digest Books.
Hall, Calvin D. 1954/1982. *A Primer of Freudian Psychology*. New York: Mentor, Harper & Row.
Halliday, M.A.K. 1967. *Intonation and Grammar in British English*. The Hague: Mouton.
Hanssen, Paula. 1995. *Elisabeth Hauptmann: Brecht's Silent Collaborator*. Bern, Berlin, and Frankfurt am Main: Peter Lang.
Harewood, Earl of. 1922/1961. *Kobbé's Complete Opera Book*, revised edition. London and New York: Putnam.
Hays, Gregory. 2017. "Found in Translation." *The New York Review of Books* 65, no. 11: 55–58.
Heemskerk Düker, W.F. van and H.J. van Houten. 1941. *Zinnebeelden in Nederland*. The Hague: Uitgeverij Hamer.
Heller-Roazen, Daniel. 2013. *Dark Tongues: The Art of Rogues and Riddlers*. New York: Zone Books.
Herbert, A.P. 1948. *Gay's London*. London: Ernest Benn Ltd.
Hermanson, Eric. 1999. "Kings Are Lions, But Herod Is a Fox." *The Bible Translator* 50, no. 2: 235–240.
Hess, David J. 1993. *Science in the New Age: The Paranormal, Its Defenders and Debunkers, and American Culture*. Madison, WI: University of Wisconsin Press.
Hinton, Stephen. 1990. *Kurt Weill The Threepenny Opera*. Cambridge: Cambridge University Press.
Hjelmslev, Louis. 1961. *Prolegomena to a Theory of Language*, revised English edition from the Danish *Omkring sprogteoriens grundlæggelse* (1943). Madison, WI: University of Wisconsin Press.
Hofmann, Michael. 2018–2019. "'A Born Contrarian.'" *The New York Review of Books* 65, no. 20: 47–52.
Holmes, James S., ed. 1970. *The Nature of Translation: Essays on the Theory and Practice of Literary Translation*. The Hague and Paris: Mouton.
———. 1988. *Translated! Papers on Literary Translation and Translation Studies*. Amsterdam: Rodopi.
———. 1989. "Translating Martial and Vergil: Jakob Lowland Among the Classics." In *Translating Poetry: The Double Labyrinth*, edited by Daniel Weissbort, 57–72. Houndmills, Basingstoke: Palgrave Macmillan.
Hubig, Christoph. 1986. "Meta-." *Encyclopedic Dictionary of Semiotics*, 3 vols, general editor Thomas A. Sebeok, vol. 1: 529–531. Berlin, New York and Amsterdam: Mouton de Gruyter.
Jakobson, Roman. 1921/1987. "Dada." In *Language in Literature*, edited by Krystyna Pomorska and Stephen Rudy, 40–34. Cambridge, MA: The Belknap Press of Harvard University Press.
———. 1932/1971a. "Musikwissenschaft und Linguistik." In *Selected Writings II: Word and Language*, edited by Roman Jakobson, 551–553. The Hague and Paris: Mouton.
———. 1935/1981. "The Dominant." *Selected Writings III: Poetry of Grammar and Grammar of Poetry*, edited by Roman Jakobson, 751–756. The Hague and Paris: Mouton.

———. 1939–1940/1971a. "Signe zero," "Das Nullzeichen." In *Selected Writings II: Word and Language*, edited by Roman Jakobson, 211–223. The Hague and Paris: Mouton.

———. 1949/1981. "Linguistics and Poetics." In *Selected Writings III: Poetry of Grammar and Grammar of Poetry*, edited by Roman Jakobson, 18–51. The Hague and Paris: Mouton.

———. 1953/1971a. "Results of a Joint Conference of Anthropologists and Linguists." In *Selected Writings II: Word and Language*, edited by Roman Jakobson, 554–567. The Hague and Paris: Mouton.

———. 1956/1971a. "Shifters, Verbal Categories, and the Russian Verb." In *Selected Writings II: Word and Language*, edited by Roman Jakobson, 130–147. The Hague and Paris: Mouton.

———. 1959/1966. "On Linguistic Aspects of Translation." *On Translation*, edited Reuben A. Brown, 233–239. New York: Oxford University Press (Reprinted in Roman Jakobson's *Selected Writings II: Word and Language*, 1971a: 260–266).

———. 1960/1964. "Closing Statement: Linguistics and Poetics" (and various comments on the propositions of other speakers)." In *Style in Language*, edited by Thomas A. Sebeok, 350–377. Cambridge, MA: MIT Press.

———. 1960/1971a. "The Kazan's School of Polish Linguistics and its Place in the International Development of Phonology." In *Selected Writings II: Word and Language*, edited by Roman Jakobson, 394–428. The Hague and Paris: Mouton.

———. 1961/1971. "Retrospect." In *Selected Writings I: Phonological Studies*, edited by Roman Jakobson, 629–658. The Hague and Paris: Mouton.

———. 1961/1971a. "Linguistics and Communication Theory." In *Selected Writings II: Word and Language*, edited by Roman Jakobson, 570–579. The Hague and Paris: Mouton.

———. 1963/1981. "Der grammatische Bau des Gedichts von B. Brecht "Wir sind sie."" In *Selected Writings III: Poetry of Grammar and Grammar of Poetry*, edited by Roman Jakobson, 660–676. The Hague and Paris: Mouton.

———. 1963a. "Parts and Wholes in Language." In *Parts and Wholes*, edited by Daniel Lerner, 157–162. New York: The Free Press of Blencoe.

———. 1971. *Selected Writings I: Phonological Studies*, 2nd expanded edition. The Hague and Paris: Mouton.

———. 1971a. *Selected Writings II: Word and Language*. The Hague and Paris: Mouton.

———. 1981. *Selected Writings III: Poetry of Grammar and Grammar of Poetry*. The Hague and Paris: Mouton.

———. 1987. *Language in Literature*, edited by Krystyna Pomorska and Stephen Rudy. Cambridge, MA: The Belknap Press of Harvard University Press.

Jakobson, Roman and Morris Halle. 1956/1971. *Fundamentals of Language*, 2nd revised edition. The Hague and Paris: Mouton.

Jakobson, Roman and Linda Waugh. 1979. *The Sound Shape of Language*. Brighton, Sussex: Harvester Press.

Johansen, Jørgen Dines. 1993. *Dialogic Semiosis: An Essay on Signs and Meaning*. Bloomington and Indianapolis, IN: Indiana University Press.

Jones, Edwin. 1989. *Reading the Book of Nature: A Phenomenological Study of Creative Expression in Science and Painting*. Athens, OH: Ohio University Press.

Jourdain, Robert. 1997. *Music, the Brain, and Ecstasy: How Music Captures Our Imagination*. New York: William Morrow and Company.

Kebir, Sabine. 1997. *Ich fragte nicht nach meinem Anteil: Elisabeth Hauptmanns Arbeit mit Bertolt Brecht*. Berlin: Aufbau Verlag.

Kerman, Joseph. 1956/1989. *Opera as Drama*, New and revised edition. London: Faber and Faber.
Kesting, Marianne. 1959/1967. *Bertolt Brecht in Selbstzeugnissen und Bilddokumenten*. Reinbek bei Hamburg: Rowohlt Verlag.
King, Julia and Laila Miletic-Vejzovic, eds. 2003. *The Library of Leonard and Virginia Woolf: A Short-Title Catalogue*. Pullman, WA: Washington State University Press (available at http://ntserver1.wsulibs.wsu.edu/masc/onlinebooks/woolflibrary/woolflibraryonline.htm).
Kirsch, Adam. 2023. "Arias of Despair." *The New York Review of Books* 70, no. 2: 19–20.
Koch, Walter A., ed. 1994. *Simple Forms: An Encyclopedia of Simple Text-Types in Lore and Literature*. Bochum: Brockmeyer.
Kockelman, Paul. 2007. "Agency: The Relation between Meaning, Power, and Knowledge." *Current Anthropology* 48, no. 3: 375–402.
Kostelanetz, Richard., ed. 1993. *Dictionary of the Avant-Gardes*. Chicago, IL: A Cappella Books.
Kramer, Lawrence. 1980. "Ocean and Vision: Imaginative Dilemma in Wordsworth, Whitman and Stevens." *Journal of English and Germanic Philology* 79: 210–230.
Kruse, Felicia E. 2011. "Temporality in Musical Meaning: A Peircean/Deweyan Semiotic Meaning." *The Pluralist* 6, no. 3: 50–63.
Kurzon, Dennis. 1998. *Discourse of Silence*. Amsterdam and Philadelphia, PA: John Benjamins Publishing Company.
Labie, Jean-François. 1990. "Berlioz, homme de lettres." *Les Troyens Berlioz. Avant-Scène Opera [French Opera Journal]* 128–129: 131–136.
Lakoff, George and Mark Johnson. 1980. *Metaphors We Live By*. Chicago, IL and London: The University of Chicago Press.
Langer, Susanne K. 1948/1980. *Philosophy in a New Key: A Study in the Symbolism of Reason, Rite, and Art*, 3rd edition. Cambridge, MA: Harvard University Press.
Langford, Jeffrey. 1981. "Berlioz, Cassandra, and the French Operatic Tradition." *Music & Letters* 62, no. 3–4: 310–318.
Leach, Maria and Jerome Fried. 1972/1984. *Funk & Wagnalls Standard Dictionary of Folklore, Mythology, and Legend*. San Francisco, CA: Harper & Row.
Lefevere, André. 1975. *Translating Poetry: Seven Strategies and A Blueprint*. Assen and Amsterdam: Van Gorcum.
Lenya, Lotte. 1956/1960. "August 28, 1938." Foreword to Bertolt Brecht's *The Threepenny Opera*, edited by Desmond Vesey. New York: Grove Weidenfeld, V–XIV.
Lévi-Strauss, Claude. 1955. "The Structural Study of Myth." *The Journal of American Folklore* 68, no. 270: 428–444.
Levy, Paul. 2017. "The Painter and the Novelist." *The New York Review of Books* 64, no. 8: 59–61.
Longyear, Rey M. 1969. *Nineteenth-Century Romanticism in Music*. Englewood Cliffs, NJ: Prentice Hall.
Lunde, Paul. 2009. *The Secrets of Codes*. London: A&C Black Publishers.
McCormick, Donald. 1980. *Love in Code: Or How to Keep Your Secrets*. London: Eyre Methuen Ltd.
MacCannell, Dean and Juliet Flower MacCannell. 1982. *The Time of the Sign: A Semiotic Interpretation of Modern Culture*. Bloomington, IN: Indiana University Press.
Mallery, Garrick. 1972. *Sign Language Among North American Indians Compared with That Among Other Peoples and Deaf-Mutes*. The Hague and Paris: Mouton.

Malmberg, Bertil. 1954/1963. *Phonetics*. Translated by Lily M. Parker. New York: Dover.
Marder, Herbert. 2001. *The Measure of Life: Virginia Woolf's Last Years*. Ithaca, NY: Cornell University Press.
McGregor, Jamie A. 2009. *Myth, Music and Modernism: The Wagnerian Dimension in Virginia Woolf's Mrs. Dalloway and The Waves and James Joyce's Finnegan's Wake*. PhD thesis, Rhodes University (available at https://www.yumpu.com/en/document/read/6625610/myth-music-modernism-rhodes-university).
McGregor, William. 1997. *Semiotic Grammar*. Oxford: Clarendon Press.
McInnes, Neil. 1967/1972. "Marx, Karl." *The Encyclopedia of Philosophy*, edited by Paul Edwards 5: 171–176. New York: Macmillan Publishing and The Free Press; London: Collier Macmillan Publishers.
McNichol, Stella. 1990. "The Waves: A Playpoem." *Virginia Woolf and the Poetry of Fiction*, edited by Stella McNichol, 117–140. London and Oxford: Routledge.
Meyer, Leonard B. 1956/1970. *Emotion and Meaning in Music*. Chicago, IL and London: The University of Chicago Press.
Miller, Jonathan. 2001. "Doing Opera." In *Doing It: Five Performing Arts*, edited by Robert B. Silvers, 47–69. New York: The New York Review of Books.
Miller, J. Hillis. 2015. "*Waves* Theory: An Anachronistic Reading." In *Communities in Fiction*, edited by J. Hillis Miller, 232–263. New York: Fordham University Press.
Minow-Pinkney, Makiko. 1987. "The Waves." In *Virginia Woolf & the Problem of the Subject: Feminine Writing in the Major Novels*, edited by Makiko Minow-Pinkney, 152–186. Brighton: Harvester Press.
Mlinko, Ange. 2020. "Water Music." *The New York Review of Books* 67, no. 12: 40–41.
Morris, Charles W. 1932/1946. *Six Theories of Mind*. Chicago, IL: University of Chicago Press.
———. 1946. *Signs, Language, and Behavior*. New York: George Braziller.
———. 1971. *Writings on the General Theory of Signs*. The Hague and Paris: Mouton.
Müller, Klaus-Detlef. 1980. *Brecht – Kommentar zur erzählenden Prosa*. Munich: Winkler Verlag.
Nettl, Bruno. 1965/1973. *Folk and Traditional Music of the Western Continents*, 2nd edition. Englewood Cliffs, NJ: Prentice Hall.
Newman, Ernest. 1972. *Berlioz, Romantic and Classic: Writings by Ernest Newman*, edited by Peter Heyworth. London: Victor Gollancz.
Nibelungenlied, The. 1965/1969. New translation by A.T. Hatto, with appendices. Harmondsworth, Middlesex: Penguin Books.
Nida, Eugene A. 1950. *Learning a Foreign Language: A Handbook for Missionaries*. New York: National Council of the Churches of Christ in the U.S.A.
———. 1964. *Toward A Science of Translating: With Special Reference to Principles and Procedures Involved in Bible Translating*. Leiden: Brill.
———. 2001. "Translations." *The Oxford Guide to Ideas & Issues of the Bible*, edited by Bruce M. Metzger and Michael D. Coogan, 494–534. Oxford: Oxford University Press.
Nida, Eugene A. and Charles R. Taber. 1969/1982. *The Theory and Practice of Translation* (prepared under the auspices of the United Bible Societies). Leiden: Brill.
Norris, Benjamin and Andrew Benjamin. 1988. *What is Deconstruction?* London: Academy Editions and New York: St. Martin's Press.
O'Hara, Daniel T. 2015. "Woolf's 'Inborn Selves' in *The Waves*." In *Virginia Woolf and the Modern Sublime: The Invisible Tribunal*, edited by Daniel O'Hara, 67–82. New York: Palgrave Macmillan.

Orrey, Leslie. 1972/1987. *Opera – A Concise History*, revised by Rodney Milnes. London: Thames and Hudson.
Ostwald, Peter F. 1973. *The Semiotics of Human Sound*. The Hague and Paris: Mouton.
Oxford English Dictionary, The. 1989. 2nd edition, edited by J.A. Simpson and E.S.C. Weiner, 20 vols. Oxford: Clarendon Press [OED 1989 followed by vol#: page#].
Panofsky, Erwin. 1954. *Galileo as a Critic of the Arts*. The Hague: Nijhoff.
Partridge, Eric. 1933/1972. *Slang To-day and Yesterday With a Short Historical Sketch and Vocabularies of English, American, and Australian Slang*, 4th edition. London: Routledge & Kegan Paul.
———. 1990/1995. *Dictionary of the Underworld*. Ware, Hertfordshire: Wordsworth Editions Ltd.
Pavis, Patrice. 1980. *Dictionnaire du théâtre: Termes et concepts de l'analyse théâtrale*. Paris: Editions Sociales.
Pavlovskis, Zoja. 1981. "Translation from the Classics." In *Translation Spectrum: Essays in Theory and Practice*, edited by Marilyn Gaddis Roser, 99–107. Albany, NY: State University of New York Press.
Pazdro, Michel., ed. 1990. *Les Troyens Berlioz. Avant-Scène Opera* [*French Opera Journal*]: 128–129.
Pearsall, Roland. 1973. *Victorian Popular Music*. Newton Abbot, Devon: David & Charles Publishers.
Peirce, Charles S. 1931–1958. *Collected Papers of Charles Sanders Peirce*, edited by Charles Hartshorne, Paul Weiss, and Arthur W. Burks, 8 vols. Cambridge, MA: Belknap Press of Harvard University Press [CP: vol# paragraph#].
———. 1976a. *The New Elements of Mathematics, Vol. II Algebra and Geometry*, edited by Carolyn Eisele. The Hague and Paris: Mouton Publishers and Atlantic Highlands, NJ: Humanities Press.
———. 1976b. *The New Elements of Mathematics, Vol. IV Mathematical Philosophy*, edited by Carolyn Eisele. The Hague and Paris: Mouton Publishers and Atlantic Highlands, NJ: Humanities Press.
———. Unpublished manuscripts. *Peirce Edition Project*. Indianapolis, IN: Indiana University and Purdue University [MS# page#].
Pike, Kenneth L. 1943. *Phonetics: A Critical Analysis of Phonetic Theory and a Technic for the Practical Description of Sounds*. Ann Arbor, MI: University of Michigan Press.
———. 1947. *Phonemics: A Technique for Reducing Languages to Writing*. Ann Arbor, MI: University of Michigan Press.
———. 1948. *Tone Languages: A Technique for Determining the Number and Type of Pitch Contrasts, with Studies of Tonemic Substitution and Fusion*. Ann Arbor, MI: University of Michigan Press.
———. 1967. *Language in Relation to a Unified Theory of the Structure of Human Behavior*, 2nd revised edition. The Hague and Paris: Mouton.
———. 1959/1972. "Language as Particle, Wave, and Field." In *Selected Writings to Commemorate the 60th Birthday of Kenneth Lee Pike*, edited by Ruth M. Brend, 129–143. The Hague and Paris: Mouton.
———. 1967/1972. "Grammar as Wave." In *Selected Writings to Commemorate the 60th Birthday of Kenneth Lee Pike*, edited by Ruth M. Brend, 231–241. The Hague and Paris: Mouton.
Perl, Jed. 2020. "The Cults of Wagner." *The New York Review of Books* 67, no. 15: 17–19.
———. 2021. "Cubism's Poet." *The New York Review of Books* 68, no. 3: 12–13.

Phythian, B.A. 1955/1979. *A Concise Dictionary of English Slang and Colloquialisms.* London: Hodder and Stoughton.
Plaza, Julio. 1981. "Reflection of and on Theories of Translation." *Dispositio* VI, no. 17–18: 45–91.
———. 1985. *Sobre tradução inter-semiótica.* Ph.D. dissertation, Catholic University of São Paulo (reprinted in 1987).
———. 1987. *Tradução intersemiótica.* São Paulo: Editora Perspectiva.
Pohl, Rainer. 1969. *Strukturelemente und Entwicklung von Pathosformen in der Dramensprache Bertolt Brechts.* Bonn: H. Bouvier & Co. Verlag.
Poizat, Michel. 1992. *The Angel's Cry Beyond the Pleasure Principle in Opera.* Ithaca, NY and London: Cornell University Press.
Popoviç, Anton. 1975. *Dictionary for the Analysis of Literary Translation.* Edmonton, Alberta: Department of Comparative Literature, University of Alberta.
Preminger, Alex., ed. 1965/1974. *Princeton Encyclopedia of Poetry and Poetics.* Princeton, NJ: Princeton University Press.
Raffel, Burton. 1971. *The Forked Tongue: A Study of the Translation Process.* The Hague and Paris: Mouton.
——— 1988. *The Art of Translating Poetry.* University Parks, PA and London: The Pennsylvania State University Press.
Rey-Debove, Josette. 1986. "Metalanguage." In *Encyclopedic Dictionary of Semiotics,* general editor Thomas A. Sebeok, 3 vols., Vol. 1: 531–532. Berlin, New York and Amsterdam: Mouton de Gruyter.
Rifkin, Jeremy. 1980/1981. *Entropy: A New World View.* New York: Viking Press.
Riley, Charles A. II. 1995. *Color Codes: Modern Theories of Color in Philosophy, Painting and Architecture, Literature, Music, and Psychology.* Hanover, NH and London: University Press of New England.
Rose, Phyllis. 2022. "I Have Quite Lost My Heart." *The New York Review of Books* 69, no. 4: 21, 24–25.
Rosen, Charles. 1996. *The Romantic Generation.* London: Harper Collins Publishers.
Rossi-Landi, Ferruccio. 1992. "Towards an Analysis of Appraisive Signs in Esthetics and Draft of an Operational Approach to Esthetic Values." In *Between Signs and Non-signs,* edited by Susan Petrilli, 111–129. Amsterdam and Philadelphia, PA: John Benjamins Publishing Company.
Sangster, Rodney B. 1982. *Roman Jakobson and Beyond: Language as a System of Signs.* Berlin, New York, and Amsterdam: Mouton Publishers.
Saules, Jacqueline. 1975. *Les Troyans d'Hector Berlioz: Du Virgil Shakespearianisé.* MA thesis, University Toulouse II, Le Mirail.
Saussure, Ferdinand de. 1949/1959/1966. *Course in General Linguistics,* edited by Charles Bally and Albert Sechehaye, translated by Wade Baskin. New York, Toronto, and London: McGraw–Hill (Originally published in French in 1949).
Scheffler, Israel. 1997. *Symbolic Worlds: Art, Science, Language, Ritual.* Cambridge: Cambridge University Press.
Schimmel, Solomon. 1992. *The Seven Deadly Sins: Jewish, Christian, and Classical Reflections on Human Nature.* New York: The Free Press.
Schmidt, Johannes. 1872 (reprint). *Die Verwandschaftsverhältnisse der indogermanischen Sprachen.* Weimar: Hermann Böhlau Verlag.
Schuhmann, Klaus. 1964. *Der Lyriker Bertolt Brecht 1913–1933.* Berlin: Rütten & Loening.

Schwab, Heinrich W. 1965. *Sangbarkeit, Popularität und Kunstlied: Studien zu Lied und Liedästhetik der mittleren Goethezeit, 1770–1814*. Regensburg: Gustav Bosse Verlag.
Sebeok, Thomas. 1974/1977/1985. "Zoosemiotic Components of Human Communication." In *Semiotics: An Introductory Anthology*, edited by Robert E. Innis, 292–324. Bloomington, IN: Indiana University Press.
———. 1976. "Drum and Whistle Systems." In *Contributions to the Doctrine of Signs*, edited by Thomas A. Sebeok, 189–200. Bloomington, IN: Indiana University and Lisse: Peter de Ridder Press.
———. 1979. *The Sign & Its Masters*. Austin, TX and London: University of Texas Press.
———. 1981. "Prefigurements of Art." *The Play of Musement*, edited by Thomas A. Sebeok, 210–259. Bloomington, IN: Indiana University Press.
———. 1984a. *Communication Measures to Bridge Ten Millennia*. Technical Report U.S. Department of Energy. Columbus, OH: Battelle Memorial Institute.
———. 1984b. "Signs of Life." *International Semiotic Spectrum* 2, June: 1–2.
———. 1994/1999. *Signs: An Introduction to Semiotics*. Toronto: Toronto University Press.
Sebeok, Thomas and Donna J. Umiker-Sebeok. 1976. "Introduction." In *Speech Surrogates: Drum and Whistle Systems*, xiii–xxix. The Hague and Paris: Mouton.
Seznec, Jean. 1953/1972. *The Survival of the Pagan Gods: The Mythological Tradition and Its Place in Renaissance Humanism and Art*. Princeton, NJ: Princeton University Press.
Shakespeare, William. 1598/1987. "The Comical History of the Merchant of Venice, or Otherwise Called the Jew of Venice." In *The Complete Oxford Shakespeare, Vol. II Comedies*, edited by Stanley Wells and Gary Taylor, 603–630. Oxford: Oxford University Press.
Shands, Harvey C. 1970. *Semiotic Approaches to Psychiatry*. The Hague and Paris: Mouton.
———. 1976. "Malinowski's Mirror: Emily Dickinson as Narcissus." *Contemporary Psychoanalysis* 12: 300–334.
Shapin, Steven. 2019. "A Theorist of (Not Quite) Everything." *The New York Review of Books* 66, no. 15: 29–31.
Sheriff, Robert E., ed. 1984/2002. *Encyclopedic Dictionary of Exploration Geophysics*, 2nd revised edition. Tulsa, OK: Society of Exploration Geophysicists.
Shipley, Joseph T., ed. 1968/1972. *Dictionary of World Literature: Criticism, Forms, Technique*, new revised edition. Totowa, NJ: Littlefield, Adams & Company.
Simonette, Lyts and Kim H. Kowalke. 1996. *Speak Low (When you Speak Love): The Letters of Kurt Weill and Lotte Lenya*. Berkeley and Los Angeles, CA: University of California Press.
Smart, J.J.C. 1967. "Time." *The Encyclopedia of Philosophy*, edited by Paul Edwards, Vol. 8, 126–134. New York: MacMillan Publishing and London: Collier MacMillan Publishers.
Spiegl, Fritz. 1997. *Lives, Wives and Loves of the Great Composers*. London and New York: Marion Boyaers Publishers.
Steiner, George. 1975. *After Babel: Aspects of Language and Translation*. Oxford: Oxford University Press.
———. 1967/1985. *Language and Silence*. London and Boston, MA: Faber and Faber.
———. 1990. "Homer and Virgil and Broch." *London Review of Books* 12, no. 13: 10–11.
Sutton, Emma. 2013. *Virginia Woolf and Classical Music: Politics, Aesthetics, Form*. Edinburgh: Edinburgh University Press.
Tallman, Susan. 2019. "'I Just Look, and Paint'." *The New York Review of Books* 66, no. 19: 17–19.

———. 2020. "What the Little Woman was Up To." *The New York Review of Books* 67, no. 5: 10–14.

———. 2021. "Knowing How." *The New York Review of Books* 68, no. 13: 4–8.

Thoreau, Henry D. 1971. *Walden*, edited by Lyndon Shanley. Princeton, NJ: Princeton University Press.

Tiersot, Julien. 1917. "Hector Berlioz and Richard Wagner." *The Musical Quarterly* 3: 453–492.

Tubeuf, André. 1962. "French Singing Reborn." *Opera Annual* 8: 33–42.

Turley, Peter T. 1977. *Peirce's Cosmology*. New York: Philosophical Library.

Umiker, Donna Jean. 1974. "Speech Surrogates: Drum and Whistle Systems." In *Current Trends in Linguistics*, Vol. 12, 497–536, edited by Thomas A. Sebeok. The Hague and Paris: Mouton.

Virgil (Publius Vergilius Maro) [19 B.C.]. 1916/1999. "Aenid I–VI." In *Eclogues. Georgics. Aeneid: I–VI*, translated by H. Rushton Fairclough, revised by G.P. Goold, bilingual edition Latin–English (Loeb Classical Library 63), 261–597. Cambridge, MA and London: Harvard University Press.

———. 1981. *The Aeneid. A Verse Translation by Allen Mandelbaum*. Berkeley, CA: University of California Press.

Voigt, Vilmos. 2015. "Zur Semiotik einiger Musikinstrumente (Vorläufige Problemstellung)." *Acta Ethnographica Hungarica* 60, no. 1: 185–199. DOI: 10.1556/022.2015.60.1.16.

Wagner, Richard. 1873/1913(?). *Der Ring des Nibelungen. Vorabend: Das Rheingold*, edited by Felix Mottl, piano score with text (PN 9800). Leipzig: C.F. Peters.

———. 1900/1995. *Opera and Drama*. Translated by William Ashton Ellis (from German original *Oper und Drama*, 1852). Lincoln, NE and London: University of Nebraska Press.

———. 1983. *Der Ring des Nibelungen (The Ring of the Nibelung): Das Rheingold*. Translated by Mark Herman and Ronnie Apter (available from the translators at mnh18@columbia.edu).

———. 1985. *The Rhinegold: Das Rheingold*. Translated by Andrew Porter, edited by Nicholas John 1976. Bilingual edition German and English, 43–92. London: John Calder and New York: Riverrun Press.

Wardhaugh, Ronald. 1985. *How Conversation Works*. Oxford: Basil Blackwell.

Warner, Marina. 2020. "Spellbound." *The New York Review of Books* 77, no. 11: 27–29.

Weill, Kurt and Bertolt Brecht. 1928/1955. *Vocal Selections from The Threepenny Opera*. Van Nuys, CA: Alfred Music.

———. 1990. *Musik und Theater. Gesammelte Schriften mit einer Auswahl von Gesprächen und Interviews*, edited by Stephen Hinto and Jürgen Schebera. Berlin: Henschelverlag Kunst.

———. 1999. *Die Dreigroschenoper / Die Threepenny Opera*, concert recording, conducted by H.K. Gruber, performed by Ensemble Modern with Max Raabe, Nina Hagen, and Chorus, translator Michael Feingold, edited by Stephen Hinton. BMG Classics 74321 66133 2.

Weiss, Paul. 1961. *Nine Basic Arts*. Carbondale, IL: Southern Illinois University Press.

Weissbort, Daniel., ed. 1989. *Translating Poetry: The Double Labyrinth*. Houndmills, Basingstoke: Palgrave Macmillan.

Wilshire, Bruce W. 1982. *Role Playing and Identity: The Limits of Theatre as Metaphor*. Bloomington, IN: Indiana University Press.

BIBLIOGRAPHY

———. 2016. *The Much-at-Once: Music, Science, Ecstasy, the Body*. New York: Fordham University Press.

Wilson-de Roze, Karen. 2018. "Have English Translations of Wagner's Ring of the Nibelung, an Icon of German Culture, Been Affected by the Changing Relationship between Germany and Britain in the Twentieth Century?" In *Key Cultural Texts in Translation*, edited by Kirsten Malmkjær et al., 53–77 Amsterdam and Philadelphia, PA: John Benjamins.

———. 2020. "Translating Wagner's *Versmelodie* – A Multimodal Challenge." In *Opera in Translation: Unity and Diversity*, edited by Adriana Serban and Kelly Kar Yue Chan, 243–270. Amsterdam and Philadelphia, PA: John Benjamins Publishing Company.

Winterson, Jeanette. 1996. "A Veil of Words (with Reference to *The Waves*)." In *Art Objects: Essays on Ecstasy and Effrontery*, edited by Jeanette Winterson, 79–99. New York: Alfred A. Knopf.

Wolf, Siegmund A. 1985/1993. *Deutsche Gaunersprache: Wörterbuch des Rotwelschen*. Hamburg: Helmut Buske Verlag.

Wolff, Larry. 2021. "Phantasms of the Opera." *The New York Review of Books* 68, no. 4: 27–28.

Woolf, Virginia. 1909/1976. "Impressions at Bayreuth." *Opera News* 41, edited by John L. DiGaetani, 22–23.

———. 1925/1933. "Modern Fiction." In *The Common Reader*, edited by Virginia Woolf, 184–195. London: Hogarth Press.

———. 1931/2000. *The Waves*, edited by Deborah Parson. Hertfordshire: Wordsworth Classics.

———. 1976. *'The Waves': The Two Holographic Drafts*, edited by J.W. Graham. Toronto and Buffalo, NY: Toronto University Press (in association with the University of Western Ontario).

Zazzali, Peter. 2018. "Consciousness in Brechtian Acting: Defamiliarizing the Self." In *Philosophizing Brecht: Critical Readings on Art, Consciousness, Social Theory and Performance*, edited by Norman Roessler and Antony Squiers, 24–46. Leiden and Boston, MA: Brill.

INDEX

acculturation, interculture, panculture 8, 10, 18–19, 21, 25, 29, 100, 144, 160; *see also* culture
Aeneas (Greek hero) 99, 102–3, 109, 111, 114–28
aesthetics 3, 14, 19–22, 26–27, 32, 38, 65, 100, 128, 170
alienation effect (*Verfremdungseffekt*) 91, 130, 134, 144, 148, 156, 158–59, 165, 170–71
Arnheim, Rudolf 10, 40–41, 44
art, fine arts 1–3, 6, 14–15, 17, 19–31, 34, 45, 49–50, 53–58, 60–61, 67, 77–78, 83–86, 90, 95, 101, 104, 114, 130, 132–34, 136, 139, 148–49, 162–65, 172
artist, artisan 4–17, 20–23, 30–34, 36, 39, 40, 45–46, 49–50, 52, 55, 57, 64, 67, 82, 91–92, 96, 98, 102, 108, 126–27
assonance, dissonance 33, 71–72, 92–94, 100, 106, 126
Auerbach, Erich 34, 51, 57, 102

ballads 21, 132, 137–38, 142–48, 150, 157, 163, 166, 170–71
beauty of literary translation 6–7, 10, 15–18, 26, 49, 71, 86, 94, 126
Berlioz, Hector 1, 13, 17, 46, 89–128, 130, 134, 171–74
Bible translation 2–4, 17–18, 61, 78, 138, 147–51, 157–59
Brecht, Bertold 1, 13, 18, 46, 120, 129–74
Bunn, James 9–10, 26, 40–41, 46, 60, 128

Cassandra (Trojan princess and prophetess) 112–15, 119, 124
chemistry, physics 5, 7, 13, 25–26, 38, 40–44, 51, 56–57, 59–60, 63–67, 74, 76, 79, 90–91

church-bells 84
Cockney slang, criminal speech 137–39, 141–44, 147, 158, 163–71
code 1, 3, 5–7, 15–20, 26–30, 33–34, 47–50, 70–71, 81, 84; *see also* encoding, decoding
conduction 7, 45–47, 56, 60, 84, 86, 91, 114, 130, 157, 162, 164, 170, 172–73
copyright 102, 145; *see also* transduction; translation
cryptology, cryptanalyst 6, 8, 24, 41, 129, 147, 161, 164–66, 171–72, 174
Cubism 18, 23, 30, 37–38, 128, 134
culture 1–2, 5, 8, 11, 14, 17, 19, 21, 25–26, 33, 37–39, 41, 51–56, 62, 66, 82, 86, 96, 101, 104, 136, 149–50, 174

degenerate signs (Peirce) 10–11, 15, 35, 103–5
Derrida, Jacques 18, 28, 48, 57, 60, 164
Dewey, John 28, 48, 57, 60
dialect 1, 10, 14, 19–20, 25–26, 31, 33, 39, 47, 52, 60–64, 130–34, 151, 163–67
Dickens, Charles 53
Dido (Queen of Cartaghe) 91–94, 102–28
double lines of human mind (Saussure) 33–34, 40, 47, 56, 73–74, 78, 99–102, 105–7, 116, 122, 126, 128, 131, 143, 149, 158–59, 161–62, 166, 169, 173–74

ecstasy 91, 110, 123, 126, 158
electricity of human mind 46, 51, 170
ellipsis, parabole, hyperbole (Peirce) 4, 9–14, 29, 41–42, 44–45, 47, 52, 68–69, 76–77, 89, 100, 108, 110, 127–28, 171–74
emotionality 6–10, 14–16, 20, 29, 35–36, 38, 44–45, 48, 50–52, 57–59, 62, 67, 76, 79, 81–89
encoding, decoding 3, 6–7, 31, 37, 39, 42–45, 102, 120, 164, 167; *see also* code

energy 2, 14, 38–47, 50, 58–61, 67, 69, 77, 79, 104, 108, 128, 136, 164, 171–72
entropy 41–42, 55, 69–70, 72, 130
epic poetry 15, 20–22, 37, 51, 53, 57–58, 70, 92, 98–101, 107–12, 114, 117, 119, 127, 134–36, 143–44, 147–48, 151, 158–65, 168–72, 174
exclamations, interjections, cries 73–75, 106–8, 110, 113, 117, 119, 123–25, 157–62, 167

feminism, women's rights 55, 57, 85–86
firstness, secondness, thirdness (Peirce's categories) 8, 11, 14–15, 27, 30–31, 35, 38, 48, 52, 85, 104–6, 150
forked tongues 1–46, 161; *see also* Bible translation
fragmentation in translation 4, 8, 13, 22–23, 37, 41, 50, 55, 63, 66–68, 86, 102–3, 123, 128, 147, 172
Freud, Sigmund 24–25, 67–68

Gay, John 132, 137–45, 148, 151–53, 163–67, 170–74

Hauptmann, Elisabeth 137, 144, 163
hexameter 99, 101, 109–10, 115
Hitler, Adolf 145, 170
Holmes, James S. 32, 50, 95, 98
Humberdinck, Engelbert 136
hypersigns 4
hypertranslation 11, 17, 20–23, 30, 32, 39, 47, 49, 64, 94, 101–2, 119, 127–29, 131, 144, 163, 172
hypothesis 38, 62, 80, 105

icon, index, symbol (Peirce) 3–5, 11, 13, 30–31, 35–36, 45, 105, 110–11, 114, 131, 135–36, 150, 152, 158–59, 162; *see also* symbol (Saussure)
interpretant (Peirce) 1–2, 9, 15, 18, 27–30, 35–36, 45, 82
interpreter as lyrical translator (librettist) 7, 9–10, 14–15, 29–31, 35–37, 43, 47, 102, 105, 128
intralingual, interlingual, intersemiotic translation (Jakobson) 18–21, 23, 28, 33, 35, 38, 47, 64, 164, 171

Jakobson, Roman 4, 6–8, 18–39, 44, 47–50, 57–74, 77–85, 94, 99, 103, 106–10, 116, 119–22, 127–31, 134, 147–51, 159–72

Langer, Susanne K. 56, 98
Lefevere, André 95
leitmotif (Wagner) 40, 56–57, 67–68, 70, 72–73, 76, 81, 86, 146, 172
Lenya, Lotte 137, 143–46, 153, 158
libretto, librettist 48, 60, 70, 76, 92–93, 96, 98, 100, 102–3, 107, 127, 136, 138, 146–48, 155, 158, 167–68, 172
lingüiculture 39
lyrical translation 1, 6, 8, 10, 20, 22, 38, 47, 51, 53, 56, 58, 69, 71, 76, 80, 93–95, 99–100, 104, 107–9, 115, 117, 119, 122, 126–29, 131, 135–37, 146–48, 153, 159, 161–63, 167–68, 170, 172–74; *see also* hypertranslation

Marx, Karl 130–35, 147, 168, 171
meaning of language 1–11, 13–22, 25–40, 43, 45, 47, 49–51, 55–60, 62–69, 71–72, 77–79, 82, 94, 99–100, 103, 105–10, 113–19, 127–28, 134, 143, 145–49, 152, 157–63, 166–71, 174
metalanguage 6, 26, 33–34, 38, 45–46, 69, 161, 163
metaphor 1, 3–6, 9–11, 17, 20, 23, 26, 29, 33, 35, 39, 41, 46, 52, 56–58, 60, 62, 64, 79–80, 82–83, 86–87, 98, 100, 104, 116, 121–22, 134, 143, 148–51, 160–61
metapoem 32, 50, 77, 80
mimesis 18, 34, 39–42, 69
Morris, Charles W. 29, 34–38, 105
musicocentrism and logocentrism 17, 48, 76–77, 100, 127
mythology, mythopoetic 4, 15, 20–21, 25–26, 31, 35, 37, 43–45, 51, 53–54, 56–57, 63–64, 70–86, 95, 97, 101–2, 116, 120–22, 127, 131, 149–50, 167, 174

Nazi symbolism 82
Nazism, political ideology of 18, 50–52, 56, 130, 133, 145, 173–74
nicknames, proper names 140, 146, 150, 165, 168
Nida, Eugene A. 2–3, 9–11, 52, 64, 66, 148–51, 160

Offenbach, Jacques 98, 136
originality, obsistence, and transuasion (Peirce) 103–6
over- and underplaying 4, 8, 14, 48, 50–52, 94, 100, 144, 157, 163, 174; *see also* quasi-semiosis (Peirce)

INDEX

parallax, parallelism 3–4, 18, 20, 26, 42, 48, 51, 58, 62, 77, 82, 84, 96, 108, 128, 130, 143, 147, 150–51, 172
parlando (Sprechstimme, Sprechgesang) 74, 80–81, 129, 136, 143
Peirce, Charles Sanders 1–2, 7, 19, 22, 26–31, 38–41, 45, 52, 82, 85, 103–6, 150, 161–63, 165
Percival or Parsifal (knight of King Arthur) 79–81
phonetics 7, 24, 27, 30–31, 33, 61–63, 65–66, 69–70, 74, 78, 81, 83, 109, 161–64, 172
Pike, Kenneth Lee 22, 61–66, 69, 84
poetics (Jakobson) 20, 22–27, 30, 37–38, 61, 70, 78, 82, 85, 94, 103, 106, 117, 119, 127, 129, 131, 171

quasi- (prefix) 5–6
quasi-mind (Peirce) 5, 15, 33, 104–5
quasi-semiosis (Peirce) 8–9, 11, 14–15, 18, 29–30, 35, 38, 104–5, 150

Raffel, Burton 3, 17, 31–32, 70, 95, 99
reactor signs (Sebeok) 2, 29, 111; *see also* symbol (Saussure)
retranslation, autotranslation or self-translation 1–2, 4, 15–16, 18–19, 33, 41, 47, 49–51, 56, 58–60, 64, 69, 76–77, 86, 89–90, 94–96, 98–106, 108, 112, 127–29, 137, 144, 161, 164, 172; *see also* hypertranslation

Saussure, Ferdinand de 7, 9, 15, 19, 21, 23–31, 38–40, 62–64, 81, 161–63, 165
Schmidt, Johannes 25, 63–65
Sebeok, Thomas A. 2–4, 31–32, 37–46, 62–64, 84, 111, 171
semiosis (Peirce) 7–9, 11, 14–18, 27; *see also* quasi-semiosis
semiotic(s) 4, 7–8, 10, 14–21, 27–29, 31, 33–46, 64, 85, 105, 161, 164, 171
Shakespeare, William 91–93, 98, 111, 114–15, 122, 128, 143
Shands, Harvey 44–45, 67
Sheriff, Robert E. 6, 9–10, 15, 40, 42, 45, 59, 72, 80, 108, 128
shifter (Jakobson) 81–82; *see also* interpretant (Peirce)
signal (Sebeok) 21, 35, 45, 55, 62, 73, 173
signifier, signified (Saussure) 7, 24–27, 29, 33, 36, 40

slang, folk- and criminal speech 62, 137–39, 143, 147, 163, 165–67, 171
source-target of translation 2–11, 14–15, 17–21, 23, 29–33, 35, 39–50, 52, 65, 68, 76, 78, 83, 95, 99–102, 105, 107–8, 119, 124, 137, 143, 149, 151, 165, 172–73
Steiner, George 32–33, 56, 76, 108, 114
symbol (Saussure) 16, 27, 57–59, 72, 77, 79, 81–82, 85–86, 91, 94, 96, 99, 108, 116–19, 158–60, 167, 169
symmetry, assymetry, parasymmetry, antisymmetry 3, 17, 41, 52, 54, 60, 74, 99
symphonic orchestra 72–73, 90, 92–93, 110, 120, 158
synonyms, parasynonyms 3–4, 7, 9–10, 17, 19–20, 28–29, 41, 52, 78, 86, 100, 103, 150, 161

telescope 6, 8–9
thermodynamics 6, 40–43, 62, 66, 128
thermostat 128
thesis, antithesis, synthesis (Marx) 136, 148, 150–52, 171
tone, token, type (Peirce) 5, 7–9, 11, 13–15, 20–22, 30–34, 41, 51, 56, 58–60, 62–63, 65–66, 68–80, 84, 86, 103–5
transcription (Jakobson) 30, 33, 45, 79, 94, 165, 170
transduction 1–2, 7–8, 10, 15–16, 22, 31, 35, 39–51, 57–60, 62–63, 66–69, 77–83, 86, 92, 98, 101–2, 106, 108, 114, 130–37, 147, 150, 161–62, 164–65, 171–74; *see also* conduction; translation
transitional genres (Jakobson) 22–23, 35, 41–42, 44
translation 23, 25–26, 28, 41–52, 58–60, 63–68, 73–75, 77–79, 84–86, 90, 94–95, 98–101, 106–8, 114, 117, 119–20, 122–25, 127, 132, 137, 144, 146, 148–50, 154, 157–65, 168–73; *see also* hypertranslation; retranslation, autotranslation or self-translation
transuasion (Peirce) 103–6

variation and invariations 6, 9, 27, 32, 34, 40, 46–47, 61, 73, 92, 95, 105, 107, 109–10, 115, 120, 129, 162, 164–67, 172, 191

Venus (Greek goddess of love) 16, 94, 111, 114–19
Virgil (Publius Vergilius Maro) 33–35, 89, 92–95, 98–119, 121–24, 126–28, 130, 172–74

Wagner, Richard 3, 47–54, 56–58, 61, 66–84, 86, 96–98, 100, 120, 133, 136, 144, 171–74

wave forms 10–11, 13–14, 22, 25–26, 32–34, 39–41, 44–87, 96, 121, 128, 172–74
Weill, Kurt 136–37, 144–47, 152–53, 155–56, 158–60, 163, 167, 170
wooden horse (dramatic symbol) 111–14, 117–18
Woolf, Virginia 1, 13–14, 17, 26, 46, 49–60, 64, 66–70, 72, 75, 100, 171–74